Whose Peace Are We Building?

African Perspectives on Peacebuilding and Leadership

Published in collaboration with the African Leadership Centre,
King's College London

Published in association with the African Leadership Centre, this unique and much-needed series brings together leading African practitioners – from leaders of peace missions to UN special envoys – in order to provide critical perspectives on current understandings of peacebuilding and leadership. Featuring unique, insider accounts of peacebuilding processes; in-depth analysis of the institutional obstacles faced; as well as theoretical and practical insights into how the present paradigm might be changed, the series presents a repository of cutting-edge knowledge for anyone interested in conflict, security and development.

The **African Leadership Centre** (ALC) is an internationally renowned academic unit based within King's College London, with a semi-autonomous research and training centre in Nairobi, Kenya. It incorporates a global community of scholars, whose cutting-edge research on peace, leadership, development and security issues aims to inform and influence intellectual debate, teaching and learning as well as policy discourses both in Africa and globally. Over the years the ALC has attracted some of the most influential African and global thought leaders, diplomats, military personnel, politicians and civil society leaders to speak at lectures and debates with its students in London and Nairobi. The ALC's overarching aim is to develop the next generation of African scholars, analysts and leaders.

The series editors are Professor 'Funmi Olonisakin, ALC, King's College London; Shuvai Nyoni, Director, ALC Nairobi; and Dr Eka Ikpe, ALC, King's College London.

Whose Peace Are We Building?

Leadership for Peace in Africa

Youssef Mahmoud
with
Albert Mbiatem

I.B.TAURIS
LONDON • NEW YORK • OXFORD • NEW DELHI • SYDNEY

I.B. TAURIS

Bloomsbury Publishing Plc

50 Bedford Square, London, WC1B 3DP, UK

1385 Broadway, New York, NY 10018, USA

29 Earlsfort Terrace, Dublin 2, Ireland

BLOOMSBURY, I.B. TAURIS and the I.B. Tauris logo are trademarks
of Bloomsbury Publishing Plc

First published in Great Britain 2021

A catalogue record for this book is available from the British Library.

ISBN: HB: 978-0-7556-1854-5
       PB: 978-0-7556-1888-0
       ePDF: 978-0-7556-1856-9
       eBook: 978-0-7556-1855-2

Typeset by RefineCatch Limited, Bungay, Suffolk
Printed and bound in Great Britain

Series: African Perspectives on Peace Building and Leadership

To find out more about our authors and books visit www.bloomsbury.com
and sign up for our newsletters

Contents

Illustrations

Foreword

We are living in particularly challenging times. Liberal and social democracies are being overrun by intolerant far right – ideologies that embrace ethno-nationalism, xenophobia, racism, exclusion and violence.

This is not only a Western phenomenon. These virulent ideologies thrive in many other parts in the world. They are dangerously undermining democracy and rule of law, fundamental freedoms and human rights.

And as if the above is not enough, since December 2019 the world has been shaken by the Covid-19 pandemic, with no clear end in sight, and a global recession without precedent is under way throwing back hundreds of millions of people into poverty.

It is against this dark international tableau that Youssef Mahmoud offers us lessons in leadership and hope.

I am pleased to have been asked by Youssef to write some words of introduction to this absolutely timely book written by someone growing up poor in a Tunisian fishermen's village and having to look after many siblings. Someone who through sheer determination and the support of benefactors was able, after many detours, to make it all the way to the United Nations where he ended up towards the end of his long career leading two UN peace operations in Africa.

We have similar life experiences. I too was born and grew up in an impoverished colonial backwater, being one of eleven brothers and sisters. But unlike Youssef, I did not arrive in New York in December 1975 to begin a dream career in the UN system. I travelled to NY as a rebel with a cause, to advocate the cause of self-determination for our people. We had declared independence unilaterally from Portugal in the closing weeks of 1975, animated by the forgivable illusion that this would deter the impending invasion of our defenceless, impoverished and betrayed country by the mighty military regime in neighbouring Indonesia.

After decades of difficult struggles in the service of peace and freedom in my own country, I found myself as a former President, the UN Secretary-General's Special Representative in Guinea-Bissau and thus can relate to much of the challenges Youssef relates in the book.

Youssef's path and mine crossed when in October 2014 he and I were invited by Secretary-General Ban Ki-moon along with several enlightened and richly experienced international diplomacy practitioners to review UN Peace Operations since the first major report fifteen years earlier that became known as the Bhahimi Report. The High Level Independent Panel on UN Peace Operations which I co-chaired with an outstanding UN leader, Ameerah Haq was tasked by the Secretary-General to propose a comprehensive review and restructuring of UN Peace operations to make them 'fit for purpose' and adaptable to the twenty-first century security challenges facing the international community.

The UN is a constellation of sovereign States led by elected and unelected leaders whose paramount allegiance is to their country's national interests. In conflict and post-conflict contexts, these interests take on at times conflicting dynamics that are rarely conducive to peace. It falls to the UN Secretary-General and the staff he appoints to represent him in these contexts to try to untangle this complicated web of interests, identify common ground and work with warring factions to help them move from violence to politics. It is no easy task as my own experience in Guinea-Bissau attests.

Youssef Mahmoud belongs to the small group of UN Envoys with solid academic backgrounds and professional experience, who spared no efforts to understand the country contexts where he was called upon to serve and listen with the intent to understand not just with the intent to help or solve problems, most of which were beyond his influence and control.

This book, *Whose Peace Are We Building?* is essentially about leadership in the service of peace. It is an invaluable guide for leaders at every level who aspire to contribute to a more peaceful, just and secure world.

In the concluding chapter of the book, Youssef eloquently shares some of the lessons he learned from his leadership journey. I quote below a short excerpt from that chapter:

> In the changing and uncertain environment we live in, context and followers have increasingly become far more important than leaders. As a manager of a UN Mission, I had to recognize the valuable benefits of drawing on the diverse expertise and perspectives of 'followers' whose values, belief systems, language and culture may be different from mine. In countries under stress, leaders emerge from many places and no society, however broken, is bereft of ideas and aspirations.

J. Ramos-Horta
Former President of Timor-Leste
Nobel Peace Laureate
Latest book: *Words of Hope in Troubled Times*, published by Longueville Media, 2018

Introduction

After a period in which armed violence and proxy wars seemed to be on the decline, it more recently appears to be again on the rise. The threats to our global security are many and varied, from health pandemics to the threat of nuclear war in the case of North Korea, to persistent and seemingly intractable conflicts in Afghanistan, the Central African Republic (CAR), Iraq, Libya, South Sudan, and Syria, among other places. The ever-growing threat of terrorism – fuelled by social exclusion, marginalization and discontent, and accelerated by radical ideologies – poses a clear and present danger to international and regional security, as well as to the Westphalian state system.

The unprecedented number of forcibly displaced persons in recent years has led to national introversion in many countries, at a moment when cooperation and proactive leadership is needed to prevent further deterioration. These evolving and multifaceted global threats pose serious challenges to the ambitions of sub-regional, regional and international organizations rendering the path to peace exceedingly difficult. The inability to prevent these threats, let alone address their devastating consequences, has raised questions about the legitimacy and relevance of inter-state governance structures. The policies of some global powers to pursue peace through strength and military prowess, or to perpetuate conflict in order to pursue their own narrow strategic interests, has made the path to durable peace even more treacherous. It has also taken us off course; away from the cooperative principles and practices enshrined in the United Nations Charter for the maintenance of international peace and security.

Within nations, conflicts are likely to persist when state institutions persistently fail to provide adequate basic services, employment opportunities, and protection for large segments of their population, particularly those in outlying peripheries. Governments are often not held accountable for their actions (or lack thereof), as oversight structures are weak or have been infiltrated by corrupt elites, criminals or other predatory, non-state actors. These hallmarks of poor governance have resulted in economic inequality and various forms of marginalization. Moreover, populations have become increasingly distrustful of public institutions, which are perceived as being under the control of governing elites who lack legitimacy.

Over the last three decades, violent intra-state conflicts have drawn the attention of the United Nations (UN) to the African continent, where 75 per cent of its peace operations personnel are deployed.[1] Although Africa is not host to the most violent conflicts in the world, the continent accommodates the five largest peace operations, and thus has had the most significant impact on the limitations and possibilities of these operations.[2]

It is against this inauspicious backdrop that my story begins. In the last years of my long career as a UN official, I was asked to head two different UN peace operations in Central Africa (which have since concluded). My first assignment was in Burundi in 2006 where, after a few months of service as Deputy Special Representative of the departing peacekeeping operation (ONUB), I was appointed Executive Representative of the UN Secretary-General (ERSG) and head of the successor peace operation in the country (the UN Integrated Mission in Burundi, known by its French acronym, BINUB). My second appointment was in Chad and the Central African Republic (CAR) in 2010, where I was UN Special Representative of the Secretary-General (SRSG) and head of an existing peacekeeping mission called MINURCAT, whose theatre of operations was confined to eastern Chad and north-east part CAR, and whose primary mandate was to protect civilians affected by the fighting in Darfur. To the chagrin of the UN Security Council, MINURCAT came to a precipitous end after host country consent for its continued presence wore thin and, eventually, it was forced to withdraw.

The leadership journey

As I made my way to higher levels of responsibility within the UN, I came to realize how well my formative years, as the oldest of nine siblings, had served me. Throughout this period, I learned that leadership is not what one does *to* others, but what one does *with* them. Over the years, through various professional training and development experiences, I gained a deeper understanding of who

[1] Van der Lijn, J., T. Smit and T. Höghammar (2016), 'Peace operations and conflict management', in *SIPRI Yearbook 2016: Armaments, Disarmament and International Security*, Oxford: Oxford University Press.
[2] Ibid., p. 273.

I am as a leader and my different leadership styles. I asked myself how it may have accounted for certain of my decisions, or how it might have affected the personal and professional wellbeing of others, in various contexts.

However, none of the above predetermined that I would take on the senior leadership positions I would go on to assume at the UN after joining it in 1981 as a junior linguist in charge of its Language Training Programme.[3] What stood me in good stead was my thirst for education, my ambition to partake in the organization's peace and security work (for which I was not academically qualified), and, above all, my willingness to draw lessons from errors I made along the way.

Context is king and listening is key

The mandates of most peace operations[4] are the result of long and protracted negotiations both inside and outside the chambers of the Security Council. Mandates are crafted on the basis of the UN's assessment of the factors driving conflict in situations judged by the Council as constituting a threat to international peace and security. It is these assessments that enable the Council to engage in complex juridical gymnastics in order to justify interventions in sovereign nations under the terms of the UN Charter.

These assessments are typically conducted from the vantage point of those who have ready-made solutions – with or without the complicity or participation of national or regional stakeholders. When such assessments involve one or more powerful members of the Security Council that have particular geopolitical interests in the country or region concerned, these members tend to steer the Council towards a particular treatment of the situation that preserves those geopolitical interests. Assessments and the subsequent response are usually influenced by ruling elites within the country or region involved, who may have already dictated the terms of the conflict settlement to ensure that the solutions prescribed by the Security Council do not negatively affect their hold on power or their other interests.

---

[3] The Language Training Programme of the UN Secretariat offered courses to UN staff members who wished to learn or enhance their proficiencies in one or more of the six official languages of the organization, assuming that those who joined spoke at least one of the working languages of the Secretariat, namely, English and French.

[4] These include peacekeeping operations and special political missions that are country specific or have a regional remit.

It is therefore not surprising when an SRSG lands in a particular country only to find that the situation is far more complex than they were informed of prior to deployment. Faced with this dilemma, how should the mission leader organize his- or herself before and during deployment, in order to better understand the reality on the ground, taking into account the activities of UN funds and programmes operating in the mission area? What kind of leadership styles, processes and strategies are required to gain a deeper understanding of the local context, while maintaining the trust and cooperation of host authorities and other stakeholders on the ground, including diplomatic missions and the UN country team of agencies funds, and programmes? It is a difficult juggling act.

My own perspective in this regard is that 'context is king and listening is key'. In this introduction, the principal aspect I will focus on by way of an entry point is the ability to listen with the intent to understand, while resisting, where possible, the urge to precipitately offer 'solutions' or provide help. Other strategies regarding the primacy of local context in conflict situations will be detailed throughout the rest of the book.

The benefits of listening are widely documented. As Ralph Nichols, credited as fathering the development of the field of listening, said, 'the most basic of all human needs is the need to understand and be understood. The best way to understand people is to listen to them.'[5] We tend to listen 'more closely to people who have control over our future' than those whose influence is judged immaterial. More importantly: 'listening attentively and mindfully'[6] without judging or giving advice takes a great deal of presence and humility. Listening with intent has been a defining practice of my leadership styles over the past two decades. Despite improvements, it is still a challenge; and I continually return to it when confronted with situations for which I have no immediate solution and over which I have little control and influence.

It is listening – as an art and a craft, even poorly practised – that helped me understand the situations I was entering, to address any preconceptions or prejudices that may have preceded my arrival, and to build, at the same time, a trusting relationship with local interlocutors and stakeholders.

As the head of the peacebuilding mission in Burundi (BINUB) and the peacekeeping mission straddling parts of Chad and CAR (MINURCAT), a proper understanding of the situation in which I was entering was also essential

[5]   International Listening Association, Listening Legend Interview, Dr Ralph Nichols, interview by Rick Bommelje, *Listening Post*, Summer 2003, Vol. 84.
[6]   Lakovic, V. (2016), 'How to Become a Mindful Listener (and Avoid Giving Advice All the Time)', Peace Blog.

for additional reasons. First, it was important to find a middle ground between what the Security Council mandate required and what the evolving realities on the ground allowed. Embarking on the implementation of the former without a deeper understanding of the latter would jeopardize the long-term dividends the mission was expected to foster. Second, it was important in terms of deciding on the appropriate leadership style to adopt in order to manage expectations and build trust. To do this, the listening skills I had learned and practised over the years would prove invaluable.

However, I should hasten to confess, it was not easy to apply my listening skills in these two mission contexts. In reality, it was extremely challenging to be a patient and impartial listener when urgent action was needed to stem societal violence or quell political tensions in Burundi, or to arrange under stringent deadlines with a defiant Chadian government for an orderly and dignified exit of MINURCAT.

The UN: attempting reforms in the pursuit of an elusive peace

During my years of service, the UN was criticized for not fully understanding the complexity of contemporary conflicts, still less preventing their outbreak. Nowadays, the wars raging in countries such as Syria and Yemen are often cited as examples of the organization's impotence, even irrelevance. The peace operations the UN deployed, while perhaps dousing the fire and creating a secure enough environment for the implementation of a negotiated peace agreement, rarely laid the foundations for self-sustaining peace. Instead, with a few exceptions, the peace operations tended to last for years.

In situations where there was little or no peace to keep, as was the case with MINURCAT, the main focus of peace operations was the protection of civilians engulfed by or fleeing from violence. This became the modus operandi for several peace operations following the UN Security Council deciding in 1999 that 'the deliberate targeting of civilians . . . may constitute a threat to international peace and security', affirming 'its readiness to consider such situations and, where necessary, to adopt appropriate steps.'[7]

In his 2012 book, *What is Wrong with the United Nations and How to Fix It*, Thomas Weiss presents the UN as remarkably ill adapted to the times. He further

---

[7]   UNSC Resolution 1270 (1999), Operative Paragraph 14, on the Mandate of UNAMSIL. Subsequent missions have used similar terminology.

notes that, in spite of a mantra of reform, the international body still struggles towards the realization of set goals.[8] Some of the UN's shortcomings are connected to limited support from member states. According to former UN Secretary-General Kofi Annan, the central problem is that the UN has 'been asked to do much with too little'.[9] It is these lingering performance deficits that, towards the end of 2014, prompted another former UN Secretary-General, Ban Ki-Moon, to order a global review of peace operations through the appointment of a High-Level Independent Panel (HIPPO), of which I was honoured to be a member.[10] In June 2015, HIPPO, under the able leadership of former President of Timor-Leste, J.Ramos-Horta, produced a report with far-reaching recommendations aimed at putting politics, partnerships and people at the centre of UN responses to conflict situations.[11] In 2017, the first year of his tenure, Antonio Guterres – Ban Ki-Moon's successor – presented an ambitious package of structural reforms in an attempt to implement some of these recommendations. Most of these reforms were approved by member states.

In turn and almost simultaneously, member states in 2015 entrusted an independent Advisory Group of Experts (AGE) with a review of the UN Peacebuilding Architecture (PBA). The PBA comprised the Peacebuilding Commission (PBC), the Peacebuilding Fund (PF) and the Peacebuilding Support Office (PBSO). The purpose of the AGE was to recommend how the PBA could be made more effective in supporting peace building in conflict-affected countries. In its report, 'Challenges of Sustaining Peace',[12] the AGE also made a number of recommendations that were the subject of long and protracted negotiations among member states. These culminated in the adoption of substantively identical resolutions by the General Assembly and the Security Council in April 2016,[13] which adopted sustaining peace as the overarching framework for revitalizing the work of the UN's peacebuilding architecture. In Chapter 1, I analyse these resolutions and the impact they have had on the peacebuilding work of the organization two years after their adoption.

---

[8] Weiss, T. (2012), *What is Wrong with the UN and how to Fix It?* 2nd edition, USA: Polity Press, 1–2.
[9] *The New York Times* (1995), 6 January.
[10] UN Press Release of 31 October 2014, SG/SM/16301-SG/A/1521-PKO/451. Available online: https://www.un.org/press/en/2014/sgsm16301.doc.htm (accessed 29 July 2017).
[11] Report presented to the Secretary-General on 16 June 2015 by the High-Level Independent Panel on Peace Operations.
[12] Advisory Group of Experts (2015), 'The Challenge of Sustaining Peace: Report for the 2015 Review of the United Nations Peacebuilding Architecture', The United Nations, June.
[13] United Nations (2016), 'Resolution adopted by the General Assembly on 27 April 2016', A/RES/70/262,12 May.

Burundi: the wounded puzzle

As ONUB completed its peacekeeping operation mandate in Burundi on 31 December 2006, the Security Council adopted Resolution 1719, authorizing the establishment of a UN Integrated Office in Burundi (BINUB), effective 1 January 2007.[14] Having acquired more than a decade's worth of experience within the UN in the area of peace and security, I was appointed by Kofi Annan as ERSG for Burundi and head of BINUB. My extensive experience did not, however, prepare me for the challenges I faced grappling with the small but complex puzzle that was Burundi. What stood me in good stead was the incipient knowledge I had gained during the last quarter of 2006 as Deputy Special Representative of the departing ONUB, becoming its de facto officer in charge after the Burundian government declared the acting head of the Mission personae non grata. This was an unexpected and double-edged development, the significance of which, as will be explained in Chapter 4, I did not fully grasp at the time.

While ERSG, I simultaneously served as UNDP Resident Representative, UN Resident Coordinator in charge of coordinating UN operational activities in the country, Humanitarian Coordinator, and Designated Official overseeing the safety and security of UN personnel working in Burundi. Each of these hats brought with it internal and external challenges that had far-reaching leadership implications and, at times, consequences for my relationship with the host government.

What brought us all together as a UN country team, despite these challenges, was the planning and operationalization of some of the peacebuilding activities mandated by the founding Security Council Resolution for BINUB cited above. These ranged from repatriation of refugees; to the disarmament, demobilization and reintegration of former combatants; to the establishment of mechanisms for transitional justice. All the members of the team were new to these fields and thus had to find ways to work across the various pillars of the UN's work to develop an integrated strategy in support of peace consolidation in Burundi. In addition to reporting to the Security Council on our collective UN-Burundi government efforts, we had to work with the newly created Peacebuilding Commission, one of whose key objectives was to facilitate the mobilization of the funds needed to implement this strategy.[15]

---

[14] United Nations (2006), 'Resolution 1719 (2006), adopted by the Security Council at its 5554th Meeting', S/RES/1719, 25 October.

[15] Nations Unies, Commission de Consolidation de la Paix. Available online: http://www.un.org/en/peacebuilding/mandate.shtml (accessed 30 July 2017).

The crisis in Burundi has historical roots that can be traced back to the deleterious German and Belgian colonial rule, leading on to the recurring political antagonisms and inter-ethnic tensions that began surfacing in the early years following on from the country's independence. The impetus for the protracted civil war was the failed October 1993 military coup, which claimed the life of the first-ever democratically elected Hutu President, Melchoir Ndadaye, just four months after he had stepped into power. Ndadaye had taken over after twenty-five years of brutal rule by a Tutsi-dominated minority government. Since the death of Ndadaye, guns had become the predominant tool for acquiring and maintaining power. While the Hutu–Tutsi divide continued unabated, armed groups of different ethnic affiliations emerged as counterforces to a government they deemed exclusionary and unresponsive to popular needs and demands. The death of another Hutu President, Cyprien Ntaryamira (together with the President of Rwanda), in a tragic plane crash on 6 April 1994, as well as the July 1996 coup initiated by the Tutsi-leader Pierre Buyoya, plunged the country into further violence. The civil war, which ran from 1993 to 2004, resulted in the death of nearly 300,000 people and the forced displacement of over 100,000 people into neighbouring Tanzania.[16]

In late 1993, the UN dispatched the former Mauritanian Foreign Minister Ahmedou Ould Abdallah to help calm the situation and restore democratic order. Initially sent as the SRSG for a three-month period, it took him almost two years to establish a semblance of stability before the regional leaders could organize inter-Burundian dialogues in the Tanzanian city of Arusha, facilitated successively by Julius Nyerere and Nelson Mandela (the former presidents of Tanzania and South Africa respectively). The dialogues culminated in the adoption of the 2000 Arusha Peace and Reconciliation Agreement,[17] which became the roadmap that made possible the organization of free and fair elections in 2005. This was done with the support of ONUB, the first UN peacekeeping mission deployed in 2004, which replaced the African Union Mission (AMIB) deployed one year previously.

Against this backdrop, BINUB was established in 2007 to help consolidate the peace gains achieved by Burundians with the support of ONUB, which had been disbanded at the end of 2006. After leading BINUB for three years, the Government of Burundi requested that I be replaced by another envoy, the political reasons of which will be delved into later.

---

[16] Project Ploughshares (2014), Armed Conflicts Report-Burundi.
[17] Arusha Peace and Reconciliation Agreement for Burundi, Arusha, August 2000.

MINURCAT in Chad and CAR: an unhappy experiment

Towards the end of 2009, at the age of sixty-two and after twenty-eight years of UN service, I was looking forward to retirement. In March 2010, however, Secretary-General Ban Ki-Moon gave me an assignment that made my Burundi tenure look, in hindsight, relatively easy. He asked me to lead a multi-departmental mission to Chad in order to negotiate a dignified and orderly exit of the UN Integrated Peacekeeping Mission for Central African Republic and Chad (MINURCAT), which the government had wanted withdrawn ahead of its scheduled end for multiple reasons. After arduous negotiations lasting nearly a month, with the support of my team I was able to strike a deal with the Chadian authorities that permitted the Mission to remain in the country for nine months later than initially requested by the government. On 1 April 2010, after assuming on an ad-interim basis the helm of the Mission for one month following the departure of my predecessor, I was appointed head of the Mission, tasked with helping implement the residual tasks of the Mission and oversee its orderly withdrawal. This came with a number of hurdles along the way that tested the adaptive leadership capacity I thought I had in abundance. Ironically, the Government of the Central African Republic did not wish MINURCAT to depart for fear it might hand the foothold it had in Birao to the marauding rebels in the embattled faraway north-eastern province of Vacaga.

MINURCAT was created by the Security Council in 2007 to help deal with the disastrous humanitarian consequences of the violent conflict raging in the Western Sudanese province of Darfur, and the cross-border warfare generated by various rebel movements that jeopardized the security of the population, many of whom found refuge in eastern Chad. This took place against a backdrop of deteriorating relations between the presidents of Chad and Sudan, each of whom accused the other of supporting armed movements against their respective regimes. Although mediation by regional leaders, including Senegal, dampened tensions between the two leaders, the humanitarian crisis in eastern Chad continued unabated, fuelled largely by untamed cross-border incursions.

MINURCAT was deployed by the Council against the advice of the UN Secretariat, which felt that the focus should be on resolving the origins of the problem, the Darfur conflict, rather than on its humanitarian consequences for which a peacekeeping mission was ill-suited. After all, there was no peace 'to keep' at the time. Under pressure from international humanitarian NGOs, the Council, heedless of the Secretariat's advice, dispatched MINURCAT and asked the European Union to provide a protection force – EUFOR – for one year, while the UN looked for troops to replace it. A year later, having not been fully successful in raising the requisite number of troops, some EUFOR contingents had to be re-hatted under the UN umbrella.

The normalization of relations between the governments of Chad and Sudan in 2009 enabled both countries to create a cross-border joint military taskforce to stem trans-border incursions, and to protect civilians. This joint venture was deemed successful enough for the President of Chad to ask for the withdrawal of MINURCAT. There were also other irritants, which will be outlined in Chapter 6, which precipitated his decision. It was under these circumstances that my time at the helm of MINURCAT began, a mission already struggling with multiple challenges and operational hurdles that had to be factored into the development of its drawdown plan. All this while at the same time laying the foundations for sustaining some of the good results the Mission had achieved since deployment, which largely involved the creation of a protective environment for vulnerable populations.

The above snapshot indicates some of the political and leadership implications with respect to a peacekeeping operation deployed in a non-permissive environment. These implications, and the difficulties of dealing with them, form a key part of the analysis developed later in the book.

Leadership for peace

Much has been written about leadership, and much has been written about peace, the latter of which is largely considered as simply the absence of violence. However, relatively little attention has been given to the nexus between the two – leadership and peace – and the paradigm shifts needed in the nature and practice of leadership in order to bring about strong, global diplomacy for peace. The few published works relating to the subject tend to depict leadership for peace as the heroic efforts of well-meaning outsiders, entrusted with carrying out short-term, liberal peacebuilding solutions. In these publications,[18] aspirations for peace tend to be depicted negatively, largely as the absence or reduction of violence, as the order that follows the end of war. This negative peace tends to shift focus away from the hard work of putting mechanisms

---

[18]   Roberts, D. (2010), 'From Liberal to Popular Peace', Opendemocracy.net, 29 October. Available online: https://www.opendemocracy.net/en/from-liberal-to-popular-peace/ (accessed 18 January 2018).

in place to repair fractured relationships and nurture resilient institutions.[19] As a result, peacebuilding is often equated with activities aimed primarily at strengthening the capacity of the state, without sufficient effort invested in empowering people to identify and strengthen their own capacities for peace.

Based on my own experience, leadership for peace is not about positions of authority and power vested in one individual. My position as the head of peace operations in Burundi and Chad–CAR had to be exercised with care. While I could exert my authority as ERSG/SRSG with some success on matters relating to the internal management of the Mission, I could not exert the same authority over national or local actors, or over the heads of the various UN agencies and programmes whose operational activities, in the case of Burundi, I was formally mandated to coordinate.

As John Maxwell, an American expert on leadership, rightly notes, 'influencing others is a matter of disposition not position'.[20] More than understanding the context, and building respectful relations through attentive listening, I soon learned that leadership was also about identifying and unleashing the potential of followers to lead.

With respect to the conflict contexts into which BINUB and MINURCAT were deployed, leadership for peace belonged to the Burundians, Chadians and Central Africans. My role was to leverage the political, human and material assets of the missions to help create an enabling environment for locally driven solutions and responses to emerge. This approach was largely inspired by significant developments in the field of leadership, some of which will be explored in Chapter 1, where context and followers were deemed far more important than the leader.[21]

However, this proved more challenging than expected, and in my attempts to exercise this empowering, servant-type of leadership I had to find imperfect answers to some of the hard questions with which I was confronted.[22] For example, how can the Mission assist the pursuit of peace without being captured by domestic ruling elites, whose concerns are mostly geared towards the interests of the few rather than those of the majority? How could I ensure that the well-

[19] Shields, P. (2017), 'Limits of Negative Peace, Faces of Positive Peace', *Parameters*, 4 (3), Autumn.

[20] Maxwell, J. (2005), *The 360° Leader Developing your Influenced from Anywhere in the Organisation*, Nashville, TN: Thomas Nelson.

[21] Kellerman, B. (2012), *The End of Leadership*, New York: HarperCollins.

[22] Trask, J. (2016), 'Servant Leaders: Empowering Followers', PennState, 15 April. Available online: https://sites.psu.edu/leadership/2016/04/15/servant-leaders-empowering-followers/ (accessed 19 January 2018).

meaning normative and paradigmatic moorings underpinning my peacebuilding and peacekeeping roles did not unwittingly erode national ownership in its plurality, or worse, do harm? How could we meaningfully involve "we the peoples" – as enshrined in the UN Charter – in the design and implementation of peace activities, without provoking the ire of a testy government that presents itself, under the banner of sovereignty, as the sole spokesperson for the wishes and needs of the people, and does not look kindly on outsiders directly consulting civil society and ordinary people? In instances of an unfinished peace process, as was the case in Burundi (a major rebel group remained outside the process), what mediation magic can one conjure up to impartially engage with conflict parties while still treating the government (in this case considered as one of the parties), to which the Mission is accredited, as a primus inter pares?

Essentially, this book aspires to offer practitioners, policymakers, as well as scholars and students of peace and conflict studies, a framework to make better sense of complex peace and conflict settings. In addition, it aims to foster new thinking about the type of leadership for effecting just change in societies under stress. It also offers some lessons learned, that might hopefully inform the future design of UN peace missions and provides practical insights for those chosen to lead them. Lastly, it put forward some ideas about the knowledge, skills and attitudes that future peace leaders need to develop in order to navigate the increasingly fractious and complex regional and global environments in which UN missions operate.

This seven-chapter book charts my leadership journey as a senior UN envoy, and my search for the appropriate relational and adaptive leadership styles with which to meet the challenging contexts in which I was deployed. It details some of the conceptual and attitudinal shifts and approaches I improvised in order to transform peacebuilding from merely a conflict-resolution tool to a strategy for building and fostering a more durable peace.

Many of the reflections I offer in this book draw on the rich, year-long exchanges I took part in in 2015 as a member of the High-Level Independent Panel on Peace Operations (HIPPO) mentioned above. I also draw on reflections from current experiences at the International Peace Institute,[23] where I serve as Senior Advisor. These reflections have emboldened me to reframe prevention, as re-introduced in the twin UN resolutions on sustaining peace,[24] not only as a

---

[23] International Peace Institute, Mission and History. Available online: https://www.ipinst.org/about/mission-history (accessed 20 January 2018).
[24] United Nations (2006), 'Resolution 1719 (2006)'.

conflict transformation tool but also as a governance and development strategy for building sustainable peace.[25]

The structure of the book

Chapter 1 seeks to provide readers from diverse disciplines with a practitioner's perspective on the evolving conceptualization and practice of peacebuilding and leadership. The chapter reviews, in particular, the evolution of the dominant, state-centric peacebuilding paradigms and some of the assumptions[26] underpinning them. It also examines the relationship between leadership and peace, and questions the relationship between peacebuilding and sustaining peace, analysing the relative pertinence of these paradigms to the complex, intra-state nature of contemporary conflicts and the impact (both negative and positive) their exercise can have on building self-sustainable peace after conflict.

Chapter 2 presents the personal and professional contexts in which my leadership abilities and styles evolved over time. It describes how at a tender age I was already entrusted with leadership responsibilities as the first child in a sibling line of nine. It then traces my uncharted journey from a small village in eastern Tunisia to New York to work for the UN, starting as a junior linguist and ending as Under-Secretary-General. It describes the main academic and professional milestones of that journey and the people who helped make it possible, including my parents. The final part of the chapter offers some life lessons that stood me in good stead in the face of the leadership challenges and opportunities with which I was faced as head of two successive peace operations.

Chapter 3 traces the genesis of the Burundian conflict and reviews the work of the successive regional and international peacemaking, peacekeeping and peacebuilding missions deployed to help manage the conflict, its consequences, and lay the foundations to prevent its recurrence. While presenting the situation in its transitional- and post-transitional periods, the chapter elaborates on the tense socio-political climate that preceded the establishment of the UN integrated peacebuilding mission, BINUB, which took over some of the residual activities of its predecessor, the UN peacekeeping mission, ONUB. It also focuses on the challenges faced by these missions and their leadership

---

[25] Mahmoud, Y. and A. Makoond (2018), 'Can Peacebuilding Work for Sustaining Peace?', IPI Global Observatory, 10 April. Available online: https://theglobalobservatory.org/2018/04/peacebuilding-work-sustaining-peace/ (accessed 8 August 2018).

[26] Ibid.

implications in terms of risks and opportunities both for the UN peacebuilding mission and for the UN Peacebuilding Architecture, which came into being a few months prior to the start of BINUB.

Chapter 4 outlines and analyses my experiences at the helm of BINUB. It describes how I prepared, soon after my appointment as ERSG, to assume leadership of the Mission and gain a deeper understanding of a country still under stress, enmeshed in political antagonism, and with a testy government bent on asserting its sovereignty after a serious run-in with the ONUB leadership. It discusses the various initiatives my senior Mission leadership team and I took to carry out the main activities of BINUB and those of the UN country team on the ground under a common peacebuilding strategy. It also describes the collective efforts of the UN and the African Union to bring into the fold the last rebel movement resisting involvement in the peacebuilding process, disarm and reintegrate its fighters, and enable its transformation into a political party. It discusses some of the challenges faced in carrying out these tasks, and the various leadership and organizational strategies, processes and mechanisms my team and I devised to address them. The chapter provides further insight on these issues through the anonymous testimonies of colleagues with whom I worked closely during the period, and concludes by speculating on the reasons the Government of Burundi asked for my replacement at the end of my three-year tenure.

Chapter 5 offers a contextual analysis of the humanitarian and security crisis in eastern Chad and north-eastern CAR, caused by the massive influx of refugees fleeing violent conflict raging across the border in Darfur (western Sudan). The crisis resulted from violent clashes between armed proxies close to the governments of Chad and Sudan, which for close to six years drove hundreds of thousands of civilians into refugee camps along the tri-partite border between Chad, Sudan and CAR. The chapter discusses the contested rationale for the dispatch of MINURCAT to protect the refugee population in the two affected regions of eastern Chad and northeast CAR, and provides an overview of the mandate and composition of the Mission. It describes the humanitarian situation I found on the ground on my arrival and the factors that contributed to the government's decision – to the consternation of the Security Council, various international stakeholders, and the CAR authorities – to ask for MINURCAT's withdrawal. Finally, the chapter describes the dispirited atmosphere within a mission shown the exit door.

Chapter 6 delves into the factors that enabled me to successfully conduct negotiations with the Government of Chad on a strategy for an honourable and orderly exit of MINURCAT, as endorsed by the UN Security Council, and the challenges faced in its implementation. Among these challenges was how to address the employment grievances of disgruntled local staff anxious about their jobs post-MINURCAT, and how to motivate all staff to continue carrying out the residual activities of the Mission, while at the same time dismantling its assets and developing a plan for handing over parts of these activities to the Government of Chad and its international partners, including UN agencies on the ground. I describe the leadership responses crafted to address these challenges, sometimes by trial and error rather than by foresight or design. Finally, the chapter lays out some of the lessons learned from a mission that has gone through the planning, deployment and withdrawal stages in a time span of less than four years.

Chapter 7 summarizes the main takeaways from the experiences detailed in the book and challenges some of the foundational assumptions that continue to inform the dominant, liberal peacebuilding agenda. The chapter proposes ways this agenda can be freed from its negative peace, conflict-management moorings so as to better build peace by reframing the peace and leadership nexus through different lenses. The starting point for outside actors and their national partners should instead be the factors associated with peaceful societies, rather than just the drivers of conflict. Lessons are also offered for future leaders of peace operations, particularly in contexts where there is no peace to keep, where host-government consent is tenuous, and where there is a trust deficit between the UN Security Council and that government. Given that many of the problems afflicting today's world are the result of a constellation of leadership and governance deficits, the chapter suggests aspects of the peace–leadership nexus which, if integrated in international relations or in leadership curricula, could better prepare students to deal with the fractious global environment in which we live. Finally, recommendations are made on peace leadership aspects that can benefit from further research.

1

Perspectives on Peacebuilding and Leadership

Leadership and peacebuilding were intrinsically intertwined throughout my experience as head of two United Nations (UN) peace operations in Central Africa. In many ways, those experiences can best be understood by appreciating the complex interactions between these two ever-evolving concepts, which are invariably coloured by the contexts in which they are applied.

Since retiring from the UN nearly ten years ago, I have reflected extensively on the normative underpinnings of leadership and peacebuilding, exploring past and current thinking in academic circles while engaging intensely in policy discourse within the UN and beyond.[1] These reflections were honed during a year-long collective learning experience which, as a member of the High-Level Independent Panel on Peace Operations (HIPPO), I was privileged to partake in.[2] This panel, to which I was appointed in 2014 by former Secretary-General Ban Ki-Moon, was tasked with examining ways that UN peace operations can be made more fit for purpose. My tenure on the Panel presented an opportunity for conceptually exchanging with scholars and policymakers alike on the encompassing notion of peace and the role leadership plays in the design and implementation of these operations.

In this chapter, using my field experiences as a backdrop, I will share what I have learned about peace and leadership. First, I will share my perspective on the origin and evolution of this nebulous and contested field called 'peacebuilding', and question some of the assumptions that have informed its liberal moorings over the past four decades. Next, I will review the ongoing policy debate on the emerging concepts of sustaining peace[3] and popular peace,[4] before embarking

---

[1]   The author is, as of this writing, a Senior Advisor at the International Peace Institute, providing support to the conceptualization and implementation of various policy forums dealing with leadership, peacebuilding and sustaining peace. See for example: https://www.ipinst.org/wp-content/uploads/2018/02/1802_Sustaining-Peace-in-Practice.pdf
[2]   United Nations (2014), SG/SM/16301-SG/A/1521-PKO/451.
[3]   International Peace Institute (2017), 'Sustaining Peace: What Does it Mean in Practice?', IPI, April.
[4]   Roberts (2010).

on a conceptual appraisal of leadership both as an art and craft, including a discussion of its relevance for the design and implementation of peacebuilding interventions. Finally, I will delve into the nexus between leadership and peacebuilding, and broach the emerging paradigm of leadership *for* peace.

Perspectives on peacebuilding

Extensively discussed in the broad field of peace studies, the concept of peacebuilding emerged over four decades ago. In his famous 1975 work – *Three Approaches to Peace: Peacekeeping, Peacemaking and Peacebuilding* – Johan Galtung argued that: 'The mechanisms that peace is based on should be built into the structure and be present as a reservoir for the system itself to draw upon.'[5] In his earlier engagement in peace studies in 1969, Galtung described peace as the absence of physical violence or the absence of structural violence. As such, he described peace from a dual perspective – 'negative peace' and 'positive peace'. Negative peace is 'the absence of violence, absence of war' and positive peace is 'the integration of human society'.[6] Thus, in order to address structural violence and promote positive peace, Galtung required that peacebuilding structures tackle the root causes of violent conflict. In addition, he argued that peacebuilding should provide justice and general security, and allow local capabilities for peace management and conflict resolution to thrive, thereby ensuring a sustainable peace.[7]

Paul Lederach conceptualizes peacebuilding from a broader perspective, arguing that it should be understood as an all-inclusive notion embodying, producing, and upholding the full range of processes, approaches, and phases needed to move conflict towards more sustainable and peaceful relationships.[8] Peacebuilding mechanisms are fundamental to building relationships that in their totality form new patterns, processes, and structures for peace.[9]

While scholars have remained attentive to the need to define peacebuilding, it is my observation that policy-makers, on their side, have spared no effort in

[5]   Galtung, J. (1975), 'Three Approaches to Peace: Peacekeeping, Peacemaking and Peacebuilding', in *Peace, War and Defence – Essays in Peace Research Vol. 2*, 282–304, Copenhagen: Christian Ejlers: 297–8.
[6]   Galtung, J. (1964), 'An Editorial', *Journal of Peace Research*, 1 (1): 2.
[7]   Galtung (1975).
[8]   Lederach, P. (1997), *Building Peace: Sustainable Reconciliation in Divided Societies*, Washington, DC: US Institute of Peace Press: 20.
[9]   Ibid.: 84–5.

establishing their own conceptualizations. From the early 1990s, the policy world began to perceive peacebuilding as a tool for responding to the needs of post-conflict societies and for attaining sustainable peace. Successive UN secretaries-general, among other top officials, shared strong views on peacebuilding processes and their objectives in various reports and speeches.

In 1992, Boutros Boutros-Ghali's policy document, 'An Agenda for Peace', identified the essence of post-conflict peacebuilding as: 'an action to identify and support structures which will tend to strengthen and solidify peace in order to avoid a relapse into conflict'.[10] Although peacebuilding was initially conceived from a post-conflict perspective, it took barely three years to acknowledge the need for engaging in peacebuilding at an earlier stage in order to avert the outbreak of violent conflict. In another document – 'Supplement to an Agenda for Peace' – published in 1995, Boutros-Ghali expanded the remit of peacebuilding to address all conflict phases, with a particular focus on the institutions buttressing peace.

Known as the *Brahimi Report*, the *2000 Report of the Panel on United Nations Peace Operations* defined peacebuilding as 'activities undertaken on the far side of conflict to reassemble the foundations of peace and provide the tools for building on those foundations something that is more than just the absence of war'.[11] The definition created awareness of the need to lay down solid foundations on which peace can rest. In February 2001, the Security Council publicly recognized that the process of building peace encompasses a wide range of political, development, humanitarian, and human rights policies and programmes, the primary aim of which is to prevent (re)lapses into armed conflict. Short and long-term actions tailored to address the needs of societies also tend to fall under the umbrella of peacebuilding.[12]

Building peace as a policy and a programmatic response to supporting fragile and conflict-affected countries gained prominence in 2005, following the creation of the United Nations Peacebuilding architecture, which comprised a Peacebuilding Commission (PBC), a Peacebuilding Support Office, and a Peacebuilding Fund. In the world of former UN Secretary-General Ban Ki-Moon, peacebuilding involved putting in place the institutions and building the

---

[10] Ghali, B. (1992), 'An Agenda for Peace: Preventive Diplomacy, Peacemaking and Peace-keeping', Document A/47/277–S/241111, 17 June, New York: Department of Public Information, United Nations.

[11] Report of the Panel on United Nations Peace Operations (2000), A/55/305–S/2000/809, 21 August.

[12] United Nations (2001), 'Statement by the President of the Security Council', S/PRST/2001/5, 20 February.

trust that, in focusing on the most pressing needs in the immediate aftermath of conflict, would carry people toward a peaceful future.[13] Chief among these needs was that of identifying and strengthening capacities that would enable a society to manage conflict in non-violent ways.[14] Mobilizing early responses to these needs on the basis of a nationally crafted peacebuilding strategy, in close collaboration with international and regional financial institutions and UN partners on the ground, was judged to be the main contribution of the PBC. Beyond the quality of national leadership, central to the effectiveness of the whole UN peacebuilding enterprise is the judicious leadership exercised by UN teams entrusted to head peacebuilding support presences in the field.

Both top-down (international, regional and national elites' agendas) and bottom-top approaches (active participation of affected communities and peoples) have been recurrent in peacebuilding narratives.[15] Thus, the PBC as originally designed was expected to serve as a forum for engaging with civil society – including women and youth groups – taking into account their diverse perspectives in the development of national peacebuilding priorities and agendas.[16] In efforts to support national processes and public dialogues, new technologies and social media were judged as indispensable tools for advancing communication and broadening participation in political processes.[17]

Liberal peace: building states to build peace

Based on the conviction that sustainable peace cannot exist without functioning states, peacebuilding has become aligned with statebuilding, with almost no substantive separation of the two concepts in many UN policy circles. Peacebuilding agendas regularly incorporate elements of statebuilding and the rule of law. As such, statebuilding becomes an 'endogenous process to enhance capacity, institutions and legitimacy of the state driven by state-society relations.'[18] "The 'order' of peace is thus promoted through law, human rights norms,

---

[13]   United Nations Peacebuilding. Available online: https://www.un.org/peacebuilding/ (accessed 10 January 2018).
[14]   Interpeace, 'What is Peace?' Available online: https://www.interpeace.org/what-we-do/what-is-peacebuilding/ (accessed 10 January 2018).
[15]   International Peace Institute (2016), 'Armed Conflict: Mediation, Conciliation and Peacekeeping', Independent Commission on Multilateralism, Paper Issue, March: 8.
[16]   Advisory Group of Experts (2015): 57.
[17]   Ibid.: 22.
[18]   OECD (2010). 'Peacebuilding and Statebuilding Priorities and Challenges. A Synthesis of Findings from Seven Multi-Stakeholder Consultations', Organisation for Economic Co-operation and Development, Paris: 21–2.

democratic representation, and (often) the 'privileging of the state.'[19] Most notably, since the 9/11 attacks on the United States and the subsequent 'global war on terrorism', stability and security in the face of organized violence have been increasingly prioritized in both national and international agendas.[20] Hence, the strong need to build states equipped with the capacity to guarantee security and control the expression of violent identities.[21]

However, some have questioned the extent to which statebuilding processes lead to sustainable peace, particularly when they are designed to strengthen state capacity without commensurate regard for the quality of its performance and in particular of the relationship it is able to maintain with its citizens (more so in periods of national or international stresses). Moreover, in the pursuit of national ownership, external peacebuilders tend to work exclusively with government elites, whether well- or ill-elected. In turn, this results in the use of peacebuilding interventions 'to enact subtle strategies of institutional capture to their own ends.'[22] As a result, this jeopardizes the legitimacy of statebuilding.

Nevertheless, the relevance of the connection between peacebuilding and statebuilding has drawn the attention of some states that consider themselves as fragile. A group of eighteen states known as the Group of Seven Plus (g7+) have come up with a broad agenda that, in seeking to attain long-lasting peace, puts statebuilding in the service of peacebuilding. These states have identified five main peacebuilding and statebuilding goals[23] on the basis of their own post-conflict experience: (i) *legitimate politics* – foster inclusive political settlements; (ii) *security* – establish and strengthen people's security; (iii) *justice* – address injustices and increase people's access to justice; (iv) *economic foundations* – generate employment and improve livelihood; and (v) *revenues and services* – manage revenues and build capacity for accountable and fair service delivery. In a similar vein, the *World Development Report 2011: Conflict, Security and Development* emphasized 'inclusive enough' politics, justice, security, and jobs as necessary foundations for building peace in conflict-affected countries.[24]

Over the past decades, 'good or good enough governance' was adopted as the overall framework under which political, economic and governance reform

---

[19] International Peace Institute (2016): 5.
[20] Ibid.
[21] Ibid.
[22] Barma, H. (2017), *The Peacebuilding Puzzle: Political Order in Post-Conflict States,* Cambridge: Cambridge University Press.
[23] Interpeace, 'What is Peace?'
[24] World Bank (2011), 'World Development Report 2011: Conflict, Security and Development', Washington, DC.

measures were benignly tucked away to pursue more state-driven securitized policies. As the sources of insecurity grew for the 'global North', so did the focus on strengthening the ability of states 'to prevent terrorist cells from operating with impunity where states are too weak to police their borders and enforce the rule of law'.[25]

Under this increasingly securitized paradigm, the prevention of violent conflict and the treatment of its root causes are presented as pathways to peace, equating the eradication of violence with peace. The recent joint UN-World Bank study on prevention is an exemplar of this approach. However, as will be explained below, empirical research has demonstrated that ending war and building peace are – while interconnected – separate processes.[26]

From liberal peace to popular peace

Over the past decade, this securitized, liberal, state-centric peacebuilding enterprise has come under heavy criticism,[27] with a lack of local legitimacy posited as the key reason that peace does not prevail as intended under this paradigm.[28] Critics argue that peace cannot be built by institutions, however reformed or capacitated, if they ignore the everyday needs and priorities of local populations, whether this be water, sanitation, healthcare or electricity. They contend that the provision of local needs is central to generating internal local legitimacy, which, in turn, is key to stability and peace. This 'popular peacebuilding', as David Roberts calls it, builds a peace that is democratically determined, strengthened from the bottom up, and nourished from the top down, a nexus that is far more likely to legitimate elite authority than momentary electoral ballots.[29] According to this perspective, the primary role of global governance institutions, whether this be the UN, the World Health Organization or the World Bank, is to respond to whatever everyday needs are enunciated locally and expressed democratically. Moreover, institutions are responsible for ensuring that 'states and other appropriately focused agencies deliver efficiently what people have identified'.[30] Popular peace, according to Roberts, is context-specific,

---

[25] Chandler, D. (2007), 'The State-Building Dilemma: Good Governance or Democratic Government?' in H. Aiden and N. Robinson (eds), *Statebuilding: Theory and Practice*, London: Routledge, 70–88.

[26] Coleman, P. (2012) 'The Missing Piece in Sustainable Peace', General Earth Institute, 6 November.

[27] Ibid.

[28] Roberts, D. (2011), 'Post-conflict Peacebuilding, Liberal Irrelevance and the Locus of Legitimacy', *International Peacekeeping*, 18 (4).

[29] Ibid.

[30] Ibid.

cannot be determined by outsiders, and – most importantly – serves the popular will over elite actors both in the Global North and South.

From peacebuilding to sustaining peace

In 2014–15, three global reviews were commissioned by the UN Secretary-General and Member States looking into how the UN peace and security work could become fit for purpose in light of the evolving nature of conflict and the difficulties encountered in addressing them, with the intent to build peace rather than just eradicating conflict. In 2015, three reports were produced as a result of these reviews: the report of the High-Level Independent Panel on Peace Operations (HIPPO), the report of the Advisory Group of Experts (AGE) on the UN Peacebuilding Architecture, and the Global Study report on the implementation of UNSCR 1325 on Women, Peace and Security.

What the HIPPO and AGE reports have most prominently in common is a series of recommendations to bring the UN's peace and security tools in line with the highest purpose of the UN Charter – that is, to maintain international peace in all its dimensions. Notably, due to the inherent weaknesses and limitations of the peacebuilding enterprise and the challenges it faces in building and fostering durable peace, both called for a fundamental shift from peacebuilding to the more holistic and integrated concept of sustaining peace.

Taking note of both reports and their far-reaching recommendations, in April 2016 the UN General Assembly and the Security Council jointly adopted substantively identical resolutions[31] endorsing the concept of sustaining peace, with all its policy and operational implications. Drawing from the AGE report, the resolutions recognized in its preamble that sustaining peace should be 'broadly understood as a goal and a process to build a common vision of a society, ensuring that the needs of all segments of the population are taken into account.... It should flow through all three pillars of the United Nations engagement in all its dimensions (peace, development and human rights).'

In one of the operational paragraphs, the resolutions reaffirm the importance of national ownership and leadership in building peace, 'whereby the responsibility for sustaining peace is broadly shared by the government and all other national stakeholders and *underline* the importance of inclusivity in order to ensure that the needs of all segments of society are taken into account'. The resolutions also underlined that the scale and nature of the challenges of

---

[31] Security Council Resolution 2282 and General Assembly Resolution 70/262.

sustaining peace can be met through strategic and operational partnership between national governments, the UN, and other key stakeholders including international, regional, and sub-regional organizations, international financial institutions, civil society organizations, women's groups, and where relevant, the private sector.

As a member of HIPPO, I struggled with the concept of sustaining peace. This is in part because I was labouring under the assumption that if I understood the pathologies of war, and the complex factors driving and sustaining violence, I would be able to foster and sustain peace. I was wedded to the notion that preventing conflict through peacebuilding prescriptions was the true pathway to peace. Very few of us on the Panel studied peace directly or developed a strategy whereby peace, rather than conflict, was the starting point.

Notwithstanding the above, the HIPPO report underscored that sustaining peace should be the ultimate objective of UN engagements in which inclusive politics and people in their plurality, including women and youth, play the central role. The report called for a number of conceptual and attitudinal shifts in order for peace operations (UN peacekeeping operations and special political missions) to contribute to sustaining peace. The first shift involved acknowledging that countries emerging from conflict 'are not blank pages and their people are not projects'. This means that efforts to sustain peace should be motivated by learning from what still works well in countries emerging from conflict, and to respect that every society, however broken it may appear, has capacities and assets, not just needs and vulnerabilities.

The second shift was the need to challenge the assumptions and values underpinning some of the supply-driven peacebuilding templates and technical approaches and solutions. These are regular staples in the mandates of a number of peace operations, such as strengthening central state institutions, which, as stated above, tend to be captured by domestic ruling elites who are more concerned with power than governance.

The third shift is legitimate politics. This means that lasting peace is not achieved through military means and technical engagement, and that juridical legitimacy derived from elections should be buttressed by performance legitimacy earned through providing everyday basic services to the population and creating an enabling environment to be active participants in decisions affecting their lives.

Through my research at the International Peace Institute, I came to understand that sustaining peace essentially involves intertwining standard conflict resolution and management approaches with the equally important endeavour of strengthening the internal and external factors known to build and foster peace. I believe this dual approach helps strike a balance between the long-term nature of sustaining peace and the short-term imperatives dictated by conflict and its aftermath.[32]

As head of a UN peacebuilding operation in Burundi, understanding these approaches to building peace and the assumptions and contradictions underpinning them is a challenge. This is all the more so when Security Council Resolution mandates indiscriminately espouse them, regardless of the specific context. Thus, a key function of leadership is not just how to interpret these mandates, but also how to carry them out in a context-sensitive way, questioning if needed the assumptions that have informed them.

I shall delve further into these assumptions in the final chapter and explain how, if unheeded, they may unwittingly lead well-meaning peacebuilding actions astray.

Perspectives on leadership

Maintaining or building peace in either a stable or unstable context requires deep understanding of the theory and practice of leadership and the assumptions informing them.

Before assessing the role of leadership in peacebuilding, it is necessary to understand the concept of leadership itself. Views on leadership are as varied and far reaching as the contexts and disciplines within which it is relevant. Our understanding of leadership has also changed over time. Leadership was, in the first three decades of the twentieth century, conceptualized on the basis of control and influence. Thus, personality traits dominated the understanding and practice of leadership, until more process-oriented approaches gained prominence in the 1970s. It thus became clear to many scholars, starting with Burns, who in the late 1970s presented leadership as a process rather than a trait-based phenomenon, that traits manifest themselves as possessions of an individual but leadership is a relationship.[33] From the twentieth century to the early twenty-first century, scholarly discussions on leadership encompassed a variety of views.

The language of leadership in the twenty-first century acquired a new vocabulary: dispersed, devolved, democratic, distributive, collaborative,

---

[32] International Peace Institute (2017).
[33] Grint, K. (2010), *Leadership: A Very Short Introduction*, New York: Oxford University Press, 85.

collective, cooperative, concurrent, coordinated, relational and co-leadership.[34] This evolution points to the fact that, as a practice, leadership is not individualistic but collective. The focus of collective leadership is on dynamic, interactive processes of influence and learning, which can transform organizational structures, norms and work practices.[35] Leadership has thus been increasingly perceived as 'shared' and distributed more than ever before. It now involves multiple actors who adopt roles both formally and informally, and, importantly, share leadership by working collaboratively.

Leadership is not exercised in a vacuum. Rather, it is fundamentally shaped by the situation – circumstances make the leader. The situational approach that gained immense attention among researchers in the mid-twentieth century is context/time-specific, with a focus on environmental factors.[36] Leaders rise and fall as situations change, with a given individual alternating between leading and following.[37] The situation induces action; the leader does not inject leadership but is the instrumental factor through which the situation is brought to a solution.[38] It is the situation that determines the qualities required of the leader and the expectations of how he or she should interact with followers. Thus, a clear understanding of the situation is crucial if leaders are to adopt a suitable leadership style and engage followers in moving toward a common goal.

Situational leaders are able to adapt their leadership style to fit their followers and the situations in which they find themselves. Irrespective of contextual variations, leadership is subject to adaptation and innovation. This means that leaders must also understand that to influence events and affect outcomes, they must be prepared to abandon policy instruments and ideas that no longer work in a new environment. They need to be able to embrace the new and re-assess the old, including previously rejected ideas and means that now might suit the new environment.[39] Inasmuch as adopted leadership approaches are informed by the prevailing situation, if effectively exercised, they will viably alter the context.

[34] Kim, J. (2011), 'Leadership in Context. Lessons from a New Leadership Theory and Current Development Practice', The King's Fund: 6.

[35] Pearce, C. and J. Conger (2003), 'All those years ago: the historical underpinnings of shared leadership' in C. Pearce and J. Conger (eds), *Shared Leadership: Reframing the Hows and Whys of Leadership*, Thousand Oaks, New Delhi: SAGE Publications, 1–18.

[36] Sternberg, J., J. Antonakis and A. Cianciolo (2004), *The Nature of Leadership*, Thousand Oaks, CA: SAGE Publications, 148.

[37] Murphy, A. (1941), 'A Study of the Leadership Process', *American Sociological Review*, 6 (5): 674.

[38] Ibid.

[39] Masciulli, J., M. Molchanov and W. Knight (2009), 'Political Leadership in Context', in J. Masciulli, M. Molchanov and W. Knight (eds), *The Ashgate Research Companion to Political Leadership*, Abingdon: Ashgate Publishing Limited, 3.

In addition, process-based understandings of leadership highlight the important relational aspects of the follower–leader dialectic. Leadership is a process whereby an individual influences a group of individuals to attain a common goal. In its relational form, leadership prioritizes the mutual exchange of influence between the leaders and the followers.[40] Notably, a leader affects and is also affected by followers, meaning leadership is not a one-way process but rather an interactive event.[41] Thus, leaders affect their followers' attitudes, beliefs, demands, and needs, while followers affect the leader's style, qualities, beliefs and motivations. Both, meanwhile, transform the environment and are thoughtfully transformed by their own actions.[42] Roles may even change, with a leader in one situation becoming a follower in another. Leadership creates an environment whereby new knowledge – collective learning – can be co-created rather than just being implemented according to a senior leadership plan.[43]

Grint, in his fourfold analysis, has sought to explain why there has been so little agreement on the definition of leadership, and what exactly leadership is from the perspective of position, person, result, and process perspective, that is: (i) it is where 'leaders' operate that makes them leaders?; (ii) is it who 'leaders' are that makes them leaders?; (iii) is it what 'leaders' achieve that makes them leaders?; and (iv) is it how 'leaders' get things done that makes them leaders?[44] Position, person and result-based approaches that do not prioritize the necessary relations between leaders and followers, as does the process approach, are limited in encompassing the practice of leadership.

Although the above fourfold analysis does not claim universal coverage, it nonetheless largely represents the day-to-day leadership settings in societies and organizations around the world. My leadership, in the context of peacebuilding and peacekeeping in conflict-affected areas, accommodated the four stated elements. For instance, in my capacity as ERSG and head of the integrated peacebuilding Mission in Burundi, I was first and foremost recognized as a leader by my interlocutors or followers on the mere basis of the position I occupied. From a person-based approach, my traits as a leader – patient listening and adaptability – undoubtedly influenced the level of people's mobilization around set goals. On the result perspective, there were clearly some achievements

---

[40] Mbiatem, A. (2016), 'Leadership Emergence and Style: Fidel Castro of Cuba', *Leadership and Developing Societies*, 1 (1): 61.
[41] Masciulli, Molchanov and Knight (2009), 3.
[42] Ibid., 7.
[43] Kim (2011): 6.
[44] Grint (2010), 4.

that I recount in later chapters in areas where I have influence or control as Head of the UN mission. The exchange of influence with my collaborators and stakeholders, respectively at mission level and within the Burundian society, was the process. However, the question here is: how much process leadership was I able to exercise, beyond the mandated short-term peacebuilding objectives in order to create the enabling conditions for the Burundians to build and self-sustain peace? I shall reflect on this question and the dilemmas underpinning it in subsequent chapters and in particular the concluding one.

Different from the other three perspectives, the process-based approach is essentially leadership in practice, and speaks to the nature of leader-followers' relations in a particular context. Current leadership literature identifies two kinds of followers: constructive dissenters and destructive consenters. Constructive dissenters are followers who dissent with the intention of protecting the collective and preventing leaders from making erroneous decisions; destructive consenters are followers who assent to what threatens the collective by acquiescing to leaders' erroneous decisions.[45] To Karl Popper, destructive consenters are generally known as 'yes people', irresponsible followers who provide flattering rather than honest feedback. On the other hand, the constructive dissenters are deemed responsible followers, as they dissociate themselves from the leader's behaviours that are perceived as being detrimental to the organizational goal.[46] These two types of followers are common in many organizations, including the UN system. Regrettably, some staff may find themselves penalised for holding constructive dissenting attitudes, while those with destructive consenting attitudes are often rewarded by the hierarchy.

At the helm of BINUB and MINURCAT respectively, I could not have exercised leadership if I had relied solely on my position and personal traits or attributes. I exercised leadership in both contexts as I interacted with my followers and other stakeholders, trying as much as possible to be mindful of both the positive and negative attitudes they may have. The demands, wants and needs of followers and stakeholders throughout the leadership process largely dictated outcomes, as I pursued the mandate entrusted to the Mission I was leading. Thus, as a leader in peace operation contexts, I exchanged influence with my followers and external interlocutors to achieve the Mission's goals. Process-based leadership is cross-cutting and so more germane to different situations where peace and conflict interact in dynamic ways.

---

[45]   Grint (2010), 133–4.
[46]   See Karl Popper's quotes cited in Grint (2010), 101–2.

Leadership is also perceived as the outcome of dynamic, collective activity, via the building of relationships and networks of influence. It is exercised as much bottom up as top down, with more equal interactions where the person labelled 'leader' behaves in a less hierarchical way than leaders traditionally have behaved.[47] In this sense, leadership is horizontal not vertical. Its non-hierarchical shape makes it inclusive, allowing more people to be involved in the process. Leadership is not limited to the mere interaction between leaders and followers but, importantly, can be transaction-based or transformation-oriented.

Transactional leadership focuses on the exchanges that take place between leaders and followers, with the latter rewarded by the former when they abide by set objectives either at the organizational or societal level. Transformational leadership, by contrast, means that leaders are attentive to the needs and motives of followers, striving to assist them in achieving their fullest potential.[48] While the exchange dimension of transactional leadership can be observed in many settings, there is need to think more of transformational leadership in contexts where social and political harmony has been fragmented, and where peace and conflict issues interact in ways that are hard for outside actors to anticipate and influence.

Thus, transformational leadership is relevant to the social change UN peace missions are expected to help bring about in conflict-affected settings. For example, the nature of leadership within a given UN peace mission is expected to positively affect the host society in which it has been implanted, with the head of mission expected to interact with all levels of local society. This is to say that an inclusive leadership approach at various levels is the best means of pushing for societal transformation. When the appropriate leadership is at the helm of such a mission, it is not constrained by the organizational structures that run it.

From a transformational standpoint, leadership operates to promote the long-term sustainability of the system as well as to help regulate its short-term performance. The effectiveness of leaders is ultimately measured by the sustainability of goals attained, not solely by the short-term results dictated by the organization. Leadership effectiveness is better judged in the context of a more democratic and inclusive system whereby the follower's wants and demands are considered as priorities, and the leader supports them in achieving their central goals. An effective leader chooses the means most likely to reach sought-for ends, but in the process also seeks to embody end-values (equality,

---

[47]   Kim (2011): 6.
[48]   Burns, J. (1978), *Leadership*, New York: Harper & Row.

freedom, justice, human rights, environmental sustainability) and modal-values (honesty, reliability, trustworthiness, fairness). Thus, leadership effectiveness is determined by the actual short- and long-term consequences of leaders' actions.

While transformational leadership is more appropriate to achieving the fundamental and long-term goals of a peace operation, it is important to elaborate on the functional similarities between leaders and managers, particularly in the context of peace missions where the person entrusted with running it is expected to demonstrate both transformational and managerial leadership.

The question therefore is: what distinguishes and connects leadership and management? In order to sustain the role of leadership in organizational or administrative settings, scholars have deemed it necessary to engage in a conceptual differentiation between leadership and management. Some scholars, such as Kotter, argue that the functions of the two are to a certain extent divergent, as the paramount function of management is ensuring order and stability in organizations, whereas leadership aims to generate change and movement.[49] Others, such as Bennis and Nanus, argue that 'managers are people who do things right and leaders are people who do the right thing'.[50]

Although conceptually different, leadership and management overlap, as their respective processes are influential in moving a group of individuals towards a common goal. Leaders and managers share extensive similarities, with effective leaders exhibiting some managerial skills, and good managers displaying leadership qualities.[51] In an organizational setting, therefore, managers more effectively influence behaviours when they show appropriate leadership qualities.[52] To be effective, organizations need to nourish both competent management and skilled leadership.[53] For instance, the UN, which plays a key role in organizational and societal constructs, needs to cumulatively depict efficient management and effective leadership in order to achieve its goals.

---

[49]   Kotter, P. (1990), *A Force for Change: How Leadership Differs from Management*, New York: Free Press.
[50]   Bennis, W. and B. Nanus (1985), *Leaders: The strategies for taking charge*, New York: Harper and Row, 221.
[51]   Hailey, J. (2006), 'NGO Leadership Development, A Review of the Literature', International Training and Research Centre Praxis Paper, 10 July: 4.
[52]   This goes in line with Kotter's argument which connects the prosperity of a given organization to the simultaneous accommodation of leadership and management. Similarly, Northouse sees in organizations with strong management and without leadership, stifling and bureaucratic outcomes. While in organizations with strong leadership and without management, outcomes are meaningless or misdirected.
[53]   Northouse, P. (2013), *Leadership: Theory and Practice*, 6th edition, SAGE Publications.

It is current practice for SRSGs in UN peace operations to operate as both leaders and managers when executing the mandate assigned them by the Security Council. In my case, managerial and leadership skills were instrumental in my peacebuilding and peacekeeping journeys in Central Africa. As head of BINUB and later MINURCAT, I was guided as a manager by the standard operating procedures directing many of the operational activities of both missions. Planning, organizing and controlling various components of the missions, among other management activities, were critical to their success. But management, in my case, could not have been productive in the absence of leadership, as both practices consistently intertwined. I exercised leadership in peace operation contexts by addressing circumstantial challenges that required contextual adaptability rather than through solutions based on standard operating procedures.[54]

Adaptability is a crucial leadership aptitude, as there is no panacea to complex and difficult situations on the ground. Rather, specific problems in peacebuilding or peacekeeping situations require specific solutions. Adaptable leaders recognize changes in task priorities and the necessity of modifying approaches and actions. Cognitive frame changing, the capacity to switch among various frames of reference, is a core skill in adaptive problem solving.[55] Adaptive leadership is ideally suited to driving creative approaches in a complex environment. Such an environment requires effective leaders to lead according to expectations. For example, while I frequently delegated responsibility and authority to my staff to carry out key managerial activities, this did not absolve me from coaching and supporting them in the execution of such activities, or, when the situation required, making the final decision and taking responsibility should things go wrong.

The following section looks at the nexus between peacebuilding and leadership by attempting to answer the question: What does leadership for peacebuilding look like for outside interveners not only entrusted with helping countries recover from conflict, but with laying the foundation for a better peace?[56]

---

[54] Grint (2010), 15.
[55] Holtkamp, M. (2014), 'Leadership Skills and the Role of Adaptability and Creativity in Effective Leadership: A Literature Review Geared toward an Integrative Model', University of Twente: 5.
[56] Olonisakin, F. (2017), 'Towards Re-Conceptualising Leadership for Sustainable Peace', *Leadership and Developing Societies*, 2 (1).

Leadership and peacebuilding: the nexus

Various leaders are always found in conflict situations, often competing for divergent, even incompatible, kinds of peace.[57] Whether possessing formal or informal authority, leaders achieve different goals in different capacities. While a leader is someone who leads, leadership, as mentioned above, is the influencing process of leaders and followers to attain objectives via change.[58] Leaders and followers in a peacebuilding situation all play crucial roles when seeking to attain set goals through genuine cooperation. This cooperation not only helps in objectively defining the problem, but also in agreeing on approaches to address the problem. Leadership should be broadly attentive, as external peacebuilders should not be seen by the local populace as concerned only with the preoccupations of government members or rebel groups. Leadership in conflict-affected contexts is only inclusive when it takes into account the preoccupations of all victims and change leaders, irrespective of gender, age, and culture.

Leadership for peace operates at different levels. It is required to set up peacebuilding blocks, and, among other things, facilitates peace negotiation processes; democratic transition arrangements; the development, implementation and establishment of a secure environment; and international cooperation.[59] When carried out systematically, leadership contributes to the enhancement and attainment of sustainable peace. Based on the fact that the attainment of peace necessitates efforts from different domains and strata of a society, those leading the peacebuilding process are expected to collaborate even beyond their own field of expertise.[60] The convergence of expertise from diverse professional backgrounds is essential, as it exemplifies the central role of leadership whereby leaders respond to followers or societal needs. Harnessing expertise or efforts in peacebuilding contexts is strategic in achieving set goals. Leadership, however, facilitates the effective convergence of relevant expertise in parallel with institutional efficiency. Breaking down the walls (bureaucratic operating procedures) that often separate UN agencies from each other is vital if such leadership is to be embraced.[61]

To John Hume and Jean Monnet, it is absolutely necessary to institutionalize positive changes in society, though institutions should not become goals in

[57] Reychler, L. and A. Stellamans (2005), 'Researching Peacebuilding leadership', 71 (2), kwartaal: 6.
[58] Lussier, R. and C. Achua (2004), *Leadership: Theory, Application and Skill Development*, Mason, Ohio: Thomson/South-western.
[59] Reychler and Stellamans (2005): 8.
[60] Ibid.: 31
[61] Weiss (2012), 199.

themselves.[62] This is because institutions have to adapt to evolving societal contexts characterized by diverse popular needs and demands. 'Nothing is possible without people,' argued Monnet, 'yet nothing is sustainable without institutions.'[63] The distinctive relevance of leadership as carried out by individuals with different competencies in no way undermines the role of institutions. Rather, leadership can more effectively respond to popular preoccupations in contexts where institutions are stable and operate within constitutional frameworks. In contexts where systems are fragmented by conflict, the role of leadership in building peace should also be programmed towards institutional establishment and consolidation. In sum, the effective functioning of institutions facilitates the attainment of peace.

As Olonisakin said: 'There is a critical need to interrogate the leadership factors and dynamics that lead to conflict as well as those that create foundations for peace.'[64] The meticulous identification of leadership gaps in the running of state affairs is an entry point to setting an effective leadership agenda. Bringing a positive response to the predicament naturally demands a clear understanding of the same predicament. Leadership deficiency has often been a root cause of socio-political instabilities in most, if not all, African countries. In Burundi, CAR, or DRC for instance, leadership gaps characterized by unequal distribution of resources have, over the years, emerged and re-emerged as root causes of the conflicts. Loss of trust and erosion of legitimacy are the results of leadership deficits, in turn resulting in unproductive relations between leaders and followers. Sustaining peace necessitates empowering people, and such empowerment can best emanate from transformative leadership. As its name may imply and as discussed above, transformative leadership is a process that transforms people and society as a whole, and involves an exceptional form of influence that motivates followers to achieve more than is normally expected from them. Followers and leaders are inextricably bound together in the transformation process.[65] People-centred leadership is extremely important in conflict-affected states where citizens across different strata of society need to feel a sense of belonging and ownership. This is only possible through collective efforts characterized by genuine cooperation between external peacebuilders and local

---

[62] Monnet, J. (1976), *Mémoires*, Paris: Librairie Arthème Fayard.
[63] OSCE (2003), Mission in Kosovo Newsletter, 3 (1): 4.
[64] Olonisakin, F. (2012), 'Leadership and Peacebuilding in Africa', ALC Working Paper, No. 3, 1 March: 16.
[65] Northouse (2013), 186.

stakeholders. Transformation sustains peace as it works from the inside out, in an inclusive manner, building on people's existing agency and capacity.

Whatever style of leadership is judged best-suited to particular circumstances and objectives, I constantly have to remind myself that peace is like a tree, growing from the bottom up, and that it is individuals and communities that are the custodians of peace. My leadership role was always to unleash the leadership potential of these communities, allowing them to draw on the capacities that kept them alive amidst devastation and build the foundations for peace, including through strengthening formal and informal governance institutions to help ensure the self-sustainability of that peace in the long term.

Leadership for sustaining peace

As detailed above, much has been written about leadership and peace/ peacebuilding. However, relatively little attention has been given to leadership *for* peace. Nor has attention been focused on the paradigm shift needed in the conceptualization and practice of leadership in global diplomacy for peace. The few publications on the market tend to depict leadership as the heroic efforts of well-meaning outsiders, entrusted with prescribing short-term, liberal peacebuilding solutions in contests under stress where the population is judged to be bereft of knowledge, expertise and agency. In these publications, aspirations for peace tend to be depicted in negative terms, largely as the absence or reduction of violence. When consultation takes place locally, it tends to be with the ruling elite, with little – if any – meaningful engagement with leaders at other levels of society. As has been noted, peacebuilding is often confused with building sustainable peace, meaning is often equated with state-centric stability, security and control, rather than unleashing the leadership potential of local actors to manage conflict non-violently, and building the institutions that will allow them to fulfil their needs and aspirations.

Leadership for peace is not about the change that outsiders can bring about in ending violence and building peace. It is about listening meaningfully and without preconceptions to 'we the peoples' – those that UN missions are intended to serve – in order to understand what local actors know and what capabilities they have that can be built upon. It also means suspending certainty and convictions about what should be considered 'right' or 'correct' for a period of time, thus allowing other ways of knowing to be experienced. In essence, this means freeing oneself from prescriptive peacebuilding paradigms and instead striving to create safe and structured spaces for listening and dialogue to take place, for societal trust building to occur, and for broken relations to be mended. Leadership for peace is about facilitating national ownership and leadership, with success not measured by short-term stabilizing results aimed at making outside intervenors look good or relevant, but rather by long-term results achieved by those at the receiving end.

The unfortunate observation to be made here is that the current peacebuilding paradigm continues to favour leadership approaches that contradict many of the nuances expounded above. Despite valiant efforts, I too succumbed, on multiple occasions, to the short-term satisfaction an un-lightened adherence of this paradigm offered. I shall return to this issue of leadership for peace in the final chapter, and in doing so offer some reflections on what I would do differently if I were to serve again as head of a peace operation.

2

An Uncharted Personal Leadership Path

The multiple paths not taken in my life journey could not have predicted the leadership experiences detailed in this book. I did not seek leadership; rather, leadership came looking for me. At the tender age of ten, I was expected to care for my younger siblings – five brothers and three sisters. In accordance with time-honoured cultural traditions which have bestowed on me considerable authority. My siblings, for example, were not allowed to use my first name without prefacing it with 'sidi' (master), aside from the occasional usage of 'brother' by those closest to me in age. The sister born directly after me, with whom there is an age-gap of barely three years, still calls me brother.

As my brothers and sisters grew older, I learned that while I could instil fear, demand respect or promise rewards to get what I wanted, my behaviour did not always have the desired effect. While in my presence there was feigned acquiescence to my commands, in my absence, there was inaction at best, sabotage at worst and even, at times, rebellion. Over the years, as each sibling married and started families of their own, my sphere of influence correspondingly shrunk, and my positional authority at the top of the totem pole, as it is now called, soon gave way to moral authority. For a few years, this enabled me to live up to the responsibilities entrusted to an older brother, helping resolve problems that posed a threat to family cohesion. As my prolonged study absences abroad became more frequent, this authority became tenuous and increasingly difficult to reclaim. Eventually, I confined myself to a facilitative role in which I created safe spaces for problems to be aired. I basically listened with the intention to understand, rather than propose solutions, as had previously been expected of me. Invariably, solutions emerged organically from those most concerned by the problem, or were proposed by another member of the extended family. Little did I know then that the meetings that I had organized in my house and the problem-solving skills I was heuristically developing over these formative years would stand me in good stead later in life as a father, teacher, supervisor, and mediator in situations of protracted conflicts in faraway places.

This chapter presents the contexts and the circumstances in which my leadership awareness, abilities and ambitions evolved, not always in predictable ways, as I assumed higher responsibilities in the United Nations. In essence, it is a broad-brush description of my personal and academic trajectory, and of professional choices I made that transformed my career path from a junior linguist to a senior UN official, retiring after nearly thirty years of service at the rank of Under-Secretary-General.

The first of nine: born into leadership

Having lost a sibling a few months after I was born, the remaining nine of us grew up as children to hardworking parents. One of my father's early jobs was water peddling. Using a rope, bucket and pulley, he would draw drinking water from deep wells situated a few kilometres from our house, pour it into clay jars that were then strapped to the back of his emaciated donkey, and trade the precious liquid throughout the village for items such as grains, fresh eggs or olive oil. In those days, money was a rare commodity. I often accompanied him, riding the donkey on the way to the wells when the jars were empty, and trailing behind him on foot once the jars were full. In summer months, once I was strong enough, I took over these duties so that my father could work as an assistant fisherman to supplement our meagre income. After a few years, we saved enough to buy a second donkey; a bigger, stronger animal that could carry more water.

I vividly remember this early phase of my life because of a treasured possession: a short-wave radio. At the age of eleven, with the little money I earned from my water peddling apprenticeship, and the occasional monetary gifts I received from uncles who had emigrated to the capital city Tunis, I was able to buy a second-hand short-wave Telefunken radio. Having no electricity, I would operate it with the help of an old car battery and listen to the BBC and several other foreign radio stations, including one that broadcast in Arabic from Communist Romania. I became so addicted to the radio's offerings that, unbeknownst to my father, one day I attempted to moor it to the stronger donkey, using a tall stick as a makeshift antenna. As for the battery, I was able to place it in one of the jar's fastenings after making some ingenious modifications. It was not a good idea and almost ended in disaster when the donkey came close to having a fall. I thereupon resigned myself to keeping the radio on my windowsill where it belonged and where the reception was almost always assured. Over the years, that radio became my reliable ticket into the world that lay beyond my village in Tunisia, Chebba.

My mother, an illiterate lady, not unlike many mothers in the neighbourhood, was an extremely hardworking homemaker with a heart as big as the village. She committed her waking hours to delivering her children into the world and caring for us, one after the other. As the oldest brother, she encouraged me to lead by example, in the hope that my siblings would emulate my behaviour. More often than not, this expectation was used to justify the more arduous house chores she would assign to me. She would, however, always offer me a reward; either a big hard-boiled egg or first go at scouring the bottom of a pot where she had deliberately left a small portion of whatever had been cooked, which usually turned out to be far tastier than what was served in the communal bowl we would all dip into at mealtime.

Until I reached the age of twelve, I lived with my parents and my then three siblings in a single-room house. Bathing and cooking took place outside in makeshift thatched sheds. In time, my father sold his water peddling business and became a shopkeeper's assistant, eventually becoming the owner of his own small grocery shop. With a few years of primary schooling, my father became one of the very few literate men in the village to whom its residents could look up to. Over the years, the shop became a destination for those who wanted to dictate letters to loved ones. Once he had entrusted what he had been told to a blank page, my father would seal the letter in a stamped envelope and hand it to the postman, who habitually stopped by his grocery shop to pick up letters and hand over others addressed to people who used his shop as their postal address. Over the years, my father became known as the 'scribe shopkeeper'.

My father was a very strict man who demanded obedience, arguing that God would frown on those who did not dutifully listen to their parents, invariably citing the Koran by heart to justify his dictates. Both parents happily saw me through my primary education, after which I received a certificate printed on expensive paper in elegant Arabic calligraphy. My certificate looked so impressive that my parents thought it should qualify me to become at least an assistant primary school teacher in the village. Indeed, they did not relish the idea of my going to a neighbouring city called Sfax, some sixty kilometres away, for secondary schooling. Our village lacked the amenities for post primary-level education.

I eventually made it to secondary school in Sfax. For the first time in my life, aged twelve, I was separated from my family. I went to live in a small room that I shared with another teenager, Hedi, who had also recently completed primary school. At that age, I could already cook and sew. This was thanks to my mother, who had deliberately trained me to be self-reliant. When things were financially tough for my father, my mother nearly always managed to conjure up money she had saved from selling the eggs from her chicken coop, or from working as a farmhand in the olive groves of wealthy villagers. My mother always behaved as though I was destined to succeed as leader of the pack, notwithstanding my many scholastic failings, which enraged my father.

Once in Sfax, I found it difficult to adapt to big city life and to the student body that came from the surrounding towns. Everything seemed far more complicated – even getting used to walking in the first real pair of shoes I had was a challenge. The shoes, which had laces, seemed too sophisticated compared to the simpler ones I had worn in the village, made out of strips of old tyre rubber sewn together with leather thread. I also had to learn how to manage the small amount of money and food items my mother sent me once a week via the man who drove the daily shuttle bus between Chebba and Sfax. Once a month, my mother would visit me and I would spend the nights nestled against her, often in tears. It was these rare moments of emotional nourishment that helped me develop the habit of being alone without feeling lonely; to be brave and 'tough it out'. Failure in the eyes of my parents was not an option.

There was no electricity in the small room I shared with Hedi. We lived near a prison with high walls and bright lights that shone through the window. After nightfall, we would wrap ourselves in oversized 'barnus' – the common name for a home-made cloak of coarse wool fabric with a hood – and cozy up under the powerful glow of the prison's lights to study. We could not afford to buy all the assigned textbooks for school, so we borrowed them from our classmates, studying them during the night before returning them the following day. During long breaks between classes, I would often sneak out of school and return to the one-room shack we called home to take a nap. Eventually, a teacher took interest in my education and bought me the books I needed for that first year of high school. I was elated. When it rained heavily, the roof of the shack leaked and my roommate and I had to take turns during the night emptying the plastic buckets we strategically placed to catch the water that made its way through invisible cracks in the roof. Though things were difficult, I gradually developed – like others left to their own devices – the capacities of self-reliance and resilience that would stand me in good stead later in life.

I did not do well at secondary school. I often fell sick and at other times was preoccupied with simply surviving. I was not good at maths or science and even had to repeat a year, to the consternation of my father. During the seven years I spent in Sfax, I would return home every summer break to assume my older brother responsibilities. This involved helping my siblings with school homework, with particular attention – on my mother's instruction – to the scholastic needs of my two eldest sisters (the third was still a baby). My mother did not want her daughters to be illiterate as she had been. In fact, she used to admonish me if she felt I was paying more attention to the boys when they reached school age. These back-home duties also involved taking care of the shop for my father during the early morning and afternoon hours, so that he could rest or supervise the construction of a new three-room living quarters.

In the absence of electricity, the rudimentary lighting system at home and at the shed I shared with Hedi began to affect my vision as I studied for qualifying exams at night. Towards the end of my secondary schooling, my French teacher, an expatriate from France, noticed that I was having trouble reading what was on the board, so she made me sit in the front row and bought me my first pair of eye glasses. I was good at languages and received very good grades in both English and French. My English teacher, who was a US Peace Corps Volunteer, also gave me extra attention and encouraged me to continue listening to BBC and Voice of America broadcasts on my beloved German-made radio, that was still in working order.

I finally, with much huffing and puffing, passed the *baccalaureat*.[1] My success was celebrated lavishly at home, with three of the best roosters from my mother's chicken coop sacrificing themselves to be the main dish for our evening meal! By this time, I was eighteen and my father, who liked to brag about the success of his now bespectacled city-boy, encouraged me to go on to university. After receiving a modest government scholarship, I did just that. Due to my proficiency in English, I was directed toward the School of Letters, where I specialized in British and American studies for my BA. From that scholarship I was able to save a little bit of money each month to send home as a symbolic contribution to the new family house that seemed to be taking forever to build. I was determined to succeed, given the harsh life conditions back in the village. In total, I ended up spending seven years at the University of Tunis, culminating in a Master's degree.

My sojourn in the land of Shakespeare

In 1968, halfway through my university studies, I travelled to Britain for one year to teach French at a secondary school – a comprehensive school, as it was called – in the northern London suburb of Muswell Hill. This teaching assignment

---

[1]   In the French-aligned education system, a *baccalaureat* is a diploma awarded at the completion of secondary school, which opens the door to university studies.

was intended as an immersive opportunity to enhance the English language skills I had acquired at university, and was a requirement for obtaining my Bachelor's degree.

It was my first-ever foray into a foreign land. Everything seemed different after I landed in London – from driving on the left-hand side of the road, to the break taken for afternoon tea. In accordance with the terms of the grant I received, I was required to live with a British family to whom I could speak only in English. I ended up living in the upstairs room of a house owned by a widower named Mr Lake, to whom I owe a great deal. Not only did he help me adapt to British life and culture, but he worked patiently on my 'less than perfect' English pronunciation. More importantly, he introduced me to – what seemed to me at the time – the arcane world of classical music.

Mr Lake, an avid opera fan and closet musician, was the proud owner of a shining vintage gramophone and a huge collection of vinyl records. He was keen to introduce me to his musical universe – which mainly comprised classical music – and which, until then, I had considered a cacophony of sounds. Knowing my background, he played scores that he thought contained some familiar rhythms, such as Rimsky-Korsakov's *Scheherazade* and Tchaikovsky's *The Nutcracker*. He was not deterred by my polite disinterest and continued playing pieces whenever I shared a meal with him or was upstairs in my room. For months on end, Mr Lake chiselled away patiently at my musical ear with the persistence of water cascading on marble. Finally, he detected an indentation in my musical proclivities and so introduced me to other classical gems such as Vivaldi's *The Four Seasons*. Suffice to say, to this day these pieces remain my favourite background music.

On the weekends, in order to supplement the meagre grant that I had been given to cover my room and board, I studied to be a French-language tour guide. The only specialty available when I signed up for classes was British history through the lens of old London pubs and churches! After intensive after-school studying and on-the-job training with a seasoned professional guide, I became a certified assistant tour guide, occasionally subbing for the principal one when she was absent. It was an odd occupation for a Muslim who did not drink and who had never visited a Christian prayer house before. The job usually entailed picking up from various hotels groups of French children who had crossed the channel for a weekend of sightseeing and shopping. I finished late on Sundays, exhausted but elated with the heavy load of coins offered to me as tips from satisfied visitors, invariably amused by a non-Frenchman chronicling in French historic characters, facts and figures from bygones eras in British history.

After my year in London, I returned to Tunisia with a newly minted British accent. This earned me the admiration of my fellow third-year university students, who ended up electing me as President of the English language club. They felt I had acquired good organizational skills, in additional to useful contacts I cultivated with the local British Council office.

My accidental journey to America and back

A year after I obtained my Bachelor's degree in British and American studies from the University of Tunis, I decided to undertake a Master's degree at the same university. This involved coursework, field trips and a thesis. As a subject for my dissertation, I chose to study existing literature on the plight of Native American Indians. In 1972, as part of an American student exchange programme, I was fortunate to receive a modest scholarship enabling me to travel to the United States and visit the Tule River Indian Reservation in California. The visit deeply troubled me due to the poor living conditions of its occupants. Even so, it enabled me to understand the corrosive transformation of a minority Indian tribe following its isolation on a reservation, all under the guise of independence and cultural preservation. One book that had a profound impact on me was Dee Brown's seminal 1971 work *Bury My Heart at Wounded Knee*, which had become well known for presenting the Native American side of the 'Indian Wars'. It remains a compelling story to this day.

In 1973, upon completion of my thesis, I received my Master's degree, after which I was hired by the American Cultural Centre in Tunis as a Programme Assistant to the American Cultural Attaché. My job entailed organizing events in Tunis and other cities across the country that showcased American culture and history through art exhibits, movies, book fairs and lectures. This road show opened my eyes to the realities of my own country, outside of the capital city Tunis. I was disheartened by the abject poverty most people living in the hinterland seemed to be locked into.

Late in 1974, the US Cultural Attaché approached me and said: 'There is a scholarship that has been awarded to a gentleman to do a Master's degree and possibly a PhD in linguistics in the United States, but, due to circumstances beyond his control, he can no longer travel. Are you interested?' I responded almost immediately by saying: 'I'll take the scholarship! But what is linguistics?' I was given the choice between the University of Texas in Austin and Georgetown University in Washington DC. I opted for the latter.

In 1977, after two challenging years adapting to a new discipline, new study habits, a competitive student life, and teaching Arabic on the side, I received my Master of Science in Linguistics. A few months later, I was awarded a supplementary scholarship to undertake a PhD in Socio-Linguistics at Georgetown. It was during this phase of my academic journey that I met my future wife, Lisa, in one of the Linguistics classes taught by an Iraqi Jesuit professor, Fr. Solomon I. Sara. After he heard word that we were considering marriage, he advised against it – he felt that a non-practising Catholic and a non-practising Muslim did not belong together. He then handed me a copy of the catechism so that I would 'know what I was getting into'. In 1978, after finishing my PhD, Lisa and I were married in a small Georgetown University chapel in a civil, ecumenical ceremony, officiated by the very same Jesuit professor who had advised against our matrimony.

My marriage to Lisa would not have been possible for me without the explicit blessing of my parents. After many valiant but unsuccessful attempts to find me a Tunisian bride who would tether me to the country so that I could look after my siblings, my parents finally relented and agreed to bless my marriage. Two major factors contributed to their decision. The first was what my father had allegedly been told after being turned down by a wealthy village family whose daughter's hand he had asked for on my behalf: that our partnership would not work as I might not even be able to afford to buy the expensive shoes she was accustomed to wearing. Even if this response attributed to the family were true, I do not believe the young lady, whom I knew and mentored, shared such sentiments.

The second factor was my wife's willingness to learn Tunisian Arabic. She also consented to visit the village where I had lived before we married, so she could see where I came from and what I would be involved in as the oldest brother. She also promised that our children would be taught Tunisian Arabic, so that they could interact with my parents without interpretation.

Sadly, my father, who had been sick for some time, passed away before he could enjoy a full conversation with my firstborn, Nura. He had, however, happily exchanged a few Arabic words with her when she was just short of three years old. My father never met my second and last daughter, Alia, who, like her sister, turned out to be fluent in the Tunisian dialect, to the immense joy of my mother.

In accordance with the terms of the Fulbright scholarship I had been awarded, I was obligated to return to Tunisia upon graduation, which I did a few months after Lisa and I were married. Shortly after settling in Tunis, I started teaching as an Assistant Professor of Linguistics at the Bourguiba Institute of Modern

Languages.[2] However, as my degree was from a university not yet recognized by the then Tunisian Ministry of Higher Education, (however prestigious it may have been in the US), it took nearly a year before the Ministry could issue the Tunisian equivalency certificate of my US-acquired PhD. Without such a certificate, I received no salary. In order to pay for the flat we rented and to make ends meet, I had to borrow money and teach at a secondary school a few hours a week. It was a difficult year. Whilst we waited for our financial situation to improve, my wife Lisa returned to the US and her former job with the Linguistic Society of America in Washington, DC.

Making it to the green glass tower: the United Nations

A few months after returning to the US, Lisa wrote to me: 'You are there and I am here; one of us is in the wrong place.' Convinced I could be of better service to my family and my country if I had a decent job elsewhere, she set out to find me a position in the US. Sure enough, a few months later, she forwarded me a job announcement from the United Nations looking for a Programme Officer to head their Language Training Programme. Lisa believed I was uniquely qualified for the job and encouraged me to apply, which I did.

On 27 June 1981, after a series of interviews and multiple delays, I joined the UN as the Head of the Language Training Programme at its headquarters[3] in New York. It was a dream come true! In the past, when I was at Tunis airport waiting for my flights, I would notice with envy the international civil servants who visited my country, breezing through the airport check points waving their blue United Nations Laissez Passer – the UN passport – as if it were a magic wand. It granted them, I was told, privileges and immunities not afforded citizens of any nation. Those observations planted the seeds for my yearning that one day I too would be working in an international organization created 'to reaffirm faith in fundamental human rights, in the dignity and worth of the human person, in the equal rights of men and women and of nations large and small', and whose intent was 'to promote social progress and better standards of life in larger freedom.'[4] Little did

[2]   The Bourguiba Institute of Modern Languages was named after the first President of Tunisia, Habib Bourguiba.
[3]   The Language Training Programme was created to afford UN staff members the opportunity to learn one of the six official languages of the United Nations.
[4]   Charter of the United Nations and the Statute of the International Court of Justice, San Francisco, 1945: 2.

I know that those ideals, as enshrined in the UN Charter, would shape my aspirations and guide my path from linguistics to peace and security

After six years as the Head of Language Training and with one promotion under my belt, I realized that my career prospects in the field of languages were limited – I could not move laterally to become a translator or interpreter as both required hands-on experience and had stringent qualifying exams. Thus, I began looking for opportunities to branch out into other professional sectors where my language skills and training experience could be put to good use.

Soon, opportunities to take professional development training in supervision and management presented themselves. I took full advantage by signing up for as many courses as I was allowed (or could afford) to take, both inside and outside the UN. These courses, which took place mostly after working hours, ranged from strategic planning and team building, to budgeting, to English drafting and problem solving and active listening. Several of these courses awarded qualifying certificates that enabled me, as the months went by, to replace an external consultant and conduct supervision training sessions in the UN staff development programme. At the same time, I was overseeing the language programme part time.

One learning experience that was particularly transformational for me was a week-long executive course on leading change in complex organizations I took in June 1990 at MIT Sloan School of Management. It was led by Professor Edgar Schein, an eminent practitioner in organizational development. I owed this opportunity to Kofi Annan, a graduate of the School, who, as UN Assistant Secretary-General for Human Resources at the time, authorized payment of the hefty course fee. I understood that Mr Annan felt that he could rely on me as an agent of change in the context of the personnel management reforms he had embarked on. Little could I imagine at the time that Annan would go on to become the seventh UN Secretary-General, and that he would appoint me sixteen years later as his Executive Representative and head of the UN Integrated Peacebuilding Office in Burundi (BINUB). Chapter 4 describes the circumstances of my appointment and the triumphs and travails of my three-year experience in Burundi as a senior UN envoy.

After dabbling in staff training and development for a year or so, I was promoted to Senior Officer and, in 1989, became Deputy to the Chief of the UN Secretariat Training and Examination Service. My eighteen-month-long stint at the Training Service connected me to UN staff members working at various levels and exercising different functions in diverse fields. Those who interested me the most and who, at my request, gave me precious time to explain their work, were the staff working in United Nations Secretariat departments and units supporting the implementation of the international organization's work in peace and security. They helped put into context the UN spokesperson briefings I consumed daily, the Secretary-General's annual reports on the work of the UN, and the copious summary records of Security Council open thematic debates.

As my interest in global peace and security matters developed over time – largely as a result of my voracious readings on the subject matter and attendance of Security Council public meetings – I set out to take short courses, as well as undertake hands-on professional training, in order to acquire the knowledge and skills that enabled my colleagues to excel in their work as political affairs officers. The courses included introductory lectures in diplomacy and workshops on conflict resolution, mediation, negotiation, listening and drafting skills. Using mostly my own resources, I engaged in these professional development experiences for almost a year while looking for opportunities that would afford me a closer inspection of, or step toward, the UN's work on peace and security, either at headquarters or in the field.

From linguistics to politics via Cambodia and Zaire

In April 1992, just such an opportunity knocked on my door. Behrooz Sadry, a veteran UN staffer, asked me to be his Special Assistant following his appointment a month earlier as Deputy Special Representative of the Secretary-General (DSRSG) for Cambodia[5] and Deputy Head of the United Nations Transitional Authority in Cambodia (UNTAC),[6] which had been established by the Security Council two months earlier. I had known Behrooz when he was Director of the Field Operations Division, and previously as Director of Personnel Administration, to whom the Training and Examination Service – of which I was deputy chief – reported. He felt that my management and organizational skills would be useful in setting up and managing the work of his new front office within UNTAC.

In addition to supervising the administration and logistical entities of UNTAC, Behrooz was entrusted with other substantive responsibilities, including political and peacebuilding responsibilities he would carry out on

---

[5] United Nations (2003), 'Secretary-General Appoints Behrooz Sadry of Iran Deputy Special Representative for Democratic Republic of Congo', SG/A/832-AFR/564, 18 February.
[6] United Nations Transitional Authority in Cambodia. Available online: https://en.wikipedia.org/wiki/United_Nations_Transitional_Authority_in_Cambodia (accessed 2 February 2018).

behalf of the head of the Mission, Yasushi Akashi. With over 21,000 military and civilian staff from thirty nations, UNTAC was the second-largest peacekeeping mission ever deployed by the United Nations (after the one in the Democratic Republic of Congo). It was an unusual mission in the sense that it had taken over the administration of an independent country while organizing and running elections, as opposed to monitoring and supervising them.[7]

Cambodia was my first peace operation mission. While my responsibilities were primarily administrative and managerial, I was able, on behalf of the DSRSG, to participate in the planning and implementation of programmes related to the training of the judiciary, the police and public defenders. A rather obscure part of my job was to oversee the work of two community liaison officers (one international and one Cambodian) whose duty it was to convey – through the proper chains of command structures – complaints or grievances they would receive from individuals or groups of Cambodians who felt harmed by the behaviour of UNTAC personnel, be they military or civilian.

This experience opened my eyes to how Cambodian political elites vied for power, and more broadly to the relative merits and limitations of elections in legitimizing how such power is acquired and exercised. I also saw up close the harm caused to a field mission's reputation when internal policy discord among its senior leadership becomes public, as well as what happens when a mission takes its relevance for granted and fails to develop contingency plans in a context where uncertainty and change are the only constants. More importantly, I witnessed first-hand the corrosive impact that peacekeeping operations can have on local communities through the injection of money and material goods, and through the obtrusive presence of UN-emblazoned, white cars which often betrayed the (comparatively) ostentatious living habits exhibited by many peacekeepers.

After nearly eighteen months in Cambodia, I returned to UN headquarters feeling enriched and, at the same time, humbled by the knowledge of what it would take to help restore a broken country traumatized by a three-year genocide in which some 1.5 to 3 million Cambodians (or 25 per cent of the population) were mercilessly massacred by their own leaders.

In September 1993, I was appointed as Principal Officer in the office of the Under-Secretary-General for Political Affairs, Marrack I. Goulding, who, in March of that year, had been appointed to head the Department of Political Affairs (DPA). The DPA had been created the previous year by the then

---

[7] Jensen, D. and S. Lonergan (2012), *Assessing and Restoring Natural Resources in Post-Conflict Peacebuilding*, USA and Canada: Earthscan.

Secretary-General Boutros Boutros-Ghali at a time when the organization was grappling with multiple crises raging in the aftermath of the Cold War.

On a visit to Cambodia when he was still in charge of the Department of Peacekeeping Operations, and on Behrooz Sadry's recommendation, Goulding had approached me for the job. An avid ornithologist who was never happier than when in the field with a pair of binoculars around his neck, he explained what the job entailed while we rode on a UN patrol boat along the Mekong River.[8] I could not have been happier when I learned that, in addition to helping him address the multitude of internal management reforms he would be embarking on, I would get to see the analyses and cables prepared by the political divisions regarding the various issues on DPA's front and back burners. More importantly, I would get to sit in on confidential meetings dealing with such issues and partake in occasional field missions to countries under the UN's watch list.

Goulding, or MIG as we endearingly called him (after his initials), was a seasoned diplomat and a proficient Arabic speaker. He and I got along quite well, despite his being a combative, demanding man, who did not suffer fools easily. It was not by accident that his 2003 book was titled *Peacemonger*.[9] Nonetheless, he was brilliant at his job and presided over the expansion of DPA with brio and ruthless efficiency. I learned a great deal from him, including how to think strategically and anticipate developments in the ever-evolving country situations we were following. I also learned how to communicate compelling ideas in simple language, and, even more importantly, how to draft with brevity and impact. The cables and other messages he would send to various UN envoys in the field or to government dignitaries were a feast to my eager eyes and thirsty brain, both for their style and substance.

With his tenure approaching its end, and staying true to his word, MIG allowed me to return to the field after three years, helping him put in place the various management structures, processes, and competencies that would give DPA its distinctive identity as the UN focal point for peacemaking, preventive diplomacy and electoral assistance.

In an interview[10] given to the Yale Oral history project in 1998 – shortly after he left the UN – Goulding drew a number of lessons from the United Nations

---

[8] Facts and Details, Mekong River Cambodia. Available online: http://factsanddetails.com/southeast-asia/Cambodia/sub5_2f/entry-3505.html (accessed 5 March 2018).
[9] The book was an insider's account of UN successes and failures in addressing global peace and security challenges of the time.
[10] Yale-UN Oral History, Sir Marrack Goulding interviewed by James S. Sutterlin, 30 June 1998, Oxford, England.

peacekeeping experience in Cambodia. These came in handy for me when, in 2010, I took the helm of a much smaller but no less complex peacekeeping operation. One of the lessons he drew is that UN officials in the field need to keep headquarters entities regularly informed about the evolving situation on the ground if they wish to lead nimbly from below, without undue interference or second guessing by these central entities. Another lesson is the need to revisit a peace agreement when the implementation of such an agreement hits an impasse.

In October 1996, just a few months before his own term came to an end, Secretary-General Boutros-Ghali appointed Raymond Chretien – a former Africa hand and Canada's Ambassador to the United States at the time – as his Special Envoy for the troubled Great Lakes Region of Africa,[11] with a particular focus on Zaire (now the Democratic Republic of Congo). I was designated to accompany Ambassador Chretien as his Senior Political Advisor.

At the time, Zaire was on the brink of civil war. President Mobutu Sese Seko's thirty-one-year-long regime was crumbling amidst ongoing attacks by rival armed factions on refugee camps in the eastern part of the country, where nearly 1 million Hutus fleeing the 1994 Rwandan genocide had found refuge. The tension had been palpable when I visited the country in June 1996 as part of a DPA-led electoral assessment mission, which had previously been requested by the embattled Zairean government in a desperate attempt to save itself through the ballot box. It was this trip that had led to me being recommended for the slot of DPA's senior representative on Chretien's team. My job was to provide political advice and ensure timely reporting to UN headquarters regarding the deteriorating situation in the country, the efforts of Chretien's office, and his evolving assessment on the need for a UN peacekeeping mission in Zaire, which at the time was being contemplated by the Security Council as a possible response to the deteriorating situation.

Thanks to the private jet and first-class logistical support the Canadian government had put at Chretien's disposal, we were able to travel in comfort and security throughout the region, as well as to southern France, where Mobutu, enfeebled by cancer, had found refuge in his luxurious villa near Nice.[12] The technology on the plane enabled us to work non-stop.

---

[11] United Nations (1996), 'Secretary-General Appoints Raymond Chretien of Canada as Special Envoy to Great Lakes Region', SG/A/624/Rev.1, 30 October.

[12] *The Irish Times* (1996), 'Mobutu Flies to Villa in South in France', 5 November. Available online: https://www.irishtimes.com/news/mobutu-flies-to-villa-in-south-in-france-1.102697 (accessed 28 February 2018).

The month-long mission was an intense learning experience for me on the politics, dramas and turmoil the Rwandan genocide had unleashed throughout the Great Lakes region. The information in the cables we had been receiving from the field paled in comparison with what we both heard and witnessed first-hand during the mission.

In early December 1996, Chretien's mission came to an end after he delivered his findings and recommendations to Boutros-Ghali and, subsequently, the Security Council. It was my first experience helping prepare a briefing to the Secretary-General and an address to the Council. Once again, what I had learned from MIG on the art and craft of writing for impact stood me in good stead, as I was able to focus on what listeners needed to hear in order to facilitate an informed decision.

The situation in the Great Lakes region continued to deteriorate rapidly and, shortly after his appointment as Secretary-General, Kofi Annan appointed veteran Algerian diplomat Mohamed Sahnoun as the Special Representative to the region for the UN-OAU (Organisation of African Unity – since renamed the African Union).[13] By this time, I had moved laterally to become the Deputy Director of the Africa II Division in DPA, monitoring and supporting UN peace and security portfolios in North, West and Central Africa.

In light of my experience with Chretien, the knowledge I had acquired of the Great Lakes, and the contacts I had established in the region, I was asked to join Sahnoun and his small team as Senior Political Advisor. By the time we landed in Zaire, the situation had further worsened. The armed rebellion against what remained of the Mobutu regime, led by Laurent-Desire Kabila (the father of Joseph Kabila who, until recently was the DRC President), had advanced considerably, with the humanitarian situation increasingly dire. It was for this reason that we had to shuttle ceaselessly (in an austere, antiquated UN propeller aircraft) between key national and regional leaders, attempting to engineer a temporary ceasefire and help create space for a less violent, negotiated transition.

During this period, I got to know and admire the work of other senior UN officials working on the ground in tandem with Sahnoun, such as the late Sergio Vieira de Mello, who at the time was the Great Lakes Region Personal Envoy of the High Commissioner for Refugees.[14] Witnessing Sahnoun engage with various

---

[13]   United Nations (1997), 'Mohamed Sahnoun of Algeria Nominated UN/OAU Special Representative for Great Lakes Region of Africa', SG/A/626, 27 January.

[14]   *The Guardian* (2003), 'Sergio Vieira de Mello High-flying UN Diplomat who Fought for Peace in Global Trouble Spots across Three Decades', 20 August. Available online: https://www.theguardian.com/news/2003/aug/20/guardianobituaries.brazil (accessed 20 February 2018).

heads of state in the region – for example, maintaining his composure while holding tense discussions with a triumphalist Kabila determined to advance on Kinshasa – was the most rewarding professional lesson in the art of diplomacy I could have hoped for. It taught me how to advocate for what you believe in without losing access to those whose cooperation is critical to advancing a cause that may not speak to their interests. It also gave me insight into understanding the world view of adversaries, however unsavoury or abject their behaviour may be.

On 17 May 1997, the Zaire conflict came to a relatively peaceful end when an enfeebled Mobutu signed his resignation papers on a South African ship under the close watch of Nelson Mandela[15] and Sahnoun, who read the final joint communiqué, outlining the various steps to be taken to ensure a peaceful post-Mobutu transition.[16] Three months prior to that, in February, I had received a call from Kieran Prendergast – who had taken over the leadership of DPA from Goulding – informing me that Kofi Annan had approved my appointment as the new Director of the Africa II division of DPA (covering North, Central and West African sub-regions). A few weeks later, having ensured that Sahnoun received a capable replacement to support him, I returned to New York to assume my new functions.

From political affairs to development cooperation via the Caribbean

After nearly seven years at the helm of DPA's Africa II Division, I came to the realization that mediation, negotiation and other political means for preventing and resolving violent conflict cannot alone create the conditions of self-sustaining peace. Over the years, as head of the Division, I developed the view that I still hold to this day – that peace is not merely the absence of violence, but the prevalence of processes, mechanisms and structures enabling people to meet their basic human needs in dignity, to reach out to others without fear, and to pursue their legitimate aspirations without coercion, with justice, and in security. I also believed – and still do – that the response to human development deficits is not wealth creation or economic growth, but the provision of justice. Seen through this lens, the pursuit of peace and security is as much about politics as

---

[15]   *Los Angeles Times* (1997), 'Zaire Peace Drive a Coup for Mandela', 9 May. Available online: https://www.latimes.com/archives/la-xpm-1997-05-09-mn-57117-story.html (accessed 20 February 2018).
[16]   https://www.youtube.com/watch?v=Bhvnobaaye.

about governance and development. However, in a department where conflict prevention was perceived solely as a peace and security matter, neither I nor any of my colleagues in the Division were equipped to translate this understanding into policies.

In order to promote this approach in the field, a senior colleague in the UN Development Programme (UNDP) and I – with the blessing of our respective principals and the support of key donors – launched a joint initiative in 2004 to enable the political and development arms of the UN to recruit and deploy peace and development advisors to the field. These advisors would work closely with UN Resident Coordinators in countries under stress to build, through development programmes, national capacities for conflict prevention[17] (as of 2019, forty-nine such advisors are deployed in the field).

Earlier that year, missing the field and wanting to experience myself what it meant to promote such an approach to prevention and peace, I sat the UN system-wide qualifying examination for the post of UN Resident Coordinator (RC). The RC is the designated representative of the Secretary-General and the Coordinator of UN operational activities in the country of assignment. The stringent, intense, three-day assessment tested my knowledge of the UN system, my field experience and – most importantly – my leadership acumen and endurance. The RC assessment contained plausible and complex humanitarian, political, development and security scenarios, which I, as a team leader, was called upon to address. This was done under the watchful eyes of seasoned examiners, representing various UN agencies. These scenarios ranged from being summoned to the office of an irate Prime Minister venting his frustration at the slow delivery of humanitarian assistance, to being greeted by an unexpected media posse, cameras at the ready, egging you to take a stand on a sensitive internal political issue.

I was the first official from a political department to sit for this exam with no development or economic background, let alone the requisite field experience. Given I had twice before migrated to different occupational groups, as well as having worked at headquarters with numerous UN agencies, funds and programmes, I was determined to make one more occupational shift before going into retirement.

I must confess, I would not have taken this major career switch from political affairs to development cooperation at the age of fifty-seven without the blessing

---

[17]   United Nations Development Programme (2016), 'Issue Brief, Peace and Development Advisors', Joint UNDP-DPA Programme on Building National Capacities for Conflict Prevention.

of my boss, Prendergast, and the financial support of DPA. Luckily, I passed the exam and my name was added to the future deployment roster of eligible RCs. After multiple false starts, I was finally appointed as Resident Coordinator and Humanitarian Coordinator in Guyana, as well as UNDP Resident Representative. Guyana was neither my choice nor that of others within the UN, who considered me a better fit for other countries. After several countries had turned me down, however, I embraced Guyana as my next destination.

I landed in Guyana in late December 2004. The country was experiencing a complex humanitarian emergency as a result of devastating rains and floods it had not known for over a century. In addition, this multi-ethnic country of fewer than 1 million people were bracing themselves for potentially violent general elections that were due to take place in 2006.

I was relieved to find a strong Peace and Development Advisory team in place. They were a tremendous help to me on the political and governance front while I attended to the urgent humanitarian situation, of which I had no prior experience. The team supported my national counterparts and I in designing and implementing the various processes and structures that would make it possible for the Guyanese to resolve conflicts non-violently, and to lay the foundations for peaceful and transparent polls – the first in over a decade.[18]

Guyana had multiple leadership challenges in store for me, all of which tested the responsibilities entrusted to me as Resident and Humanitarian Coordinator. However, with the help of a good country team, we were able to overcome these obstacles. This can be attested to by the unprecedented mobilization of resources through various flash appeals[19] addressing the disastrous consequences of the floods.

The national conversations we spent more than a year organizing had a tremendous impact. They calmed the nerves of many during times of national uncertainty and stress, and steered Guyanese of different ethnic and religious stripes to settle their differences through non-violent means both before and during the elections. We were even able to innovate during this tense period. One such innovation was a unique partnership between UNDP and the Guyanese private sector that enabled the mobilization of local and regional entrepreneurs in creating economic incentives for peace and stability.

---

[18] GUYANA. A case study prepared by the Social Cohesion Programme (UNDP Guyana) for the UNDESA expert meeting on dialogue, New York, 21–3 November 2005.
[19] European Union, Emergency Humanitarian Aid Decision. Available online: https://ec.europa.eu/echo/files/funding/decisions/2005/dec_guyana_01000_en.pdf (accessed 28 February 2018).

I was expecting Guyana to be my last assignment before retiring. Little I know that Secretary-General Annan, in the last few months of his term, had a different plan in mind for me. In 2006, one year shy of my sixtieth birthday, he appointed me his Deputy Special Representative in Burundi.[20] My leadership experiences in Burundi, a country far more wounded than Guyana, are the subject of Chapters 3 and 4 of this book.

In 2010, after my three-year assignment in Burundi, Annan's successor, Ban Ki-Moon, appointed me his Special Representative for Chad and the Central African Republic, and the head of the embattled peacekeeping mission, MINURCAT. This experience, with its share of triumphs and travails, is detailed in Chapters 5 and 6.

Concluding thoughts

In concluding this chapter, I wish to share the two main lessons I have learned from my personal and professional journey, and that have informed the choices I made in responding to the leadership challenges outlined in Chapters 4 and 6.

The first is that if you are a lifelong learner you will be better prepared to recognize and seize opportunities when they arise. From my experience, luck is earned rather than given, and once you have it, you cannot take it for granted. You must nurture it with humility. Most of the seemingly fortuitous miracles that dotted my life journey were either the result of deliberate choices or brought closer to my peripheral vision by those who were witness to my efforts to be better and do better. In my language, we say that those who try and succeed get two points, and those who genuinely try and do not succeed still get one point. I was raised in a culture where what is prized is effort and the ambition to serve, not necessarily the reward that may or may not await you at the end of the journey.

The second lesson is that leadership is defined not by the positional authority or power afforded you at birth or – deservedly or not – conferred upon you. Rather, leadership is defined by what you do *with* others, not *for* others; by the actions you take to unleash others' potential to lead; by the conscious effort to ensure that what you say and do does not unwittingly jeopardize such potential, or negatively impact the personal and professional wellbeing of those who may look up to or rely upon you.

---

[20] United Nations (2006), 'Secretary-General Appoints Youssef Mahmoud of Tunisia as Deputy Special Representative for Burundi', SG/A/1021-BIO/3809, 22 September.

As such, the most valuable life skill I learned from the professional training courses I took was active listening. Listening in this sense is the simple but hard-to-acquire act of lending a genuine ear to someone with the intent of understanding, as opposed to attempting to solve their problem or putting across your own point of view, however valid it might be. In these training courses, I was taught how to suspend certainties when faced with familiar or unfamiliar realities. After years of practice, and as I assumed greater responsibilities, I began to appreciate the value of this precious skill. I felt increasingly at ease with subjects I did not understand or situations I could not influence or control, and I was able to accept that often they were not mine to address alone. Through active listening, I was also able to build trust where none had previously existed, and to create safe and structured spaces for others to hear themselves in my presence without being judged. 'Listening,' Sahnoun used to tell me, 'is a lifelong practice; stop practising it and you will stop learning.' I did not fully understand the depth of his words until I faced my own leadership challenges and began learning the art and craft of mediation in intractable conflicts.

I will refer back to this autobiographical sketch in the last chapter of this book, where I further reflect on these lessons and how they have guided my actions as I endeavoured – not always with success – to support countries in recovering their self-organizing capacities for restoring and sustaining peace.

3

Burundi: A Wounded Puzzle

In September 2006, I was appointed by then Secretary-General Kofi Annan as his Deputy Special Representative (DSRSG) for Burundi, just as the UN peacekeeping mission (ONUB) there, which had been in operation for two years, was coming to a close. A few months later, on January 2007, I became Executive Representative of the Secretary-General and head of a successor presence called the UN Integrated Office in Burundi, known by its French acronym (BINUB). Soon after my appointment as DSRSG, I started reading as much as I could about the country and its tortuous and violent history, with which I had become somewhat familiar when serving as Director in the UN Department of Political Affairs covering central and western Africa. While I knew I was embarking on a challenging mission, I had no idea of the extent to which the multi-layered Burundian context would exhaust the limits of my leadership mettle, something I thought I had honed during my previous, similarly challenging, posting in Guyana. The following chapter details the nature of these challenges and my efforts to address them in the course of implementing the mandate entrusted to BINUB by the Security Council. The purpose of this one is to set the context.

Burundi's protracted civil war had resulted in deep divisions among its population along political and ethnic lines. Relations had been destroyed and avenues for dialogue narrowed, making the establishment of a solid peace foundation difficult. The lingering, visceral mistrust among former enemies now sharing power under a new constitution and weak governance institutions had largely shaped the difficult situation prevailing in Burundi prior to my arrival in early October 2006. Sadly, it is a situation that continues to this day.

Known to be a peaceful country during its pre-colonial history, Burundi became socio-politically divided under colonial rule. The division took a violent turn after independence, which was largely fuelled by overambitious political and military elites. Exclusive governance and the longstanding divide between the majority Hutu and the minority Tutsi segments of the population ignited like dry tinder in 1993 following the assassination of the first-ever democratically elected Hutu President, Melchior Ndadaye. A decade-long, brutal civil war ensued for the remainder of the twentieth century and continued sporadically into the early years of the twenty-first, despite the regionally brokered Peace and Reconciliation Agreement signed in Arusha, Tanzania in 2000.

The processes of securing peace in Burundi during conflict and post-conflict periods have known many reversals. This is unsurprising given the multifaceted problems afflicting the country and the deep enmities among key national actors determined to achieve politically what they could not do through violent confrontations. Successive UN and AU missions in Burundi found it difficult to navigate this tense political atmosphere in which the incumbent government and opposition were highly suspicious of one another, engaging in divisive politics that paralysed governance institutions. Despite a decrease in armed hostilities that could be observed during the power-sharing arrangement put in place following the signing of the Arusha Agreement, the platform for peacebuilding was far from clear.

While preparing for my deployment, two questions troubled me most: first, why did a conflict that included inter-ethnic massacres and cost the lives of over 300,000 people? And, second, why, after the signing of a peace agreement and substantive international support peaceful, pre-colonial country descend, after independence, into a decade-long violent, was Burundi continuing to experience a prolonged period of no war and no peace, with intermittent conflicts that did not always devolve into violence? In this chapter, I hope to provide some insights that might help provide answers to such questions. This is done in the full knowledge that any such insights may be subject to over-simplification.

A peaceful and resilient, pre-colonial Burundi

In contrast with a good number of sub-Saharan African countries, pre-colonial Burundi, a land-locked country almost the size of Belgium, was a monarchy. From the seventeenth century until the early years of the twentieth, Burundi as a kingdom expanded in size by annexing smaller neighbours, competing with Rwanda as it did so. The growth was particularly remarkable during the reign of King Ntare IV Rutaganzwa Rugamba,[1] who ruled the country from about 1796

---

[1]   History of Burundi#Kingdom of Burundi (1680–1966).

to 1850 and saw the kingdom double in size.[2] That of his successor Mwezi Gisabo (1850 to 1908)[3] was also foundational in the statebuilding process.

The country's inhabitants, currently a little over 11 million, hailed from three ethnic groups – Hutu (85 per cent), Tutsi (14 per cent) and Twa (1 per cent).[4] Uniquely, all three groups speak, to this day, the same language (Kirundi), share a common culture and Burundian identity, look up to a traditional common monarchy, and for centuries lived peacefully alongside each other, occupying the same hills and communes. Although some physical distinctions have been used to differentiate members of each group, significant levels of inter-ethnic marriage progressively rendered the physical predictor of ethnic identity imperfect.[5] The negligible degree of ethnic discrimination that did exist under the monarchical system did not undermine peace during the pre-colonial period, with stability prevailing despite the fact that monarchs largely originated from the minority Tutsi ethnic group.

Cultural differences in the past were linked to production skills: Hutu were associated with agriculture, Tutsi with cattle, and Twa with hunting.[6] Before the arrival of Western colonizers, Burundi was ruled by a princely oligarchy – Ganwa. The Ganwa clan provided a unifying reference point for all Burundians. Based on the assessment of historian Rene Lemarchand – as well as that of others – status, not ethnic identity, was the principal determinant of rank and privilege during pre-colonial times.[7] Ethnic tensions in Burundi were less pronounced, to the extent that political divides were not centred on Hutu–Tutsi distinctions but on competition within the princely Ganwa clan.[8] Despite some leadership related tensions, pre-colonial Burundi was predominantly peaceful and unified. It is therefore not surprising that Chapter 1, Article one of the Arusha Peace and Reconciliation Agreement of August 2000[9] made reference to the pre-colonial situation as follows:

---

[2] Newbury, D. (2001), 'Precolonial Burundi and Rwanda: Local Loyalties and Regional Royalties', *International Journal of African Historical Studies*, Vol. 34, No. 2: 280.

[3] Vansina, J. (1967), 'Note sur la Chronologie du Burundi Ancient', *Bulletin de l'ARSOM* 38: 7.

[4] Ndikumana, L. (2005), 'Distributional Conflict, the State, and Peacebuilding in Burundi', Research Paper No. 2005/45, United Nations, University World Institute for Development Economics Research (UNU-WIDER).

[5] Wolpe, H. (2011), 'Making Peace after Genocide. Anatomy of the Burundi Process', United States Institute of Peace: 7.

[6] Newbury (2001), 268.

[7] Lemarchand, R. (1996), *Burundi: Ethnic Conflict and Genocide*, Cambridge: Woodrow Wilson Center Press and Cambridge University Press, 9.

[8] Wolpe (2011): 7.

[9] Arusha Agreement for Peace and Reconciliation in Burundi.

During the pre-colonial period, all the ethnic groups inhabiting Burundi owed allegiance to the same monarch, Umwami, believed in the same god, Imana, had the same culture and the same language, Kirundi, and lived together in the same territory. Notwithstanding the migratory movements that accompanied the settlement of the various groups in Burundi, everyone recognized themselves as Barundi.[10]

Under the monarchy, there was a patron–client relationship in which the populace received royal protection in exchange for tribute and land tenure. Political culture in the evolving monarchical system was reinforced from within and was subject to very little influence from outside.[11]

During this period, Burundians, regardless of their ethnic origins, displayed a remarkable resilience that enabled them to peacefully address any socio-economic and political conflicts that emerged. Although suspicion between Tutsi and Hutu was not entirely absent, there was no overt ethnic division. The state construction process, while not free from some age-old ethnic animosity, did not betray a pattern of tribal warfare.[12] In the eastern and southern areas in particular, widespread community interaction encouraged the exchange of material goods, with livestock, agricultural produce, salt and iron among the more important commodities.[13] During the pre-colonial stage, Burundi was thus the main driver of its own development.

The peaceful and resilient Burundians witnessed a different form of leadership following the infiltration of colonial powers. Socio-political divisions chiefly based on ethnic superiority originated from discriminatory colonial administrations successfully run by the Germans and the Belgians. The previously existing social contract was upended, with exploitative exogenous powers pushing forward their own colonial interests.

The origins of the festering wounds

In fomenting a racist ideology and ethnic hierarchy bias against Hutus, the colonial administrations of the Germans (1889–1918) and later the Belgians (1918–62) exacerbated divisions among the Bahutu, the Batutsi and the

---

[10] Ibid., Art. 1.
[11] Newbury (2001), 282.
[12] Ibid., 283.
[13] Chrétien, J.-P. (1978), 'Le Commerce du Sel de l'Uvinza au XIXe Siecle: De la Ceuillette au Monopole Capitaliste', *Revue Française d'Histoire d'Outre-Mer* LXV.

Batwa[14] that naturally resulted in more rigid identities,[15] which in turn led to ethnic tensions.[16]

On 8 July 1966, Burundi deposed its penultimate monarch – King Mwambutsa – and a few months later, on 28 November 1966, the country was declared a republic when Tutsi Captain Michel Micombero finally took power. A de facto military regime was established, triggering civil unrest which continued unabated until the early 1970s. From late April to September 1972, following a Hutu-led armed rebellion that killed hundreds of Tutsis,[17] a period of bloodletting ensued, with an estimated 200,000 to 300,000 Hutu killed by the Tutsi-dominated Micombero government.[18] About 300,000 people became refugees, with most of them fleeing to neighbouring Tanzania.[19] Lemarchand noted that, while crushing the rebellion was the first priority, the mass killings systematically targeting existing and rising Hutu elites turned the army, police and gendarmerie into a Tutsi monopoly. This prevented the potential return of the monarchy following the assassination of Ntare V, the last king, who ruled from July to November 1966.

In 1976, Colonel Jean-Baptiste Bagaza, a Tutsi, took power in a bloodless coup against Micombero. Having spent over a decade in power, Bagaza was deposed in 1987 by another Tutsi, Major Pierre Buyoya. The latter dissolved opposition parties, suspended the 1981 constitution and instituted a military regime. Under Buyoya's rule, clashes between the army, the Hutu opposition and the Tutsi hardliners were recurrent. Even in the post-Cold War period, power in Burundi continued to revolve around the head of the executive, with little or no consideration for institutional checks and balances. In many developing societies across the world, the collapse of the Berlin Wall and the advent of democracy were seen as a strong foundation for good governance and the beginning of the end for predatory states, unequal distribution of resources, and discrimination. This popular democratic wind of change briefly landed in Burundi, resulting in the election of its first Hutu President, Melchior Ndadaye, in 1993. However, he was assassinated just three months after assuming power.

---

14 The plural forms of the three ethnic groups.
15 Lemarchand (1996), 42.
16 Arusha Peace and Reconciliation Agreement for Burundi, Art 2.
17 https://en.wikipedia.org/wiki/Burundian_genocides
18 Lemarchand, R. (2009), *The Dynamics of Violence in Central Africa*, Philadelphia: University of Pennsylvania Press, 129.
19 International Crisis Group (2003), 'Refugees and Internally Displaced in Burundi: The Urgent Need for a Consensus on Their Repatriation and Reintegration', 2 December: 2.

Protracted civil war

On 21 October 1993, a group of officers in Bujumbura assassinated President Ndadaye, together with high-ranking officials of the FRODEBU Hutu party, among whom were the speaker and deputy speaker of the parliament.[20] The political-ethnic violence that subsequently engulfed the country prompted the UN to dispatch a small political mission to Burundi later that year.

This mission was entrusted to the very first Special Representative of the Secretary-General to the country, Ahmedou Ould Abdallah,[21] urgently dispatched[22] in November 1993 to help stabilize the situation at the tail end of a devastating surge in mass killing. The initial three-month assignment given to this seasoned diplomat was to lay the foundations for the return of a modicum of democratic order.[23] It took him almost two years to bring a semblance of stability through the institution of a power-sharing arrangement he was able to broker, called la Convention de gouvernement.[24] The tragic plane crash of 6 April 1994 that led to the death of another Hutu President, Cyprien Ntaryamira,[25] re-ignited politico-ethnic strife and plunged Burundi into further bloodshed, jeopardizing the gains made due to Ould Abdallah's valiant efforts.[26]

After the death of Ntaryamira, the Hutu presidency and Tutsi military continued to operate the Convention until 1996, when Tutsi Pierre Buyoya removed the Hutu interim president in a coup. In response, Hutu rebels killed approximately 300 Tutsis on 20 July 1996[27] and army soldiers killed at least 126

[20] Boshoff, H., W. Vrey and G. Rautenback (2010), 'The Burundi Process: From Civil War to Conditional Peace', Monograph 171: 6.

[21] Centre for Strategies and Security for the Sahel Sahara, Biography Ahmedou Ould Abdallah. Avaiilable online: http://www.centre4s.org/en/index.php?option=com_content&view=article&id=47&Itemid=55 (accessed 5 March 2018).

[22] When Ahmedou Ould Abdallah was appointed, I was at that time the head of the office of the Under-Secretary-General for Political Affairs that would back stop him from New York. His appointment was so rushed that all Ould Abdallah was able to take was a Secretary, the UN flag and a few copies of the UN Charter.

[23] Ahmedou Ould, A. (2016), *Plutôt Mourir que Faillir*, Tunis: Sud Editions, 237.

[24] *Liberation* (1996), 'Entretien avec Ahmedou Ould Abdallah, Ancien Représentant de L'ONU au Burundi. "il Faut Imposer la Cohabitation"', 26 July. Available online: https://www.liberation.fr/evenement/1996/07/26/entretien-avec-ahmedou-ould-abdallah-ancien-representant-de-l-onu-au-burundi-il-faut-imposer-la-coha_176189 (accessed 2 March 2018).

[25] *The Washington Post* (1994), 'Two African Presidents Are Killed in a Plane Crash', 7 April. Available online: https://www.washingtonpost.com/archive/politics/1994/04/07/two-african-presidents-are-killed-in-plane-crash/38ee6e5e-ba11-4d21-b17c-50a0c1d88516/ (accessed 2 March 2018).

[26] See Ould Adallah's reflections on the promise and limitations of preventive diplomacy in his book *Burundi on the Brink 1993–1995* (2000). Available online: https://bookstore.usip.org/books/BookDetail.aspx?productID=51265 (accessed 10 March 2018).

[27] International Archive (2007), 'Chronology for Hutus in Burundi', 10 January.

Hutu refugees on 5 January 1997.[28] In 1998, Buyoya and the opposition-led Hutu parliament reached an agreement to sign a transitional constitution and Buyoya was sworn in as President.

Following other inter-ethnic clashes and a crippling economic blockade imposed by neighbouring countries on Burundi, pressure mounted on all sides to put an end to the incessant carnage and finally sit down at the negotiating table. It fell to the historic African political figure, Mwalimu Julius Nyerere, former President of Tanzania, to be the facilitator of the inter-Burundian peace process, which officially began on 15 June 1998.[29] However, the venue for the negotiations, the Tanzanian town of Arusha, was considered problematic, particularly for hardline Tutsis who were suspicious of Tanzania's impartiality given that the country had been refuge to hundreds of thousands of Hutu Burundian refugees since 1972.

Despite serious challenges, Nyerere's facilitation team managed to set up a relatively solid foundation upon which former South African President Nelson Mandela strongly relied when he assumed facilitation responsibilities following the demise of Nyerere in 1999.

On 28 August 2000, Mandela succeeded in persuading thirteen of the belligerent parties, including the main protagonist parties UPRONA (mainly Tutsi) and FRODEBU (mainly Hutu), to sign the Agreement,[30] together with eleven smaller parties. Two major rebel movements declined to participate in the Arusha process. Despite the Agreement, persistent internal political antagonisms resurfaced, threatening the integrity of the hard-won Arusha peace gains. Already in 2000, an estimated 200,000 people had been killed as a result of the most recent ethnic clashes and reprisals, with 550,000 citizens (9 per cent of the population) forcibly displaced, some for as long as six years.[31]

As a framework agreement for ending conflict and restoring stability in Burundi, the 2000 Arusha Peace and Reconciliation Agreement called for ethnically and regionally balanced military and government, and for the holding of democratic elections following an interim, power-sharing, transitional period. According to the Agreement, executive power was to be shared between the

---

[28] *The New York Times* (1997), 'Burundi Army Admits It Killed 126 Hutu Refugees', 12 January. Available online: https://www.nytimes.com/1997/01/12/world/burundi-army-admits-it-killed-126-hutu-refugees.html (accessed 11 March 2018).

[29] Wolpe (2011): 9.

[30] Jackson, S. (2006), 'The United Nations Operations in Burundi (ONUB)-Political and Strategic Lessons Learned', External Independent Study, Conflict Prevention Peace Forum, New York: 7.

[31] GlobalSecurity.org. (2000) 'Burundi Civil War'. Available online: http://www.globalsecurity.org/military/world/war/burundi.htm (accessed 11 March 2018).

President and two Vice-Presidents, with each of the latter hailing from a different political party and ethnic background – the first would be nominated from the mainly Tutsi-dominated party; the second, from the mainly Hutu-dominated party. With respect to the security sector, the agreement made, under Protocol 3, provisions for the various armed groups to be integrated into the existing army in such a way that a single ethnic group would not comprise more than 50 per cent.[32] However, the question of army reforms had to be put on hold until the other warring parties that had remained outside the peace process – such as *le Parti pour la liberation du peuple Hutu-Font national de liberation* (PALIPEHUTU-FNL) – were finally coaxed into either signing the Arusha Agreement or signing subsequent negotiated agreements.

The Arusha Agreement in Chapter one, Article four, describes the conflict in Burundi 'as fundamentally political, with extremely important ethnic dimensions', and stemming 'from a struggle by the political class to accede to and/or remain in power'.[33] The three-year transitional government, which was formed a year after the signing of the Agreement, struggled to find a point of common ground. Despite the agreement, a jockeying for power dominated the political landscape. Power accession or maintenance remained a point of discord among parties. This power-driven attitude had, to a large extent, overshadowed pressing societal needs.

In November 2003, the power-sharing arrangements foreseen by the Arusha accord were finally implemented and a transitional multi-party government was inaugurated with, for the first eighteen months, *Union pour le Progrès National* (UPRONA) leader Pierre Buyoya as President and Domitien Ndayizeye of the *Front pour la Démocratie au Burundi* (FRODEBU) as Vice-President.[34] After this eighteen-month period, Mr Ndayizeye became President and an UPRONA nominee was appointed Vice-President.[35]

Following the signing of the Arusha Agreement and during this interim period, external aid, on which Burundi had been heavily dependent, started flowing back into the country. In 1999, donors had pledged $410 million for post-conflict reconstruction, with a further $832 million pledged in 2001. However, these respective amounts were not completely transferred.[36]

---

[32] Bouka, Y. (2014), 'Status and Dynamics of the Political Situation in Burundi', Central African Report, Institute for Security Studies, Issue 1.

[33] Arusha Agreement for Peace and Reconciliation in Burundi.

[34] UK Foreign and Commonwealth Office (2005), 'Country profiles: Burundi'.

[35] Bentley, K. and R. Southall (2005), *An African peace process: Mandela, South Africa-Burundi*, Cape Town: HSRC Press, 91.

[36] Daley, P. (2006), 'Ethnicity and political violence in Africa: The challenge to the Burundi state', *Political Geography*, 25 (6): 674.

Additionally, grants from the IMF ($54 million) and the European Union ($191.25 million) had been given from their respective post-conflict programmes in order to tackle economic priorities and engage in civil service reforms.[37] These structural reforms were judged harsh and had deleterious effects on the accessibility of critical social services policies, engendering multiple civil servant strikes.

On 3 and 4 September 2004, President Ndayizeye convened an extraordinary session of the Council of Ministers to discuss the text of an interim constitution,[38] which he later submitted for legislative deliberation. On 20 October the draft constitution was signed into law and subsequently validated following a referendum held on 26 November 2004. After a short extension of the transitional government, the first post-transition democratic election finally took place during the first half of 2005, under the watchful eye of the UN peacekeeping mission ONUB.

An unstable situation of no peace no war, prior to my arrival

The election of Pierre Nkurunziza as President on 19 August 2005 effectively marked the end of the power-sharing transitional period in Burundi, and the beginning of the end for the UN peacekeeping mission (ONUB), which had been dispatched over a year earlier to help stabilize the security situation and support free and fair elections. As mentioned above, the mission eventually withdrew at the end of December 2006.

Pierre Nkurunziza, former leader of *Conseil national pour le defence de la democratie-Forces de defence de la democratie* (CNDD-FDD)[39] and Minister of Good Governance in the post-Arusha transitional government, emerged as the first post-transitional president following his appointment by the newly elected National Assembly. CNDD-FDD won a resounding majority with 58 per cent of seats in parliament and 57 per cent in communal councils, as well as twelve of the twenty government ministries.[40] Sadly, the elections and their aftermath did not usher in, as had been hoped, a period of political and institutional stability.

[37] International Monetary Fund (IMF) (2002) 'IMF Approves US $13 Million in Emergency Post-conflict Assistance for Burundi', Press Release No.02/48, 9 October.

[38] United Nations (2004), 'Second Report of the Secretary-General on the United Nations Operation in Burundi', S/2004/902, 15 November: 2.

[39] Wolpe (2011): 9.

[40] International Crisis Group (2006). 'Burundi: Democracy and Peace at Risk', Africa Report No. 120, 30 November 2006: 1.

Instead, the climate of suspicion and mistrust that cut across the political class in Burundi remained palpable after the elections.

According to the post-transitional constitution, the President is to be assisted by two Vice-Presidents – a Hutu and a Tutsi – and the government is to include 60 per cent Hutu and 40 per cent Tutsi. The same proportion is applicable at the National Assembly, whereas the Senate – one of the main missions of which is to monitor the application of the ethnic equilibriums stipulated in the constitution – consists of an equal number of Hutu and Tutsi. The security forces, likewise, include Hutus and Tutsis in equal number. At the communal level, it is stipulated that no more than 67 per cent of mayors are to belong to either group. Meanwhile, women must make up at least 30 per cent of the members of the National Assembly.[41]

Even though these quotas were largely observed after the elections, political elites continued to compete for power in the executive branch. The incumbent government was bent on maintaining the status quo, while the opposition consistently clamoured for reforms, attempting to discredit government actions with a view to triggering a fairer form of the power-sharing arrangement.

The dominant presence of the ruling party, CNDD-FDD, in state institutions was judged a contravention to the law regulating the distribution of ministerial positions proportionate to seats in parliament. President Nkurunziza gave FRODEBU three ministries, not the five this influential party formation was entitled to, and one ministerial post to the Union for National Progress (UPRONA), instead of two. In response to what it labelled governance abuses, FRODEBU in March 2006 decided to withdraw from the government and join the opposition. Undeterred, the ruling party remained steadfast in pursuing its agenda of 'institutional monopoly.' The government replaced all FRODEBU directors of state companies, as well as all-but-one UPRONA director, with its loyalists.[42] The placing of many CNDD-FDD officials in the court system undermined judicial independence, with several newly appointed Supreme Court judges reportedly close to the party.

In addition to the political instability caused by the perceived unbalanced composition of the government, significant human rights violations took place. Local human rights groups reported serious cases of torture in the first six

[41]   Lemarchand, R. (2006), 'Consociationalism and Power Sharing in Africa: Rwanda, Burundi, and the Democratic Republic of the Congo', *African Affairs*, 106 (422): 8.
[42]   Ngaruko, F. and J. Nkurunziza (2000), 'An Economic Interpretation of Conflict in Burundi', *Journal of African Economies*, 9 (3): 386.

months of 2006.[43] Suspects were deprived of the right to fair trial, with Burundian judges denying access to the jails where many of them were tortured.[44]

On 15 December 2005 and 2 February 2006, in a stadium in Bujumbura, detainees were forced to parade wearing signs describing the crimes they had been accused of and subsequently asked to declare that they had not been mistreated.[45] Despite the questionable means it had itself employed in attempting to gain legitimacy, the government recognized that its internal security service – the National Intelligence Service (SNR) – had gone too far, and asked the UN to provide training for its staff. However, severe ill treatment of suspects continued with impunity.[46]

Economic recovery, reconstruction, reconciliation, governance, trade, education and environmental protection were announced by President Nkurunziza as government priorities for 2006.[47] Unfortunately, this plan of action – which raised huge expectations among Burundians – was soon dampened down by egregious governance deficits, thus hindering the implementation of development initiatives. Lemarchand, in depicting the situation in Burundi during this period, quotes a Hutu resident of Bujumbura, the Burundian capital who said: 'We thought Nkurunziza and his men were serious when they attacked corruption, human rights violations, bad governance, ethnicism and nepotism as a mode of government. We believed they wanted to change things, we have been duped. They have been doing the opposite of what they preached since they came to power'.[48] Although such personal testimony does not speak to the perception of every Burundian regarding the Nkurunziza's government during the post-transitional period, many were still waiting for the government to deliver on the multiple promises it had made at the beginning of its term.

Corruption was indeed rife, particularly in Burundi's public administration. Official statements announcing a firm anti-corruption policy and the establishment of an anti-corruption brigade and tribunal in 2006 failed to stem rampant corrupt practices during the first year of Nkurunziza's rule.[49] That same year, the illicit sale of the presidential plane, a Falcon 50, assessed well below its

---

[43] United Nations (2006), 'Sixth Report of the Secretary General on the United Nations Operation in Burundi', S/2006/163, 21 March: 8.
[44] United Nations (2006), S/2006/163.
[45] Ibid.
[46] International Crisis Group (2006): 5.
[47] United Nations (2006), S/2006/163: 2.
[48] Lemarchand (2006): 4.
[49] Bouka, Y. and S. Wolters (2016), 'Battle for Burundi, Is there a Viable Solution?', Central Africa Report, Institute for Security Studies, Issue 7: 12.

market value, not only provoked internal dismay but triggered a crisis with the country's main donor partners. The government faced mounting pressure from the World Bank, which requested an audit and a parliamentary investigation[50] into the matter. The minister of finance and the President's Chief of Staff were identified as having had a clear intention to embezzle profits from the plane sale, with proceeds going to key government officials' private accounts.

Moreover, revelations about the misdeeds by government officials exposed a form of state patronage that entertained corruption networks. In February 2006, the state granted exclusive licences for wholesale sugar to seven businessmen, four of whom were CNDD-FDD parliamentarians.[51] Despite numerous reports by NGOs and state auditing bodies, the Ministry for Good Governance, parliament, and the courts failed to launch investigations, and were therefore judged complicit in enabling corruption to prosper unhindered in a country that was, at the time, witnessing an increasing degree of structural deterioration.

The highly reputed anti-corruption and civil society activist, Ernest Manirumva, strongly argued for greater accountability in the Burundian system of governance. As the Vice-President of the most assertive anti-corruption nongovernmental organization, known as the *Observatoire de la Lutte contre la Corruption et les Malversations Economiques* (OLUCOME), Manirumva organized multiple seminars and workshops aimed at raising awareness of the negative effects of corruption.[52] He was assassinated in April 2009 after having started an investigation into an illegal shipment of small arms, allegedly by individuals close to the regime. This assassination will be revisited in Chapter 4, due to its implications for the implementation of the mandate I had been entrusted with as Executive Representative of the Secretary-General and head of BINUB. Despite external pressures and half-hearted, internal investigations, the perpetrators of the Manirumva assassination are still, at of the time of writing, at large.

The strong corruption networks sustained by prevalent legal impunity and the government's failure to meet societal needs severely eroded whatever juridical legitimacy the government had gained through elections. Further, it aggravated the existing climate of mistrust among political actors and the population at large.

---

50   République du Burundi, Assemblée Nationale, Commission d'Enquête Parlementaire sur la Vente de l'Avion Présidentiel 'Falcon 50', Bujumbura, July 2008. Available online: www.arib.info/An_RAppORT_venTe_FAlCOn50.pdf (accessed 16 March 2018).
51   République du Burundi, Assemblée Nationale: 6.
52   Schiavo-Campo, S. (2006), 'Fighting Corruption and Restoring Accountability in Burundi', United States Agency for International Development: 13.

Notwithstanding such dismal governance performance, a positive development took place on the security front. On 7 September 2006, a month prior to my arrival, a Comprehensive Ceasefire Agreement between the PALIPEHUTU-FNL – the last active rebel movement that had remained outside of the Arusha peace process – and the Government of Burundi (GoB), was signed in Dar-es-Salaam, Tanzania, after intense and sustained mediation by South Africa, acting on behalf of a regional initiative led by Uganda. The salient points of the agreement included: a complete cessation of hostilities; temporary immunity for FNL fighters, the demobilization of its troops, and their subsequent integration into the armed forces of Burundi; and, not unlike other peace agreements, power-sharing arrangements in the security sector.[53] Issues relating to the possible participation of the FNL in the government and modalities for the integration of its elements into regular security forces were not clearly addressed. It was left to the South African facilitation entrusted with following up the ceasefire agreement to help address any political issues arising and to ensure its implementation.[54]

This ceasefire agreement between the GoB and the FNL, which came into force on 10 September 2006, was initially hailed as a significant breakthrough. However, it was marred in the ensuing months by multiple violations, for which each party blamed the other. The month of November 2006, a month after my arrival, was far from peaceful. These violations escalated from armed skirmishes to open clashes between the two protagonists in various provinces, as well as occasional shelling of the Burundian capital Bujumbura.

On 3 and 14 November respectively, the FNL, through two different letters to the chairperson of the Regional Peace Initiative for Burundi and the Secretary-General Kofi Annan, accused the government of violating the ceasefire agreement in various ways, including the continued detention of FNL members.[55] During a meeting with the diplomatic corps in Bujumbura on 28 November, the government accused the FNL of not engaging in the implementation of the ceasefire engagement in good faith.[56] It highlighted criminal offences allegedly perpetrated by FNL combatants against the population, and accused the rebel

---

[53] Wielenga, C. and S. Akin-Aina (2016), 'Mapping Conflict and Peace in Burundi, An Analysis of the Burundi Conflict Terrain', ResearchGate: 16.

[54] United Nations (2006), 'Eighth Report of the Secretary-General on the United Nations Operation in Burundi', S/2006/842, 25 October: 2.

[55] United Nations (2006), 'Eighth Report of the Secretary-General on the United Nations Operation in Burundi': 2.

[56] United Nations (2006), 'Ninth Report of the Secretary-General on the United Nations Operation in Burundi', S/2006/994, 18 December: 1–2.

movement of willful delaying the disarmament, demobilization, and reintegration of its combatants.[57]

In addition to uncertainties on the security front, political uncertainties continued to unfold with unrelenting frequency on the governance front. The alleged August 2006 coup that led to the resignation[58] of the second Vice-President, Alice Nzomukunda – who accused the government of gross human rights violations and a lack of respect for the rule of law – continued to raise doubts about the nation's political stability. The alleged coup also led to the arrest of former high-level government officials, among them former transitional Vice-President, Alphonse-Marie Kadege, and former transitional President, Domitien Ndayizeye.[59] Pressure and outcry from political parties, civil society organizations, human right organizations, and other external actors culminated in a decision on 6 October by the Supreme Court to release on bail the seven alleged coup detainees. The decision was ultimately overturned by the Attorney-General.

This decision added another blow to the already questionable separation between the executive and legislative branches of government. In parliament, political parties had accused the CNDD-FDD of using its majority status to flout parliamentary rules and regulations and declared a three-week boycott of the 2006 second parliamentary session. On 12 October, members of Parliament from the FRODEBU, UPRONA and CNDD (an early splinter group of the CNDD-FDD) parties addressed a letter to President Nkurunziza, complaining about the irregularities in the National Assembly and requesting that the Assembly's voting system be improved.[60]

On 21 November, in an attempt to defuse the political situation, the government convened a meeting presided over by the Minister of Interior and Public Security, during which twenty-four representatives of the then thirty-six registered political parties raised a number of concerns on the socio-economic and political situations at the time. UPRONA – one of the political parties represented in this meeting – decided to remain in the government, taking the position of first vice-president, despite the disapproval of some its party's leaders.[61] These relatively positive developments took place amidst the continued

57   Ibid.: 2.
58   Ibid.: 4.
59   United Nations (2006), 'Ninth Report of the Secretary-General on the United Nations Operation in Burundi'.
60   Ibid.: 4–5.
61   Ibid.: 3.

detention of the seven alleged coup plot suspects and several failed attempts to put six of them on trial.[62]

In addition to the uncertain political situation, freedom of expression was further compromised after the arrest of two journalists – Serge Nibizi, and Domitille Kiramvu – on 22 November, for allegedly threatening state security and broadcasting information on political detainees while their case was under judicial investigation. Similarly, the director of the Isanganiro radio station, Matthias Manirakiza, was jailed on 29 November for allegedly broadcasting information that could disturb public and security order.[63] Furthermore, strained relations between the government and international non-governmental organizations came under further scrutiny when the Director of the National Office for the Coordination of International Non-Governmental Organizations revealed that thirty-two out of ninety-five organizations operating in Burundi could be asked to leave the country for not complying with the government's regulations on mandatory reporting of their activities.[64]

Even so, following internal and external pressure, some improvements on the human rights front were observed. Activities toward the establishment of a national independent human rights commission were initiated on 20 December. On 22 December, the President, by decree, commuted all death sentences, and also reduced sentences for some categories of prisoners and released others, including elderly and terminally ill prisoners. The President also ordered the release of all prisoners whose detention violated legal procedure. In total, 2,588 prisoners were freed and the sentences of 862 were reduced.[65]

Concluding observations

A few months after my arrival in Burundi, I asked some of my UN colleagues working in outlying provinces to seek the views of ordinary Burundians as to what peace meant to them. My curiosity was inspired by the work of Peter Uvin,[66] who had come to Burundi around the time I was there to ask similar questions for his research project.

[62] Ibid.
[63] International Federation of Journalists (2006), 'Journalist Summoned by Prosecutor Goes Missing; IFJ Calls for End of Intimidation Campaign against Independent Journalism', 11 December.
[64] United Nations (2006), S/2006/994:4.
[65] United Nations (2007), 'First Report of the Secretary-General on the United Nations Integrated Office in Burundi', S/2007/287, 17 May: 9–10.
[66] Campbell, S. (2015), 'What Burundi's Crisis Tells Us About UN Capacity to Build Peace', *The Washington Post*.

What came out of this rudimentary exercise was enlightening, with most of those interviewed expressing that better governance institutions and elections were not a priority. Peace for them was a roof over their heads that did not leak, the ability to go about their daily business without being robbed, raped, or killed, and the pursuit of their legitimate aspirations without fear, with justice, and in security.

Had I engaged in understanding the history of this tormented country from the eyes of those who had engaged in violence, those who had been victim of it, or simply those who had helplessly observed its horrors, I would probably have acquired a richer understanding of Burundi's troubled history.

It is against this background that the UN Integrated Peacebuilding Mission in Burundi (BINUB) that I had been asked to lead came into being on 1 January 2007, replacing the peacekeeping mission, ONUB. How did I prepare to assume the helm of this new mission? How did we, as a UN system (BINUB and the various UN agencies, funds and programmes) attempted to organize ourselves strategically and programmatically in order to help Burundians consolidate the gains they had achieved and avert reversals? How did the principled stand that BINUB took with respect to governance issues, including corruption and human rights violations, affect its relationship with governing elites? What role did BINUB play as part of the regionally-led peace process? What assessment can be offered of BINUB's peacebuilding contributions in light of the instability and intermittent violence the country continues to experience to this day? What can be learned from BINUB's experience that might inform current and future UN peacebuilding engagements in conflict and post-conflict-affected countries? The following chapter will attempt to provide elements of response to some of these questions.

4

Leading BINUB in a Fragile Context

'I was awakened early this morning by my Security Advisor asking my permission to use the UN helicopter to evacuate to the Burundian capital, Bujumbura, a French woman working with the NGO, Action Contre la Faim, who was seriously injured following an assassination attempt in one of the provinces. She died upon arrival to the hospital. It was a sad morning for me. It left a bitter taste on the dawn of a new year.'

The text quoted above was part of a message I sent to my family on the first day of 2008, a year after I took the helm of the UN Integrated Office in Burundi (BINUB). At that time, armed clashes between the last remaining rebel movement and government forces were taking place amid mutual accusations that the Comprehensive Ceasefire Agreement signed in September 2006 was being violated. Regardless of who was culpable, the victims were invariably innocent civilians.

Before coming to Burundi in early October 2006, I had served as UN Resident Coordinator and Humanitarian Coordinator in Guyana at a time when the country was experiencing a severe humanitarian crisis and was bracing for potentially violent, inter-ethnic clashes ahead of the 2006 general elections. It was my first long-term mission away from UN headquarters, as well as my first experience promoting prevention and social cohesion as governance and development functions rather than simply crisis management tools.[1]

When in September 2006 the then late UN Secretary-General Kofi Annan appointed me as his Deputy Special Representative (DSRSG) of the departing UN peacekeeping operation in Burundi (ONUB),[2] and several months later as his Executive Representative (ERSG) and head of the UN Integrated Office in

---

[1] Lund, M. and S. McDonald (2015), *Across the Lines of Conflict: Facilitating Cooperation to Build Peace*, Washington, DC: Woodrow Wilson Center Press with Columbia University Press.

[2] The UN Operation in Burundi (ONUB) was a peacekeeping mission that was active from June 2004 till 31 December 2006, numbering over 5,000 military, 200 military observers, 120 police force and 443 civilian staff. BINUB staffing as of 1 January 2007 was 471 civilian posts, both national and international.

Burundi (BINUB),[3] I thought my sojourn in Guyana would stand me in good stead. More importantly, I believed that my familiarity with Burundi from the time I managed the Central Africa portfolio as a Director in the UN Department for Political Affairs (DPA) would accelerate my learning curve. However, Burundi turned out to a very different challenge from what I had imagined, rendered more complex by divergent regional and international agendas. This was despite its small size and the apparent lack of geopolitical status.

This chapter describes how I prepared for and exercised my leadership responsibilities throughout my tenure in Burundi. It also examines the multi-faceted challenges my senior mission leadership team and I encountered in implementing key components of BINUB's mandate (from an integrated perspective), as well as the various strategies, processes and mechanisms we devised to address them. The chapter also assesses BINUB's contributions, as well as my own, to the tortuous implementation of the Comprehensive Ceasefire Agreement between the Government of Burundi (GoB) and the last remaining rebel movement, the PALIPEHUTU-FNL.[4] The final section speculates on the main reasons behind the GoB asking that I be replaced as the third year of BINUB drew to an end. This was despite the Security Council's decision to extend BINUB for an additional year and the Secretary-General's continued confidence in my work.

An ounce of preparation is worth a pound of immersion

Soon after my appointment as DSRSG for Burundi – as well as Resident Coordinator, Humanitarian Coordinator, and head of United Nations Development Programme (UNDP) – was announced in September 2016, I proceeded to learn as much as I could about what was awaiting me in Burundi. I was warned that I would have to hit the ground running: As DSRSG I was expected to help manage the transition from ONUB[5] to BINUB, while at the same time contributing, as Resident Coordinator, to the ongoing development of

---

[3] The UN Integrated Office in Burundi, known by its French acronym, BINUB, was the successor peacebuilding arrangement to the UN Operation in Burundi (ONUB). See https://www.un.org/press/en/2007/sga1030.doc.htm

[4] Comprehensive Ceasefire Agreement between the Government of the Republic of Burundi and the PALIPEHUTU – FNL, Dar ES Salam, 7 September 2006.

[5] *UN News* (2006), 'As Blue Helmets Prepare to Leave Burundi, UN Officials Pledge Continued Support', 20 December. https://news.un.org/en/story/2006/12/204102-blue-helmets-prepare-leave-burundi-un-officials-pledge-continued-support

the transitional United Nations Development Assistance Framework (UNDAF)[6] for Burundi. I was also expected to lead the process of putting in place strategies and structures for the implementation of BINUB's mandate (to begin on 1 January 2007), which the UN Security Council had approved on 25 October 2006.[7] As will be shown, such an ambitious agenda would have been impossible to carry out in such a short timeframe without the invaluable support and leadership of the team I started working with during ONUB's drawdown.

In addition to the briefings I received from the UN Department of Peacekeeping Operations (DPKO) on the overall situation in the country, I sought and received, from various independent sources, analytical information on key national and regional stakeholders. This included governing elites that came to power after the first internationally supervised democratic elections of 2005 and Burundian political opposition figures. A supplementary brief was made available to me on the main donors active in the country, their interests, their contributions, and the relationships they enjoyed with key political figures both inside and outside government. I also acquired knowledge on the then ongoing ceasefire negotiations between the GoB and the last active rebel movement, the PALIPEHUTU-FNL (FNL), which were taking place in Tanzania, as well as on the personalities of various heads of UN agencies, funds, and programmes operating on the ground whose operational activities I was expected to coordinate. More specifically, I sought advice on which senior staff I should retain and which physical assets should remain with BINUB following ONUB's departure in order to ensure a seamless transition between the two missions. Finally, I inquired about the circumstances that had generated the palpable tension between the GoB and the top leadership of ONUB in the final months of its operation.[8]

One of the first people to guide me into the labyrinth of Burundian politics was Ambassador Mamadou Bah, a distinguished diplomat[9] from Guinea who, in 1997, was appointed as the Special Representative of the AU Commission Chairperson in Burundi. From 2002, Ambassador Bah was a major actor in the implementation of key provisions[10] of the 2000 Arusha Peace and Reconciliation

---

6   United Nations Development Assistance Framework Guidance 2017.
7   United Nations (2006), 'Resolution 1719 (2006)'.
8   Security Council Report (2006), 'Africa Burundi', March 2006 Monthly Report.
9   GCI (2011) 'In Memoriam: Mamadou Bah, le Représentant De L'UA au Burundi N'est Plus', 28 June. Available online: http://www.guineeconakry.info/article/detail/in-memoriam-mamadou-bah-le-representant-de-lua-au-burundi-nest-plus/ (accessed 25 March 2018).
10 Reliefweb (2002), 'Burundi: Interview with Mamadou Bah, AU Representative', 12 December. Available online: https://reliefweb.int/report/burundi/burundi-interview-mamadou-bah-au-representative (accessed 25 March 2018).

Agreement, which put an end to Burundi's decade-long, brutal civil war.[11] After the departure of ONUB, he took on greater responsibility for the implementation of the 2006 Comprehensive Ceasefire between the GoB and the FNL. Ambassador Bah had intimate knowledge of the tangled webs connecting the various national and regional political protagonists, their strengths and weaknesses, their shifting alliances, and their relative influence on Burundi's fractious politics.

Ambassador Bah and I worked closely together throughout my three-year tenure as ERSG. I consulted him on major decisions, sometimes waking him up in the middle of the night. I have written elsewhere[12] about the exemplary partnership we established and the difference it made in managing the peace and security challenges facing Burundi at that time, and in building the foundations of a less reversible, albeit fragile, peace. Enfeebled by illness, he ploughed on undeterred until his last days. On 23 June 2011, he passed away and I paid him homage in a local Burundi newspaper.[13] He had and has my undying gratitude for being both a friend and mentor throughout my Burundi journey.

During my stint as DSRSG I became familiar with most of the senior staff of ONUB and was able to gauge their suitability regarding staying on with BINUB and filling some of the positions allocated to the new mission. Two of these staff members, Boubacar Kane and Mbaye Faye, had been in Burundi for a number of years and had an intimate understanding of the political and security situation, as well as being closely acquainted with the main political and security protagonists. It was my good fortune that both accepted to stay on after ONUB's departure as, respectively, heads of the political and security sector reform sections of BINUB. They contributed tremendously to my education on the country, and without their unparalleled competence, wise counsel and unfailing loyalty, I would not have been able to steer the mission in the right direction, particularly during turbulent times.

BINUB's evolving mandate

The last three months of 2006, as ONUB was drawing down, were a whirlwind of activity both within and outside the UN family of agencies, funds and programmes. It was during this early phase of my tenure that the major planning

---

[11] Arusha Peace and Reconciliation Agreement for Burundi.
[12] Mahmoud, Y. (2010), 'Partnership for Peacebuilding in Burundi: Some lessons Learned', in H. Besada (ed.), *Crafting an African Security Architecture,* London: Ashgate, 129–42.
[13] IWACU (2011), 'Hommage à l'Ambassadeur Mamadou Bah', *La Voix du Burundi,* 27 July.

for setting up BINUB and its programmatic and structural integration mechanisms and processes took place.

One of the staff positions that I was able to wrench from the jaws of the departing ONUB was that of a Best Practice/Lessons Learned Officer. This is a mid-level position created within certain peace operations to engage in after-action reviews, its purpose being to inform senior mission leaders of what went well and what could have been done differently, and to offer best practices and lessons learned. A year into my new mission, I asked the position's incumbent, Zenja Basagic,[14] whom I had attached to my front office, to review the planning and programming phase of BINUB's work, with a view to evaluating its effectiveness.

The review conducted by Zenja covered a period stretching from June 2006, when the recommendation was made to establish an integrated peacebuilding mission (BINUB), until November 2007, when the major planning phase had ended and implementation had begun. The report, which was made public in early February 2008,[15] provided an excellent overview of the critical activities I facilitated as DSRG and later as ERSG, to prepare the ground for implementation of BINUB's mandate.

The following sections of this chapter, largely inspired by this review, provide a synopsis of how my team and I exercised strategic, catalytic leadership[16] to: (1) develop a common vision around peace and peace consolidation in Burundi, as well as a shared practical understanding of how the UN system should organize itself strategically, programmatically, and operationally; (2) secure and cultivate the buy-in and continued engagement of the host government, civil society and other key national stakeholders throughout the planning and implementation phases; and (3) nurture and cultivate good working relationships with the various heads of UN agencies, funds and programmes both on the ground and at their respective headquarters.

The integrated peacebuilding office in Burundi[17] was created in response to a November 2005 request by the newly elected leadership for a successor

---

[14] Basagic, Z. (2007), 'The Role of the United Nations in Making Progress Towards Peace In Burundi' Available online: https://www.diplomacy.edu/sites/default/files/23082010104120%20Basagic%20 %28Library%29.pdf (accessed 25 March 2020).

[15] United Nations Peace Operations (2008), 'UN Integration in Burundi in the Context of the Peacebuilding Office BINUB Taking Stock and Lessons Learned from June 2006 to November 2007', BINUB Bujumbura, February.

[16] Catalyst for Peace, Building Peace from the Inside Out. Available online: https://www. catalystforpeace.org/ (accessed 25 March 2020).

[17] Throughout the first three years of its existence, BINUB had an average of 420 staff members, 239 of whom were local civilian staff. Its budget hovered around the $70 million figure.

arrangement to ONUB that could support peace consolidation and reconstruction efforts. After consultation with the GoB and the UN Country Team, in his June 2006 report to the Security Council on the work of ONUB,[18] the Secretary-General recommended the establishment of an integrated office that would sustain adequate level of delivery in the areas of human rights, transitional justice, security sector reform, and peace and governance. The recommendation was welcomed by the Security Council in Resolution 1692[19] and, on the basis of the Secretary-General's June 2006 report and its August 2006 Addendum,[20] BINUB was established. Its purpose was to harness the collective capacities of the UN system in an integrated and coherent manner in order to help Burundi respond to its peace consolidation priorities, paving the way towards development-oriented engagement with the support of the UN and other international partners.

These peacebuilding priorities and the structure, functions and resources of BINUB were based on the recommendations of the August 2006 Addendum and the Memorandum of Understanding, which were in turn based on the May 2006 consultations between the GoB and the Secretary-General. More specifically, the mandate and objectives of BINUB were designed to support the government in the following areas: peace consolidation and democratic governance; disarmament, demobilization and reintegration; security sector reform; promotion and protection of human rights; measures to end impunity; and UN agency coordination.

BINUB was expected to fulfil its mandate in three ways. First, by strengthening UN capacities for system-wide strategic planning, including through joint monitoring and evaluation, political analysis, reporting, communication, capturing best practices, and mainstreaming cross-cutting issues such as youth and gender. Second, by hosting three major joint programmes that would leverage the comparative advantages and, where possible, the staffing and financial resources of the main UN entities on the ground in the areas of peace consolidation and democratic governance, security sector reform/small arms (SSR/SA) and justice/human rights. These programmes, as explained below, were supported by a series of joint mechanisms aimed at ensuring the

---

[18]   United Nations (2006), 'Seventh Report of the Secretary-General on the United Nations Operation in Burundi', S/2006/429, 21 June.
[19]   United Nations (2006), 'Resolution 1692 (2006), adopted by the Security Council at its 5479th meeting, on 30 June 2006', S/RES/1692 (2006), 30 June.
[20]   United Nations (2006), 'Seventh Report of the Secretary-General on the United Nations Operation in Burundi', S/2006/429/Add.1, 14 August.

coordination, monitoring and evaluation of their implementation. Third, by providing strategic and programmatic support as well as political advice to the government and other national stakeholders, with the aim of peacefully managing political differences.

After its first year of operation, BINUB was entrusted by the Security Council with a 'robust political role'[21] supporting regionally-led efforts for implementing the 2006 Ceasefire Agreement between the GoB and the FNL, after the process had stalled and armed clashes between the two parties had increased. As this last leg of the peace process continued to stumble throughout 2008, the Security Council reiterated the need for BINUB to step into this role in Resolutions 1858 (2008)[22] and 1902 (2009),[23] which renewed the Mission's mandate for, respectively, the third and fourth consecutive year. I shall return to this specific task in the latter part of this chapter.

As the political and security integration of the FNL progressed satisfactorily throughout 2009 and Burundi began preparing for its crucial 2010 general elections, BINUB's mandate further evolved. After taking note of a multidisciplinary assessment report sent to Burundi in early 2009, the Security Council encouraged BINUB to direct its attention toward supporting political dialogue among contending political parties and other key actors ahead of the elections, and to providing logistical and financial support to the National Independent Electoral commission.[24]

On exercising my integration hat as ERSG

As alluded to earlier, the nearly three-month assignment as Deputy Special Representative of the Secretary-General, deputy head of ONUB (and simultaneously Coordinator of UN operational activities in Burundi), afforded me a unique opportunity to deepen my knowledge of the Burundian context. This was no easy task, as I had to suspend most of the certainties I had gained from my preparations prior to landing in Burundi. This interim assignment also enabled me, soon after the adoption of BINUB's founding resolution, to lay the

[21] United Nations (2007), 'Resolution 1791 (2007), adopted by the Security Council at its 5809th Meeting, on 19 December 2007', S/RES/1791 (2007), 19 December.
[22] United Nations (2008), 'Resolution 1858 (2008), adopted by the Security Council at its 6057th Meeting, on 22 December 2008', S/RES/1858 (2008), 22 December.
[23] United Nations (2009), 'Resolution 1902 (2009), adopted by the Security Council at its 6245th Meeting, on 17 December 2009', S/RES/1902 (2009), 17 December.
[24] Ibid.

foundation for achieving my first objective: namely, to collegially craft and disseminate a shared vision of the UN peacebuilding agenda, post ONUB, and develop a common and practical understanding of how the UN system should organize itself to implement that vision once BINUB's mandate became effective on 1 January 2007.[25]

An implicit objective I pursued throughout this preparatory phase was to ensure that the frayed relations between the GoB and the senior leadership of the departing mission did not negatively colour the image and actions of the incoming senior team I would be leading. I tried to do this without appeasement or overly ingratiating myself with governing elites, while at the same time being mindful of their views and legitimate needs and aspirations. Whether I succeeded in this balancing act, without being captured by this elite, is a subject I will return to in a later in this chapter.

The functions of the Executive Representative of the Secretary-General (ERSG) were clearly outlined in the Addendum to the Secretary-General's June 2006 report.[26] In addition to heading BINUB, the ERSG would also serve as the UN Resident Coordinator and Humanitarian Coordinator, the UNDP Resident Representative, and the Designated Official for Security. The Executive Representative 'would be responsible for integrating United Nations activities and engaging the government at the most senior political level'. In addition, the Executive Representative was expected to serve as the primary UN interlocutor with the government, including on all political and development matters. In his or her capacity as Resident Coordinator, the Executive Representative would have overall responsibility for resource mobilization with respect to the UN common action plan, as well as the provision of technical assistance and support to the government's National Committee on Aid Coordination, in collaboration with other development partners.

In carrying out these functions, the Executive Representative would be supported by a small office, including a political unit, and would have responsibilities in the areas of coordination, planning, analysis and assessment, conduct and discipline, legal affairs, gender mainstreaming and the empowerment of women, and child protection. The Executive Representative would also be

[25] Reliefweb (2008), 'UN Integration in Burundi in the Context of the Peacebuilding office BINUB – Taking Stock and Lessons Learned from Jun 2006 to Nov 2007', 29 February. Available online: https://reliefweb.int/report/burundi/un-integration-burundi-context-peacebuilding-office-binub-taking-stock-and-lessons (accessed 5 May 2018).
[26] United Nations (2006) 'Seventh Report of the Secretary-General on the United Nations Operation in Burundi', S/2006/429/Add.1.

supported by a Deputy Executive Representative of the Secretary-General.[27] Clearly, taken together the above tasks represented a tall order, one I would not have been able to measure up to without the leadership and dedicated work of the team I was fortunate to have around me.

As set out in the founding resolution, the initial duration of BINUB's mandate was for one year. Its renewal beyond this was contingent on progress on specific performance benchmarks national actors were expected to achieve with the support of BINUB.[28] These included:

- the cessation of armed conflict in Burundi between the government and the FNL, and the implementation of both the political and military aspects of the comprehensive agreement between the two parties signed in September 2006;
- full respect for constitutional provisions such as power-sharing arrangements by the government and all political actors in the country;
- progress to made in the establishment of mechanisms for conflict prevention, management, and resolution, and the creation of a political environment conducive to the conduct of free and fair national elections in 2010;
- the adoption of legislation and the achievement of progress in reforming public administration;
- the adoption and launching of a national plan for the reform of the security sector and an adequately resourced, structured, and trained Burundi National Police force that would assume responsibility for ensuring law and order;
- a reformed intelligence service whose main responsibilities would be limited to gathering and analysing intelligence in conformity with international standards and under civilian oversight;
- the development, adoption, and launching of a comprehensive strategy against the proliferation of small arms and light weapons, as well as the completion of the disarmament and demobilization of former combatants, and;
- the implementation of programmes providing comprehensive training in human rights standards. This was judged as an overly ambitious, long-term and eminently internal endeavour that would require longer-term international support rather than a short-term peacebuilding mission such as BINUB could offer.

---

[27] United Nations (2006), 'Seventh Report of the Secretary-General on the United Nations Operation in Burundi' Addendum.
[28] Ibid.

Despite genuine efforts, various delays and reversals in the peace process rendered progress on most benchmarks slow, which prompted the Security Council to renew BINUB's mandate for two more years, before it morphed into another political configuration called BNUB in 2011.[29]

One challenge I was not fully prepared for was how to secure the cooperation of the various heads of UN agencies, funds and programmes (AFP) operating on the ground, many of whom considered themselves as *primus inter pares* in their respective fiefdoms, and whose operational activities I was mandated to coordinate for the purposes of consolidating peace. A related challenge was how to communicate the integration approach to these AFPs without raising concern that a temporary Security Council-mandated political mission was attempting to merge under one umbrella UN development and humanitarian entities that pre-dated BINUB and would presumably continue to operate long after its closure.

Understanding and communicating BINUB's mandate

Soon after the approval of BINUB's mandate by the Security Council in October 2006, my team and I set out to listen to the expectations, concerns and prejudices of the GoB and other key stakeholders, including the UN country team, with respect to the impact the integration approach would have on their work. In this regard, Ambassador Bah, as well as two senior colleagues, the heads of UNICEF and UNHCR (see under (b) below) provided me with helpful insights as to the challenges awaiting me as the newly appointed ERSG.

Having fully internalized what BINUB's mandate was all about, my small team and I designed and conducted a series of sensitization campaigns to explain the mandate and the operational, programmatic and structural steps needed. We carried out these campaigns with the help of well-designed presentations prepared by my competent strategic coordination officer Vincent Kayijuka. We also held public workshops to build a collective understanding of the mandate and how it would contribute to the achievement of Burundi peacebuilding priorities, as reflected in various national planning documents prepared with the support of the UN[30] or the Bretton Woods institutions.

Those that are noteworthy include the bilateral discussions, held both publicly and privately, with individual government officials – including ministers – who had embraced the establishment of BINUB as well as those who had doubts

[29]   United Nations Security Council Resolution 1959 (2010).
[30]   United Nations (2008), 'Annual session 2008 16 to 27 June 2008, Geneva Item 4 of the provisional agenda UNFPA – Country programmes and related matters', DP/FPA/2008/6, 28 March.

about its relevance. Both as DSRSG, and after I assumed my new responsibilities as ERSG, I held several press conferences during which I spelled out the mandate of BINUB and its modus operandi.

The centerpiece of this intensive information campaign was a high-level round table on 20 January 2007, presided over by the then First Vice-President of Burundi with the participation of a number of relevant ministers, during which BINUB's mandate and structures were explained. This was followed by a long and exhaustive question-and-answer session addressing the government's concerns. This session, which was a major icebreaker, was appreciated for its transparency and frankness. Presentations were subsequently organized for donors, civil society, the private sector, NGOs, religious organizations, the media and for local and provincial authorities. Additionally, BINUB produced a CD with the presentation materials (of the new mandate and the integrated structures) for UN agencies to disseminate to their respective staff.

Alongside these activities targeting key stakeholders in Burundi, there were simultaneous efforts throughout my tenure to explain BINUB's work to the UN community at Headquarters in New York. Moreover, my colleagues and I missed no opportunity to speak at various fora outside of New York, where we were invited to showcase the planning and programmatic activities of BINUB, with a focus on the special partnership it had established with the Peacebuilding Commission through the Peacebuilding Strategic Framework for Burundi.[31]

Internally, similar efforts were made to sensitize UN system staff. During one of the town hall meetings we polled both national and international staff to come up with a catchphrase encapsulating the purpose and objective of our collective work. 'Together for the consolidation of peace' was selected from the proposed entries. Peace – or *'amahoro'* in Kirundi, the local language – is a salutation commonly used in personal encounters. The slogan was used when opening and closing meetings and adorned the front pages of the French monthly bulletin of BINUB, called 'BINUB Info'.[32]

Forging a common understanding of integration

'Integration' was the middle name of this new UN entity called BINUB, which was the second such entity (and it turned out to be the last, as will be explained

---

[31]   United Nations Integrated Office in Burundi (2008), 'Strategic Framework for Peacebuilding in Burundi Highlights and key lessons learned', Tokyo, 25 July.

[32]   Bureau Intégré des Nations Unies au Burundi (2009, 'La Réinsertion durable des Soldats Démobilisés, Gage de Stabilité', BINUB, No. 026, February.

later), after the one in Sierra Leone (UNIOSIL) established a year earlier.[33] In fact, before agreeing to BINUB's mandate,[34] Burundian government officials were afforded the opportunity to travel to Sierra Leone to see for themselves what a UN integrated successor arrangement to a peacekeeping presence would look like.

Much has been written since these early experiments on the successes and travails[35] of 'integration' as a guiding principle in the design and implementation of peacebuilding activities. For example, strategic and structural integration was the subject of several guidance notes by UN Secretaries-Generals Kofi Annan[36] and Ban Ki-Moon.[37] The former concentrated on the responsibilities and working relationships between the Special Representative of the Secretary-General and members of his/her senior mission leadership teams, while the latter focused on the need to link different dimensions of UN peacebuilding engagement (political, social, economic, humanitarian, human rights and the rule of law) into a coherent support strategy. In Directive 2008/24, Ban Ki-Moon stated that the main purpose of integration is 'to maximize the individual and collective impact of UN response, concentrating on those activities required to consolidate peace'.[38]

Integration goes against the grain of the fragmented nature of UN work. Heads of UN entities on the ground representing various AFP tended to act as *primus inter pares*, answerable only to their regional and hierarchical superiors[39] and through them to the disparate, Member State-led governance structures overseeing these AFP.[40] As a result, amidst the team I was expected to lead toward the virtuous path of integration, there was only a reluctant adherence to the above guidance notes. Furthermore, where such adherence existed, there was no agreement on its practical implementation as an overarching framework for organizing UN operational activities.

Faced with this lukewarm attitude towards integration, I spent a substantial amount of time studying the lessons learned from other integration attempts,

[33] United Nations (2005), 'Security Council Establishes UN Integrated Office in Sierra Leone to Further Address Root Causes of Conflict', SC/8487, 31 August.

[34] United Nations (2006), 'Seventh Report of the Secretary-General on the United Nations Operation in Burundi'.

[35] Campbell, S. and A. Kaspersen (2008) 'The UN's Reforms: Confronting Integration Barriers', *International Peacekeeping*, 15 (4).

[36] United Nations Development Operations Coordination Office (2017) 'Interim Technical Guidance. The Assessment of Results and Competencies for Resident Coordinators and UN Country Teams', September.

[37] Panel Discussion: Panelist Presentation 1 The UN Integrated Approach –Toward Effective Humanitarian Assistance Tomoya Kamino (Gifu University).

[38] Ibid.

[39] I shall return to this upward accountability where agency success and visibility as well as personal ambitions competed with efforts to make a peacebuilding difference on the ground (downward accountability).

[40] Mahmoud (2010).

with a particular focus on the reasons these attempts did not fully succeed, as had been the case with ONUB.[41] One insight I gained was that I should articulate the added value of integration regarding individual UN entities visibility in the eyes of the government and donors. 'Integration,' I hammered home, 'did not mean merger.' I assured the relevant parties that during and after BINUB each agency would end up more relevant to the post-conflict peacebuilding context, long after BINUB had folded up its tent. After a series of mini internal workshops where I repeated the same message, we were able to agree that during the lifetime of the political missions we would be 'all BINUB'.

This meant that each agency would identify activities within their mandated programmes, which, in addition to their intrinsic values (humanitarian, development, human rights, etc.), would have value-added contributing explicitly to the drivers of peace. For example, UNHCR and the World Food Programme identified items such as rugs for refugees or wooden pallets for food storage that could be procured or manufactured locally instead of imported. This could provide income for local artisans or manufacturers, thus generating employment opportunities for young people, particularly those going through the DDR programme. This would be achieved without jeopardizing humanitarian principles, which I was entrusted to uphold.

During one of these workshops, I was able to identify among the heads of UN agencies change agents who, despite some lingering doubts, had embraced the spirit and letter of integration, and to whom I could delegate some of the coordinating functions assigned to me as ERSG. For example, I asked the head of UNHCR, Bo Schack,[42] to act on my behalf as a Humanitarian Coordinator, and thus take the lead in encouraging humanitarian actors to carry out their activities from a peacebuilding perspective. He was instrumental in fostering development-oriented reintegration of Burundian refugees returning from Tanzania.

Another able person was Bintou Keita, the UNICEF representative, whom I was able to have appointed as my Deputy (DERSG). In her capacity as the overall custodian of the peacebuilding projects being designed and implemented through the UN Peacebuilding Fund, some of which will be described later, Bintou communicated with other agencies in ways I was incapable of doing. She knew how to gain and cultivate the trust and cooperation of some recalcitrant

---

[41] Jackson (2006).
[42] United Nations (2010), 'Secretary-General Appoints Bo Schack of Denmark Deputy Special Representative for Central African Republic', SG/A/1214-AFR/1928-BIO/4157, 5 January. Bo Schack is a Danish lawyer. On 5 January 2010 he was appointed by the United Nations Secretary-General Ban Ki-Moon as Deputy Special Representative of the Secretary-General in the Central African Republic.

Burundian political actors, whose partisan politics stood in the way of BINUB's peacebuilding agenda. She was truly a catalytic leader both within and outside the mission. In hindsight, this was one of the happiest decision I took as ERSG.

Engineering integration

With these modest gains achieved, BINUB, despite some stubborn challenges, managed to make significant advances in the area of integration by engineering various processes to make it a reality at the strategic, programmatic, operational and structural levels. In this endeavour we were guided by Ban Ki-Moon's 2008 policy guidance which *inter alia* states that 'country level arrangements can take different structural forms, but all integrated presences should include, shared objective, closely aligned or integrated planning, agreed results and agreed mechanisms for monitoring and evaluation among UN components'.[43]

To illustrate the degree of integration we were able to achieve, this section provides an overview of how the various UN agency heads and chiefs of BINUB sections organized themselves under one structure to provide common strategic leadership and programmatic guidance.[44] This overarching structure was named the UN Integrated Management Team (UNIMT).

UNIMT met weekly under my leadership or that of my Deputy, Bintou Keita. We made a point of holding the meeting away from the imposing BINUB headquarters, with, for various reasons, UNICEF's conference room ending up being our preferred venue. In addition to articulating and nurturing a common vision of integration, UNIMT supervised the work of a number of joint programmatic and operational mechanisms, including:

- the Integrated Planning and Programming Task Force (IPPTF), whose primary focus was to spearhead integrated peacebuilding planning and programming;
- the Administrative Support Group, which looked into issues pertinent to operational integration, including common services;
- the Information, Communications and Advocacy Committee (InfoComm), responsible for the coordination of all UN communication activities and

---

[43] Metcalfe, V., A. Giffen and S. Elhawarydf (2011), 'UN Integration and Humanitarian Space. An Independent Study Commissioned by the UN Integration Steering Group', Humanitarian Policy Group Overseas Development Institute, December.

[44] United Nations (2006), 'Seventh Report of the Secretary-General on the United Nations Operation in Burundi' Addendum.

strategies and for the contents of the monthly BINUB Bulletin.[45] It operated under the guidance of the ERSG and the Head of Media and Communication, BINUB;

- the Integrated Monitoring and Evaluation Group, which comprised UN system staff hailing from different agencies;
- the UN Integrated Service Center (UNSIC), which operated under my guidance in my capacity as Resident Coordinator/UNDP Resident Representative. It provided administrative, human resources and financial support to all peacebuilding and community recovery projects funded by the Peacebuilding Fund (PBF),[46]and;
- the Integrated Welfare Services Committee, which oversaw facilities and activities aimed at enhancing staff wellbeing;
- Last but not least there was the entity that integrated and coordinated the UN system's activities in the area of gender equality and women's empowerment, pursuant to paragraph three of BINUB's founding resolution.[47] UNMIT and the various subsidiary structures that report to it have been amply described elsewhere,[48] and have been the subject of various information and advocacy campaigns both within and outside BINUB.

The integrated GoB-BINUB planning and programmatic structures created to follow up on the implementation of the Strategic Framework for Peace Consolidation[49] (negotiated with the PBC and the related UN peacebuilding support strategy), were also the subject of a great deal of negotiation between the UN system, the GoB and legitimate society representatives. It was felt that the time and effort invested in setting up these structures were necessary in order to achieve national, inclusive leadership and ownership. This national ownership strengthened our advocacy when seeking funds for implementing the peacebuilding projects we had submitted to the Peacebuilding Fund (PBF). For example, PBF ended up

---

[45] Bureau Intégré des Nations Unies au Burundi (2009), 'La Réinsertion durable des Soldats Démobilisés, Gage de Stabilité'.

[46] Campbell, S. (2010), 'Independent External Evaluation of Peacebuilding Fund Projects in Burundi'. Available online: https://reliefweb.int/sites/reliefweb.int/files/resources/CABFEA3AB9A416D 34925779C000EAE96-Full_Report.pdf (accessed 2 June 2020).

[47] United Nations (2006), 'Resolution 1719 (2006), adopted by the Security Council at its 5554th meeting, on 25 October 2006'.

[48] Reliefweb (2008), 'UN integration in Burundi in the context of the peacebuilding office BINUB – Taking stock and lessons learned from Jun 2006 to Nov 2007'.

[49] United Nations (2007), 'First session Burundi Configuration Identical letters dated 21 June 2007 from the Chairman of the Burundi configuration of the Peacebuilding Commission to the President of the Security Council, the President of the General Assembly and the President of the Economic and Social Council', PBC/1/BDI/4, 22 June.

approving a first tranche of $35 million.[50] In this connection, I cannot emphasize enough the catalytic role these funds played in galvanizing UN agencies in favour of the integration agenda, given many of them were executing agents of the projects, and thus were able to skim funds to meet some of their overhead expenses.

The creation and performance of these and other pioneering structures, such as the Partners Coordination Forum led by the GoB to follow up on the implementation of the Poverty Reduction Strategy Paper (PRSP),[51] were amply documented by the Lessons Learned Officer[52] and the UN Secretary-General's first report on BINUB.[53]

Security Council Resolution 1858 (2008), which renewed BINUB's mandate for the second consecutive year, noted BINUB's integration efforts and, in paragraph 17, encouraged the Executive Representative of the Secretary-General to pursue his action to enhance the integration and effectiveness of United Nations efforts on the ground in support of the implementation of the Strategic Framework for Peacebuilding in Burundi and of the recovery and development priorities of the government and people of Burundi."[54] This explicit mandate strengthened my hand in dealing with the GoB, as well as giving me the added incentive in my capacity as UN Resident Coordinator and UNDP Resident Representative to help create conditions for recovery and sustainable development, through, *inter alia*, the support I gave to the planning and organization of several donor conferences, inside and outside Burundi.

The quotations that follow and those interspersed in other parts of the book are the oral testimony of colleagues inside and outside BINUB, who watched my style of leadership evolve during my first two years at the helm of BINUB as I struggled with integration and other challenges. I felt it was important to elicit these testimonies, given that leadership for peace is as much about the leader as about followers. Some are admittedly favorably biased towards my Deputy Bintou, and me, others were somewhat critical. These testimonies, some of which were in French, were anonymously collected and edited for style and clarity.

---

[50]   In early 2007, the PBF allocated US $35 million to fund Burundi's first Peacebuilding Priority Plan (PBFI), which ran from 2007 to early 2010 and covered four key areas: governance, rule of law and the security sector, protection of human rights, and land issues, with a focus on the reintegration of returning refugees and resolution of land disputes. See United Nations Peacebuilding Fund, 'Burundi Overview', www. unpbf.org/ countries/burundi

[51]   International Monetary Fund (2007), 'Burundi: Poverty Reduction Strategy Paper', IMF Country Report No. 07/46, February.

[52]   United Nations Peace Operations (2008), 'UN integration in Burundi in the Context of a Peacebuilding Office BINUB Lessons Learned from June 2006 to October 2007'.

[53]   United Nations (2007), 'First Report of the Secretary-General on the United Nations Integrated Office in Burundi'.

[54]   United Nations (2008), 'Resolution 1858 (2008)'.

1. My Leadership in the Service of Integration: The Perspectives of Others

'The team was consenting with the vision of Mr Mahmoud. He trusted all team members. On certain issues there was dissent and some will go behind his back to discuss things, while others will not confront him for further explanation. However, in the UN system when a decision is taken, one has to abide with it and move ahead. Mr Mahmoud had displayed throughout responsible managerial qualities as head of mission ... Apart [from] weekly meetings that were held to assess the work of all agencies, more should have been done. The fact that he was the head of the mission, the head of country team among other tasks, it became very cumbersome for Youssef to be much more effective in delivering. Sometimes it was even impossible to hold weekly meeting because of excessive responsibilities. Although he was really good at gathering people, it was not always possible to do that because there was a lot of work on his desk. As a result, some people felt side-lined because their voices could not be heard.

'As his career was from within UN system, he knew how it worked. He knew how to interact with different departments of the UN. He is not someone who is very strong on hierarchy; he will have no problem sharing some issues with a desk officer. I won't say there were big initiatives but he was open and ready to discuss with Headquarters in New York. If headquarters had something to say he will listen, but he would also take bold decisions when needed. He used to present the report of the SG twice a year; he was greatly instrumental in letting the others know how the Peacebuilding Commission (PBC) supported by the Peacebuilding Fund (PBF)) should operate. In terms of relations with the PBC, he delegated a lot of to his Deputy Bintou Keita with a background from UNICEF, who really knew how to handle peacebuilding projects funded by the PBF. PBF projects were very instrumental in achieving PBC goals. She was good at working with various nationals on PBC projects.

'The main challenge in implementing BINUB's mandate comes from the host country key political actors. Mahmoud provided a direction on how to prioritize activities to be supported by the PBF. There was an attempt to really look what were the root causes of the conflict in order to consolidate peace. Decisions on the approach were reached jointly by the UN and the government. Bintou Keita played a very instrumental role in the process on ensuring inclusive dialogue, with everyone who mattered present at the table. Even though the government at the end had asked him to leave as it did with two of his predecessors, he succeeded in establishing collaborative working relations with the government for a considerable time of his mandate.

'The process he took in terms of joint operation and joint implementation of different mandate contributed to the enhancement of the mission. His direct engagement around the activities of the PBC and PBSO has also enhanced the performance of the mission on the ground.'

Championing gender equality and women's empowerment

In paragraph 3 of BINUB's founding resolution,[55] the Security Council urged the Mission:

> to take account of the rights of women and gender considerations as set out in resolution 1325 (2000) as cross-cutting issues . . . including through consultation with local and international women's group, and *requests* the Secretary-General, where appropriate, to include in his reporting to the Security Council progress on gender mainstreaming throughout the Integrated Office and all other aspects relating to the situation of women and girls, especially in relation to the need to protect them from gender-based violence.

In pursuit of this provision, and to send the unmistakable message that gender mainstreaming is not an ancillary frill or expendable add-on, I championed the full implementation of the above paragraph by chairing BINUB's integrated gender with Bintou Keita as Deputy Chair. Both Bintou and I agreed that Security Council Resolution 1325 on women, peace and security, was not about women only. It concerned everyone in the mission. We also agreed that both gender equality and women's empowerment were critical to ensuring the long-term impact of the peacebuilding initiatives we were embarking on.

Even though this paragraph was no longer a prominent feature in subsequent resolutions, I continued to provide every six months – in the margins of my presentation of the SG reports on the work of BINUB – a separate informal report to the members of the Council on major developments relating to the implementation of Resolution 1325. These included BINUB's monitoring and training activities on women's protection, human rights as women's rights and political empowerment.[56] These ranged from training women elected at the local[57] and national levels to granting livelihood subsidies to women associated with FN combatants; supporting the government to increase the number of women in the security forces through gender-sensitive recruitment campaigns to helping the Electoral Commission develop a gender-sensitive strategy enabling women to play their rightful role as informed voters and motivated candidates in anticipation of the 2010 elections.

---

55   United Nations (2006), 'Resolution 1719 (2006)'.
56   Nations Unies, '6236e Séance', S/PV.6236, Thursday 10 December 2009.
57   Bureau Intégré des Nations Unies au Burundi (2009), 'Journée Mondiale des Réfugiés', No. 030, 20 June.

Women with national identity/voting cards

With respect to political empowerment, I wish to focus on one particularly important initiative where the UN system in Burundi acted as one, and of which my team felt particularly proud. This relates to the provision of voting cards in record time to Burundian women and men who could not afford them. This was done as part of BINUB's overall effort to support the creation of a conducive environment for inclusive, free, and fair elections.[58]

One of the provisions of the new electoral law was the requirement that eligible voters be in a possession of a National Identity Card (NIC), without which they could not register on the electoral roll, let alone run as candidates. In Burundi, over 70 per cent of the population – mostly women and vulnerable groups – lived beneath the poverty line and could not afford a NIC, which cost about three dollars. The failure to provide women – who represented 51 per cent of the population – with NICs would exclude them from the elections and lower their representation below the required minimum quota of 30 per cent at the national (Parliament, Government) and local levels (Communes).

After the Secretary-General received a letter from the Burundian Minister of the Interior requesting financial and material support for issuing and distributing those cards, I established a BINUB and UNDP taskforce led by my Senior Gender Advisor to plan and execute – in close consultation with the GoB, the Independent National Electoral Commission and civil society organizations – an urgent project addressing this request. It was felt that a rapid response would help alleviate the concerns of some political parties, who were alleging that cards were being distributed in a way that favoured the ruling party. This was something the government denied.

However, there were some key challenges to overcome. The first was that the government did not want women to be the only beneficiary of NICs. It was then agreed that the key criteria would be level of poverty, meaning that rural poor women and men who could not afford an NIC would be included. This amounted to about 1 million potential beneficiaries. The second challenge was the task force had only two months to issue these 1 million NICs.

After discussion with the government, it was decided to organize 129 decentralized centres in order to assure timely issuance of the NICs. In record time, the issuance centres were properly equipped with forms and adapted material, including digital cameras enabling the development of photos on the

---

[58] United Nations (2009), 'Fifth Report of the Secretary-General on the United Nations Integrated Office in Burundi', S/2009/270, 22 May.

spot without using electricity. The required equipment had to be procured in record time. Because it was decided, following consultations with the government, to target men as well, over 1,000 additional local staff had to be recruited, trained and deployed to provide the centres with sufficient human resources and technical knowhow. This was in addition to the 4,000 volunteers who had been mobilized to support the campaign. Moreover, an additional amount of US$ 3 million had to be mobilized,[59] to accommodate both the needs of women and men.

I should hasten to add that not all the decentralized card registration and issuance centres performed optimally. The lack of electricity in some areas, weather hazards, long travel distances and limited transportation meant additional challenges had to be overcome.

All of the above notwithstanding, the outcome of this unprecedented mobilization was nothing short of miraculous. The necessary funds were mobilized in record time and the entire project was implemented within one month, resulting in the issuance of nearly 1 million NICs. Critical to the success to the operation were not only the integrated structures that enabled us to act as one UN but also the full ownership of the process taken by local actors at the national, provincial, local levels. The establishment of joint government-UNDP technical monitoring committee and involvement of the Civil Society and Women organizations were also key to this success.

The outcome of this collective effort contributed to a notable increase in female representation in public institutions at both the local and national levels. In his seventh report to the Security Council on BINUB, the Secretary-General conveyed his satisfaction by saying:

> A rate of representation by women in the National Assembly of 32% was attained without co-optation; that rate is above the 30% required by the Constitution. With regard to the Senate, representation by women now stands at 46%, positioning Burundi as the first country in Africa and second in the world in terms of representation by women at this level. Overall, 706 women were elected, representing 34% of all elected officials. That is a substantial increase from the 23% following the 2005 elections. Representation by women in the Government has also increased, from 32% in 2005 to 42% in 2010, with nine women holding Cabinet positions. In addition, more than 10,000 women served as election observers.[60]

---

[59] *Independent News* (2009), 'Burundi's Election Needs International Support', United Nations Press Release, 11 December.

[60] Bouka, Y. (2017), 'Burundi: Between War and Negative Peace', in G.M. Khadiagala (ed.), *War and Peace in Africa's Great Lake Region*, Switzerland: Palgrave Macmillan, 17–31.

2. How My Colleagues Perceived Gender Mainstreaming Efforts

'The first initiative was a systematic effort for integrating a gender perspective in our peacebuilding work. Our work in this area was regularly brought to the attention of the UN at Headquarters. Another initiative was the training in gender equality targeting top military official who were looking at that time for effective ways to recruit women in the Burundi armed forces. The Minister of Defence decided to have all senior military officers (at least major in rank) undertake a two-week gender training after which they will also be able to train junior military officers. According to those who took part, this training had a positive impact on the army.

'We adopted a transformative approach in an integrated manner. For example, we were not only working with victims of sexual violence but also with perpetrators of the violence. This is because we wanted perpetrators to understand the need of henceforth using their strength to protect women rather than assaulting them. This had a transformative impact as sexual violence issues were discussed both with men and women. This was an added value. Taking into consideration a country which had engaged in violence for almost two decades, young men knew more the language of violence than any other one.

'Another example is our contribution to increase women's participation in elections by assisting them in receiving their ID cards. It was decided to engage the UN in this massive undertaking to avoid measure fraud usually associated with establishment of national ID cards. We thus pleaded with the donors to provide the necessary resources after securing the blessing of the government. The opposition appreciated our support a lot.

'While this exercise was carried out successfully, we could have done certain things differently. For example, we should have kept a certain distance vis-a-vis some national actors whose vision was not encouraging. You know when national actors do not have a vision, our actions can be counterproductive. Mr Mahmoud was so anxious to obtain results to the extent he was trying to work with everybody, including unfortunately some people who were not of good faith. Also needed was an organization of the work that served the country rather than serving careers.'

Epilogue on integration

Long after I left Burundi, the Secretary-General in his last report on BINUB[61] expressed his gratitude to my predecessor, myself and all UN personnel for our 'dedication and tireless efforts to implement the mandate of BINUB in a truly integrated manner'.

---

[61] United Nations (2008), 'Seventh Report of the Secretary-General on the United Nations Integrated Office in Burundi', S/2010/608, 30 November.

I should hasten to add unfortunately that integration was the proverbial victim of its success. It was not totally embraced by several influential members of the GoB, despite appearances to the contrary. Nor was it universally accepted at Headquarters in New York. Several heads of humanitarian agencies had expressed concern about the depth and breadth of the endeavour, fearing that the integration of some structures might blur agency mandate lines, and even drive the system apart.[62] It came therefore as no surprise when the 'I' for 'integration' disappeared from the name of the UN presence succeeding BINUB – it was simply called BNUB.[63] Also joining the annals of history was the designation of the 'all-powerful' triple-hatted ERSG as the head of integrated missions and the overall Coordinator of UN operational activities on the ground. I was the second and last to be so called. This UN Secretary-General has now reverted to the standard nomenclature of Special Representative (SRSG) for appointees heading political presences.

What apparently precipitated the demise of this innovation was the appointment by the UN Secretary-General of a competent colleague at the helm of the UN Integrated Mission in Sierra Leone (UNIOSIL) who had not served as UN Resident Coordinator before (as his predecessor had done), nor passed the qualifying assessment/exam for such a position, as I had. Passing the exam was one of the requirements that must be met in order for UN officials to be designated as ERSG (see Chapter 2). There were also other reasons, too long to recount here, relating to turf battles between certain UN entities.

I shall revert to the lessons learned from this integration endeavour and its leadership implications in the final chapter.

Promoting inclusive dialogue

One of the painful legacies of violent conflict is broken relations between members of affected societies, distrust of formal governance institutions at all levels, and the weakening of autochthonous, traditional mechanisms for dialogue. Such mistrust tends to reach new heights at times of national stress, whether on the occasion of elections or in the wake of natural disasters.

---

[62] Boutellis, A. (2013), 'Driving the System Apart? A study of United Nations and Integrated Strategic Planning', International Peace Institute, August.
[63] Ibid.

Burundi, which had experienced over a decade of inter-ethnic massacres, was no exception.

Coming fresh from my last posting in Guyana, where I had organized a series of national conversations to promote social cohesion after years of social and political strife, I was gratified to find an appetite for a similar experience in Burundi. Among the eighteen peace consolidation projects approved by the Peacebuilding Fund (PBF),[64] there was one project in which we had invested a great deal of time and energy. Like several other peacebuilding projects, this was hailed as a model for ensuring inclusive national ownership in terms of its design, implementation and evaluation. It was called the Cadres de Dialogue,[65] or 'Support to putting in place frameworks for dialogue and consultations among social partners', and was financed to the tune of $3 million dollars. Due to its sensitive political nature, my Deputy Bintou and I supervised the project throughout its various phases of planning, execution and evaluation in close consultation with the Minister of Good Governance and the office of the then First Vice-President. Not unlike other PBF-financed projects, this one benefited from the overall monitoring and guidance of a joint UN-GoB steering committee.

The overall objective of the project was to restore trust among national partners through permanent, participatory and inclusive dialogue. More specifically, it aimed at enhancing knowledge and skills in participatory democracy, as well as creating spaces for debating key issues and strategies related to peace consolidation.

The project took nearly two years to design and implement. After intense preparation of the methodology and rigorous training of local facilitators, under the leadership of an international lead facilitator, the project was launched in February 2008 and ended in November 2009. It galvanized, across the country, government officials, parliamentarians and other elected officials at the local level, political parties, civil society, women and youth, the media, and the private sector. One of the concrete results of this project, following nine national and regional forums, was the establishment of a permanent framework for dialogue among political parties to debate issues of national importance. It was political parties themselves that pushed for this outcome.

---

[64]   United Nations (2007), 'First Session Burundi Configuration Identical letters'.
[65]   See Annex.

Reflections on dialogue

The question I am now asking is why such an investment in dialogue and the commendable results the project achieved did not prevent the 2010 electoral crisis, the attempted coup of 2015, and the ensuing eruption of violence that has had devastating consequences for the economy, for people's lives and for the rule of law. I shall return to this question in the final chapter of this volume and offer some elements of an answer, drawing lessons for the enterprise of peacebuilding in post-conflict contexts. In the meantime, I reproduce below the reflections of one of my anonymous colleagues, which might shed some light on this question.

---

3. The Perspective of a Junior Colleague on 'Cadres de Dialogue' Project

'What I will say, is that the cadres de dialogue was informed by his experience in Guyana. He insisted on having this project implemented at local level. He emphasized that inclusive dialogue that was to bring about trust among the population. He tirelessly pushed for this agenda both from the peacebuilding and development perspectives, as head of United Nations Development Programme (UNDP).

'He took the opportunity offered by this project to strengthen civil society organizations so they can play a watchdog role. He was very good at trying to ensure that all the actors have understood the goals and objectives of this and other peacebuilding initiatives. Although he left about six months before the 2010 elections, he managed to support the Burundians achieve in a very short time the goals set by the project. He boosted the country's capacity to go through the path to peace. We trained many government organs on political dialogue, decentralization, and anti-corruption, all funded by the Peacebuilding Fund.

'I don't think we were successful from the long-term perspective. I think we could have sat down and talked about what we wanted to achieve in 2008, or in ten years. Youssef himself persistently talked about sustainable foundation for peace. When I looked at what we implemented, it was for a here and now. We should have built foundations for a long-term peacebuilding. The problem is also the way mandates are issued by SC. These are for very short durations; it is usually one year or maximum fifteen months. That is the difference between the politics of the fifteen members of the SC and the reality on the ground. The ideal is to balance the short-term perspective and long-term perspective to achieve positive results.

'Leading a peace process for two years, he relentlessly boosted the idea of sustainable peace. But the big question remains: how do you achieve sustainable peace in such a working environment? Look at Burundi now – the sustainability is not there. This is maybe because we failed to address some key priorities that should have been addressed between 2005 and 2010.'

The peace process with the FNL: learning to lead from behind

Prior to my becoming ERSG, the implementation of the 2006 Comprehensive Ceasefire remained stalled.[66] As a result, the last active rebel movement – the FNL – increased its activities, including recruiting new members in Bubanza, Cibitoke and Bujumbura Rural provinces. Exactions against the population attributed to the movement, such as looting, extortion, ambushes, kidnappings and robbery, were still taking place as 2006 drew to an end. In some areas, FNL combatants were also reportedly conducting law and order activities, which many observers felt was the prerogative of the central government, however absent it may have been. Meanwhile, national security forces continued to arrest and detain individuals accused of FNL membership or collaboration. In December 2006, the South African Facilitation team, led by Charles Nqakula, Minister of Safety and Security, organized a meeting in Dar-es-Salaam at which the two parties reached an agreement overcoming key stumbling blocks. These included the granting of provisional immunity for the FNL, as well as the release of detained FNL members who had been nominated to participate in the Joint Verification and Monitoring Mechanism (JVMM) foreseen by the Agreement.

Throughout 2007 and early 2008, the peace process witnessed many additional setbacks, including breakouts of violence amidst increasing political demands from the FNL laid down as conditions for the resumption of the peace process. As 2008 progressed, however, significant advances in the peace process began to take place, the most important of which was the return to Burundi of the FNL leadership on 30 May 2008. These advances were the result of consistent pressure by the Security Council, as well as commendable and sustained efforts by the South African Facilitation and Regional Initiative led by Uganda and Tanzania.

Other key positive developments included a direct meeting between the President of Burundi and the FNL leader in Tanzania on 17 June 2007, followed by another in August 2008 in Burundi under the aegis of the South African Facilitator. Following these, significant decisions were taken, including the release of FNL prisoners. Ambassador Bah, the AU Special Representative, and I all actively participated in the public portions of those meetings, and, where appropriate, lent support to the drafting of the final communiqués.

---

[66] Comprehensive Ceasefire Agreement between the Government of the Republic of Burundi and the PALIPEHUTU-FNL.

Another milestone event was the 4 December 2008 summit of regional heads of state under the chairmanship of President Museveni of Uganda. During this summit, a clear road map for addressing the outstanding peace process issues was agreed, including the DDR process and the political integration of the FNL.[67] I read out the Secretary-General message to the summit.[68]

Two additional mechanisms are worth mentioning which, in my view, greatly contributed to bringing the Burundian peace process to a successful conclusion. These were the creation by the South African Facilitation of the Group of Special Envoys on Burundi (GSEB) and the Political Directorate (PD). Both were chaired by South Africa's Envoy to the Great Lakes region, Ambassador Kingsley Mamabolo, who made frequent visits to Bujumbura on behalf of the Facilitator, Minister Nqakula. In the absence of the latter, Ambassador Bah chaired meetings of the GSEB, which met as needed and was designed to coordinate international efforts in support of the Facilitator's mandate,[69] extended by the Regional Peace Initiative to run until 31 December 2008.

On 9 June 2008, shortly after the return of the FNL head Rwasa to Burundi, the Facilitator convened what was to prove to be one of the most important meetings of the GSEB. It took place in Magaliesburg (near Johannesburg), with both the leadership of FNL and high-level representatives of the Burundian government participating. The outcome of the meeting was the 10 June 2008 Magaliesburg Declaration, which outlined the commitments of all those present to resolving outstanding issues, with a view to laying the foundations for a less reversible peace in Burundi by the end of the year.[70]

The Political Directorate (PD) was created during an earlier February 2008 meeting of the GSEB in Cape Town, and, in addition to the GESB, included the two Burundian parties to the peace process among its membership. The PD's main mission was to serve as a listening forum to help address contentious political issues – which could not be addressed by the Joint Verification and Monitory Mechanism (JVMM) overseeing the disarmament and reintegration

---

[67] Bureau Intégré des Nations Unies au Burundi (2008), 'Célébration de la Journée Internationale des Droits de l'Homme', No. 024, 10 December.

[68] United Nations (2008), 'Secretary-General Urges Parties to Burundi Ceasefire Agreement to Summon "Political Will and Courage" to Overcome Outstanding Issues, in Message to Regional Summit', SG/SM/11983-AFR/1785, 4 December.

[69] Reliefweb (2008), 'Mandate of the Burundi Peace Process Facilitator Extended', 8 February. Available online: https://reliefweb.int/report/burundi/mandate-burundi-peace-process-facilitator-extended (accessed 7 July 2018).

[70] Institute for Security Studies (2008) '23 June 2008: The Return of Agathon Rwasa Could Signal Permanent Peace in Burundi', 23 June. Available online: https://ucdpged.uu.se/peaceagreements/fulltext/BUI%2020080610.pdf (accessed 1 July 2018).

of FNL combatants – arising between the FNL and GoB in the context of the peace process' implementation. A phased Programme of Action to Take Further the Peace Process in Burundi was agreed, with the PD entrusted to support the Facilitator to implement it by the end of 2008.

Since its launch, the PD met regularly on the premises of BINUB, which served de facto as its secretariat, including helping set the agenda and summarizing its deliberation.[71] With respect to the Magaliesburg meeting, BINUB was able to secure a small aircraft from the neighbouring UN Mission in the DRC in order to transport PD members there, including the GoB and FNL delegations. Confined together in the plane and having to stop several times for refuelling along the way, the Burundian protagonists exhibited considerable camaraderie – an art that Burundians in general excel at publicly, despite deep differences. This spirit of camaraderie enabled the Burundian parties to issue a joint declaration on 8 June 2008 expressing their determination to move forward together on the path of peace for the benefit of all Burundians.

These developments, in particular the support BINUB provided to the South African Facilitation, have been well documented in the third[72] and fourth[73] reports of the Secretary-General to the Security Council. Such support ranged from providing technical assistance to the JVMM to securing an office for facilitation on BINUB's premises, all the way to facilitating the work of the GSEB and PD.

---

4. How Others Perceived BINUB's Contributions to the Peace Process

'Most of Mahmoud's work was behind the scene[s]. For example, he was able to get funding from flying government representatives and the FNL leadership to South Africa for meetings. This is because the logistic[s] was also a challenge. The other contribution was to help design the meetings, and help facilitate the process towards some of the concrete recommendations.

'For the FNL in the peace process, the thing we missed which was very clear on the table, was when the FNL accepted in South Africa to join the peace process and

---

[71] United Nations (2008) 'Third Report of the Secretary-General on the United Nations Integrated Office in Burundi', S/2008/330, 15 May.

[72] United Nations (2008) 'Third Report of the Secretary-General on the United Nations Integrated Office in Burundi'.

[73] United Nations (2008), 'Fourth Report of the Secretary-General on the United Nations Integrated Office in Burundi', S/2008/745, 28 November.

disarm later on in 2009. They were promised (actually the leader of the FNL kept reminding people in the room) to be helped to be transformed from a rebel movement to a political party. He kept telling people in the room that you promised to transform its movement into real political party. To my understanding that was not properly done. And today as you can observe we are still paying consequences of that. Because had we helped the FNL to be a true political party [which it today is] but had we helped it with professional expertise, it would have been positively different.

'One of the opportunities which seemed very obvious was the strong presence of the African Union. Burundi is one of the few countries in Africa in which the AU as an organization has been engaged for many years. So Having Ambassador Bah as the AU representative for over a decade was a huge opportunity for Mahmoud. Mahmoud did not come as this UN arrogant SRSG, pretending to know it all. He sat there with Bah in order to reap key information from his extensive experience in Burundi.

'One day [in April 2008] while we were in a meeting, when "des obus" [mortar shells] were directed towards our sites in Bujumbura. Mahmoud disappointedly exclaimed to himself by saying: "Ils m'ont eus", meaning in this context "I was had" He continued by saying "this is FNL ... they promised to drop their weapons but I am realizing the opposite" [A promise I thought had been secured from the FNL leadership]. In the space of twenty minutes about seven "obus" were aimed at us [On 22 April the Vatican Embassy sustained structural damage during one of the raids]. In responding to that, Mahmoud decreed a security emergency plan to protect the staff as per the UN procedure. He and others have however subsequently succeeded to convince Rwasa [the FNL top leader] to drop their arms and return to Burundi.' [Key to this happy turn of events was pressure exercised by President Kikwete of Tanzania where the rebel leader had been in exile for years].

'He closely worked with the international community and specifically with [the] lead mediator, which was South Africa at the time, as well as with the Peacebuilding Commission in order to bring all actors on board. His inclusive approach in building peace enabled him to remarkably help bring on board the last rebel movement (FNL) to the negotiation table in 2008. This rebel movement was later on transformed into a political party. This was thanks in part to his good offices. Aghaton Rwasa, who was the leader of that rebel movement, is currently a member of the Burundian parliament.'

Reflections on my contributions with respect to the FNL

My own contributions as ERSG to the peace process led by Minister Nqakula were guided by the spirit and letter of paragraph 4 of Security Council Resolution 1791 (2007), in which the Secretary-General was requested, 'including through BINUB, to play a robust political role in support of the peace process, in full coordination with regional and international partners.'[74] This request was

[74] United Nations (2007), 'Resolution 1791 (2007)'.

reiterated in the Council's Presidential Statement of 24 April 2008, after the breakout of violence occurring earlier that month.

I robustly carried out the role entrusted to me, while fully recognizing and respecting that the main facilitator for the process was Minister Nqakula and his South African mediation team. Even during periods of heightened insecurity – such as during late 2007/early 2008,[75] when the FNL declared its lack of confidence in Mr Nqakula – my initiatives toward unblocking the situation were invariably coordinated with Nqakula's deputy, Ambassador Kingsley Mamabolo. This included faithfully reporting, both in writing and orally, on my private meeting in Dar-es-Salaam with the FNL leadership, as well as subsequent telephone conversations with them, usually initiated by either Pasteur Habimana, the FNL spokesman, or the movement's Chairman, Agathon Rwasa. I invariably toed the agreed line at the conclusion of our deliberations inside the Political Directorate.

I was therefore stunned to learn towards the end of 2008 of a memo from Minister Nqakula addressed to the Secretary-General accusing me of undermining his efforts. In a meeting with DPKO senior management in November 2008, in the margins of a briefing to the Security Council, Minister Nqalula repeated his grievance. I can only speculate as to the underlying causes of these sentiments, but even so we were subsequently able to iron out whatever misunderstanding had occurred, continuing to work together in perfect synergy until my departure. This culminated in the positive results witnessed after the FNL returned to the country and transformed into a political party.

Why was I asked to leave Burundi?

What can be observed in the case of Burundi, as elsewhere, is that tension at times arises between a UN presence and the host nation when the initial consent granted – whether willingly or under duress – is put to the test following the deployment of the mission. In other words, while adhering to the juridical legitimacy, a host government may not fully cooperate with the implementation of whatever mandate has been entrusted to the UN entity (as will be illustrated in Chapter 6 with respect to MINURCAT). This often depends on whether the host government perceives such implementation as infringing on its sovereignty

---

[75] UMOYA, Grandes Lagos; Semaine du 28 janvier au 1er février 2008, 05 Février. Available online: https://umoya.org/2008/02/05/grandes-lagos-semaine-du-28-janvier-au-1er-fie.r-2008 (accessed 4 August 2018).

or as safeguarding and enlarging it. Thus, as an ERSG or SRSG, you may find yourself caught between mandate expectations and power politic realities on the ground.

While I felt mandated to bring on board other key political stakeholders – including the political opposition, civil society and the FNL – the Government of Burundi viewed it differently, particularly as the 2010 elections drew near and the active involvement of BINUB on the political front had become more visible.

As my third year in Burundi drew to an end, I sensed that I had probably overstayed my welcome, having survived longer than my predecessor (or, for that matter, those who have succeeded me). Though the President had always been courteous to me, my meetings with him had become less frequent, and our rarer encounters shorter. With the exception of the then First Vice-President, who hailed from the minority party UPRONA, I could also sense the discomfort of government officials in my presence.

With each report that the UN Secretary-General produced on the general situation in Burundi and the work of BINUB, which occurred every six months, I am usually asked to travel to New York to present it on his behalf to the Security Council. The sixth report[76] in December 2009 was no exception.[77]

On this occasion, the Minister of Foreign Affairs and International Cooperation, Mr Augustin Nsanze, travelled himself to New York to present to the Council the GoB's point of view on the report's contents. Previously, this task had been performed by the Permanent Representative of Burundi to the UN, or a high functionary dispatched from the capital.[78] Rather than simply relaying his government's comments, Mr Nsanze gave a robust rebuttal to some of the observations and recommendations contained in the sixth report.

One of the Secretary-General's observations read as follows: 'The opposition parties continued to report attempts at intimidation by [the ruling party] CNDD-FDD and restrictions on the freedom of assembly imposed by local authorities throughout the country. They also accused Radio Télévision Nationale du Burundi of being biased and criticised the continuing media coverage of CNDD-FDD activities while the activities of the opposition parties received less media coverage.'[79] This observation echoed a recommendation contained in

[76]   United Nations (2009), 'Sixth Report of the Secretary-General on the United Nations Integrated Office in Burundi', S/2009/611, 30 November.
[77]   United Nations (2009), '6236th Meeting,' Thursday 10 December.
[78]   United Nations Official Document. Available online: http://www.un.org/en/ga/search/view_doc. asp?symbol=S/PV.6138 (accessed 2 August 2018).
[79]   United Nations (2009) 'Sixth Report of the Secretary-General on the United Nations Integrated Office in Burundi'.

the previous report where the Secretary-General stated, 'I am concerned about the numerous reported instances of disruption of the activities of opposition political parties by officials affiliated to the ruling party. I encourage the authorities to treat all political parties equally under Burundian law and respect the right to freedom of expression and assembly enshrined in the Constitution and in accordance with international standards.'[80]

Mr Nsanze latched onto these observations as a rationale for saying the following at the end of his rather long intervention:

> A paragraph of the report [of the UN Secretary-General] refers to the absolute need to carry out the election process according to the principle of fairness, and our Government welcomes that recommendation. In this regard, I recall that the success of the process will depend in part on respect for the principle of fairness in the implementation of the BINUB mandate.
>
> The Government of Burundi has observed that, for some time now, the principle of fairness highlighted in the report has, regrettably, not been upheld on the ground. The desire of some to incriminate the ruling party as if it did not have the same rights as the other political parties in the coming elections, and to assert that, having been entrusted with the mission of organizing elections, the Independent National Electoral Commission's is mandated to replace the authority in charge of territorial administration, represent two good examples of the lack of respect for the principle of fairness. It would be unfortunate and greatly damaging for the United Nations-Burundian Government partnership if the latter partner asks for the replacement of the sitting representative.[81]

Mr Nsanze's statement came as no surprise to me. What did surprise me, however, was that he had felt it necessary to take the unusual step of bringing his government's displeasure with me to the Security Council's attention at a public meeting, when he had already intimated it to UN Secretariat officials at headquarters. On 24 December 2009, Mr Nsanze sent a *note verbale*[82] to the Secretary-General formally requesting my replacement as head of BINUB, arguing that given the mission's future direction, a person with a different profile was needed. This was done with the full knowledge that my yearly contract was nearing its end. It is only fair to point out that the *note* duly expressed the GoB's

---

[80]   United Nations (2009) 'Fifth Report of the Secretary-General on the United Nations Integrated Office in Burundi'.

[81]   United Nations (2009), '6236th Meeting'.

[82]   PressAfrik (2009), 'Burundi: Le Gouvernement Burundais Demande le Départ du Représentant de l'ONU', 20 November. See Annex 1 of the actual *note verbale* requesting my replacement as ERSG in Burundi.

appreciation for my services and my active involvement in the consolidation of peace in Burundi.

Knowing that the GoB employed similar pretexts to justify the replacement of both my predecessors and successors, and to explain, after the fact, the departure of the German Ambassador less than a year after me,[83] I later set out to uncover what was really behind the GoB's animus. What follows is what I learned from former high-level Burundian officials who had since fallen out of favour with the government, and from other national and international sources who wish to remain anonymous.

Was it all about human rights?

In addition to getting rid of an inconvenient witness on the eve of the 2010 elections, the real reason, I was told, that what really unleashed the ire of the President and of the CDD-FDD generals who keep him captive was my consistent reporting on human rights violations and the GoB's inaction to bring perpetrators to account. A few months after my departure, the Human Rights Watch Representative in Burundi, Neela Goshal, having urged the government in one of her reports to combat political violence and ensure peaceful conditions, saw her work permit unceremoniously revoked and was asked to leave the country.[84]

In one of my early audiences with the President, I clearly but respectfully conveyed that while I would endeavour to be impartial in my interactions with Burundian political parties and leaders, it should not be expected that I would be neutral in matters of human rights violations. I further made it clear that I would bring verified violations to his attention before reporting on them to the Secretary-General and the Security Council, with the hope that I would be informed about actions being taken to shed light on such violations and bringing their perpetrators to justice. This, I added, would enable me to present a balanced picture of the human rights situation in the country.

One egregious act that shook the conscience of Burundi and its international partners was the brutal assassination in early April 2009 of Ernest Manirumva, Vice-President of '*l'Observatoire de lute contre la corruption et les malversations*

[83]   IWACU (2011), 'Chronique d'un Désamour', 30 July. Available online: https://www.iwacu-burundi. org/chronique-dun-dsamour/ (accessed 6 August 2018).
[84]   Peace Insight (2010), 'Human Rights Watch Representative Asked to Leave Burundi', 20 May. Available online: https://www.peaceinsight.org/blog/2010/05/human-rights-watch-representative-asked-to-leave-burundi/ (accessed 7 August 2018).

econonomiques' (OLUCOME)[85] and a well-respected, anti-corruption militant and human rights defender. It was alleged he was investigating a case of arms trafficking by individuals close to the ruling party. Despite calls from all quarters for a credible investigation into the exact circumstances of the assassination, no serious action was taken. I raised my concern about the lack of movement in addressing the issue several times with the highest authorities, including the President himself, receiving no satisfactory answer. I also reiterated on these occasions the lack of progress in establishing a credible National Independent Human Rights Commission.

In his report of 30 November 2009 on the situation on Burundi, the Secretary-General, stated that he remained deeply concerned about human rights abuses and the prevailing climate of impunity, including a number of serious crimes that remain unaddressed. He added 'In this regard, an early and just conclusion of the case involving the killing of the Vice-President of OLUCOME would be an important step in the right direction.'[86] It was this very report that Mr Nsanze criticized in his 10 December 2009 intervention alluded to above.

Notwithstanding Mr Nsanze's prevarications, the Security Council adopted Resolution 1902 (2009), renewing BINUB's somewhat modified mandate for another year. In paragraph 18 of that resolution, the Council called upon 'the Government of Burundi to pursue its efforts to broaden the respect and protection of human rights, including through the establishment of a credible National Independent Human Rights Commission' and encouraged it to end impunity and to take the necessary measures to ensure its citizens fully enjoy their civil, political, social, economic and cultural rights without fear or intimidation.

It was the principled stand taken on human rights violations in general and the OLUCOME case in particular that rankled the gaggle of generals surrounding the President, whom many observers accused of being implicated in these violations. It was '*la dernière goutte qui a fait déborder le vase,*'[87] [the last drop that made the vase overflow] according to my informant. Shortly after the publication of the 30 November 2009 report, the GoB decided to write to the Secretary-General requesting a new ERSG be at the helm of BINUB for the fourth and final year of its mandate. As the time of writing, and despite the establishment of three commissions investigating the murder of Manirumva – the last of which

---

[85] Observatory for the Fight Against Corruption and Economic Embezzlement.
[86] United Nations (2009), 'Sixth Report of the Secretary-General on the United Nations Integrated Office in Burundi'.
[87] "The last straw that broke the camel's back".

was assisted by the US Federal Bureau of Investigation (FBI) – proceedings have failed to deliver justice.[88]

There were other contributing factors that, I was told, may have stacked the deck against me. These included the successful campaign for the issuance of ID cards in record time, which the Minister of Interior would have liked to have taken credit for due to narrow partisan reasons. There was also the tussle at UN headquarters between DPKO (through which BINUB reported on its activities) and DPA, which wanted to take over responsibility for BINUB, given that the mission had no military component and was carrying out 'eminently political tasks'.

Among other possible factors cited was my even-handed treatment of the FNL as a partner in the tortuous implementation of the ceasefire agreement. The GoB reportedly felt it should have been considered the *primus inter pares*, rather than being treated as on equal footing with the FNL. Yet another possibility was the difficult relation BINUB had with the government-picked Chair of the joint Burundian-BINUB-civil society Commission, which was entrusted with the national consultations on implementing the three transitional justice mechanisms foreseen by the Arusha Peace Agreement.

As I have not been able to independently verify these and other hypotheses, I shall refrain from speculating further on their veracity.

Saying farewell

I returned to Bujumbura early in January 2010 to pack my bags and say farewell to the Burundi government, the diplomatic corps and my UN colleagues. In a town hall farewell to the latter, in which I reviewed all that we had accomplished in support of Burundi, I ended my remarks by saying:

> All good things come to an end and there is not a perfect ending. Why do I have to go now? There are many speculations about the reasons for my departure. Don't listen to these speculations. Diplomats and international civil servants come and go. And my time has come, even though you might think it had been precipitated.
>
> I leave feeling serene and proud of what we have accomplished together in support of the Burundian people in their legitimate pursuit of peace. I depart for other shores but you will continue your mission. I know that you will spare no

---

[88]   Imburi Phare Media (2016), 'Burundi: Justice pour Ernest Manirumva, 7 Ans après sa Mort', 10 April.

effort to sustain what we have achieved together. I leave you in the capable hands of my deputy Bintou Keita, until a new Representative is appointed. *Murakoze Cane, genda n'amahoro.*[89]

I left Burundi on 1 February 2010. As noted in a previous chapter, in March 2010 I was entrusted by the Secretary-General with another, no less challenging assignment with uncertain outcomes, but thankfully with a clear exit goal.

5. How my UN colleagues perceived the circumstances of my departure

'He left as he was asked to leave. The instruction was clear, "I am leaving," he said, "but the work of the UN continues." Other UN workers were left behind to continue the work of the UN and his deputy took over. The UN kept on working to the best of its ability ... We tried different things. When the government asked Youssef Mahmoud to leave some of us still thought that the decision could be reversed. Different groups initiated talks with the government to convince the latter that Youssef was working for a good cause. In the end the government decided to stick to its decision.

'Headquarters really messed up. They instigated the process of the transition from one department to the other, (from DPKO to DPA). The Government of Burundi used that [transition] to ask for the replacement of Youssef. That could have been done differently. The reasons of why he was pushed out were so blurred. In Burundi, his position was a unique one: instead of SRSG, he was ERSG. That position was never replicated although it could produce more positive results in other missions.

'But I also wonder why he did not foresee the government was not comfortable with him due to his political activism. Because he used to be very aware of everything ... When he left so many things fell apart. Was it because of his strong leadership? Or maybe he was not getting enough support? It was too complex to understand. Even though the UN was somehow effective in Burundi it did not build a solid platform for sustainable peace in Burundi.

'However, there shouldn't have been a lack of support from the UN Security Council when the government asked Mahmoud to leave. He should have never left. The UN needed to protect its ERSG because his performance on the ground was very positive.

'I think the government was mad about the fact that Mahmoud wanted to integrate the FNL. But government considered the FNL as very small and felt that it was not really representative of the society. While Mr Mahmoud looked forward to implementing a consensual democracy, the government did not see it that way. I think that is really when he became hated by government. Mr Mahmoud was very

---

[89] Kirundi for "Thank you very much, be in peace".

active and passionate about consensual democracy. New elections were coming, the government felt threatened. I am also sure some people in the UN were not happy with his consensual democratic inclination. There was some resistance within the UN with regard to the integration [approach] . . . When he was removed it came as a surprise to me. Although I suspected that . . . it came so fast.

'Mahmoud was very successful in implementing but less in achieving the yearned sustainable peace. In contrast with his predecessor, in the face of the government he was too humble to the extent they easily kicked him out. Meanwhile Carolyn Mcaskie the former SRSG [Head of ONUB] was feared by the government for her stand. She knew they wanted to kick her out, she could anticipate their moves and said she would go only at the end of her term. She did leave but on her terms.'

Epilogue

I learned after my departure that individual members of the diplomatic community in Bujumbura did express concern about the ease with which the GoB continued to ask for the recall of the highest ranking UN officials in Burundi under the guise of sovereignty, all without protest from the Security Council. They felt this could have a negative impact on the independence and neutrality of the Secretary-General's representatives.

However, I also learned that some individual Security Council members privately expressed displeasure at the Burundian authorities' actions, as they were concerned about this becoming an acceptable course of action whenever disagreement occurred between Secretary-General representatives and the host government. From my perspective, I am unsure whether any overt or discreet demarche on my behalf by Security Council members, individually or collectively, would have made a difference. This is particularly so, given the ease with which the same government requested the removal of my successors without consequences, and the cavalier way it rejected the July 2016 resolution by the same Council,[90] which approved the deployment of over 200 UN police to help mitigate the violence engulfing the country after the President won a third term.[91]

I have no regrets about leaving Burundi in the manner it was orchestrated. I left Bujumbura with my head held high, without rancor, secure in the knowledge

---

[90]　*The East African* (2016), 'Burundi Rejects UN Police Force after Security Council Vote', 4 August. Available online: https://www.theeastafrican.co.ke/news/Burundi-rejects-UN-police-deployment-after-Security-Council-vote/2558-3330100-r7xmuy/index.html (accessed 20 August 2018).
[91]　United Nations (2016), 'Adopting Resolution 2303 (2016), Security Council Requests Secretary-General Establish Police Component in Burundi to Monitor Security Situation', SC/12469, 29 July.

that I had executed my duties as ERSG to the best of my abilities. At the same time, I am fully aware there were many things, in hindsight, I could have done differently in the service of peace in Burundi, including questioning the liberal assumptions that informed my peacebuilding actions. I shall return to this and other related issues in the final chapter of the book.

5

A Trans-Border Humanitarian Crisis and a Contested Response

I could not have predicted that barely two months after departing Burundi in February 2010 I would be asked to lead a UN team to Chad, to negotiate the terms of the premature departure of a UN peacekeeping operation that had straddled eastern Chad and north-eastern Central African Republic (CAR). The operation, known by its French acronym MINURCAT (*Mission des Nations Unies en Centrafrique et au Tchad*), had been sent in 2007 to protect civilians who had fled the Darfur conflict in neighbouring Sudan and help deal with the humanitarian situation it had created.

This chapter provides a brief overview of the causes and magnitude of the complex humanitarian crisis that gripped eastern Chad and north-eastern CAR, leading the UN Security Council to dispatch a peacekeeping operation under less than optimum conditions. It also analyses the factors that contributed to Chad's decision to request the early departure of the mission. The chapter next describes the evolving multi-faceted situation prevailing on the ground following my arrival in Chad, highlighting some of the internal management challenges my senior leadership team and I faced during my nine-month tenure as Special Representative of the Secretary-General and head of the mission. These challenges and the efforts deployed to address them are discussed in detail in the following chapter.

An evolving crisis

State authoritarianism underpinned by non-inclusive leadership has, over the decades, been a source of frustration among various strata of the population in independent Chad, Sudan and CAR. These three countries share extensive similarities in the manner of governance, with the asymmetric distribution of resources leaving a huge part of these countries' populations in abject poverty. In Chad and Sudan, the level of rights enjoyed by their nationals has been to a considerable extent proportionate to their respective political and ethnic affiliations. Recurrent class discrimination and elite capture of the state has given rise to the formation of various internal armed groups, often forging alliances with kindred ethnic groups living across borders. These problems were not new developments in the region, but rather the continuation of earlier crises whose causes emanated from tumultuous socio-political pasts.[1]

Over the years, the once separated conflicts increasingly became intertwined with widespread trans-border consequences. Thus, worrisome as the internal situation in each country was, the humanitarian crisis that eventually attracted the attention of the UN Security Council could not be fully understood without close examination of the relationships between the countries sharing porous border lines around Chad's eastern region.

The strained relationship between the regimes of Khartoum and N'Djamena from the early 2000s onwards gradually contributed to violence escalating across these shared borders. Additionally, the fast deteriorating relationship between some former Chadian mercenaries and President François Bozizé after the latter took power in CAR in 2003 led to huge migration flows, with vulnerable civilians seeking refuge in eastern Chad.

The rivalry between President Omar al-Bashir of Sudan and President Idriss Déby of Chad, which emerged as a result of the Darfur conflict, exacerbated the already tense situation on the ground. Having earlier initiated the overthrow of President Hussène Habré from Darfur, Déby – who was expected to remain grateful and thus loyal to the Khartoum regime, which had supported him – turned his back on al-Bashir after over a decade in power. On top of growing domestic pressures, Déby fell out with the Sudanese government, which allegedly gave strong support to Chadian rebels bent on bringing to power a more collaborative regime in N'Djamena. Threatened by desertion in his army and presidential guard, Déby started giving tactical and logistical support to the Sudan Liberation Movement (SLM) and the Justice and Equality Movement (JEM),[2] both aligned against the Khartoum regime. As the enmity between the former allies grew, the situation on the ground further deteriorated. In April 2006 and later February 2008, Chadian rebels allegedly supported by the

---

[1]   Berg, P. (2008), 'The Dynamics of Conflict in the Tri-Border Region of Sudan, Chad and Central African Republic', Friedrich Ebert Foundation.
[2]   Ibid.

Khartoum regime stood at the doors of the capital city N'Djamena, coming close to overthrowing Déby in their second attempt.[3]

In Sudan, the fight had ceased to be solely between the government and its militias against Sudanese rebel groups. A strategic game for regional dominance that required going beyond its borders was being played by the Khartoum regime, the intention being to overcome all rivalries masterminded by neighbouring Chad's regime. Besides supporting the loyal Janjaweed militias with modern weapons and giving them a guarantee of escaping legal prosecution for atrocious crimes committed against civilian populations in Darfur, the central government in Khartoum concurrently supported the activities of Chadian rebels against the government of N'Djamena.[4] The masked and unmasked roles of the two sovereign entities against one another continued to deepen the crisis long after the famous Comprehensive Peace Agreement of 2005 between the Northern and Southern parts of Sudan.[5]

In the meantime, as part of its counter-insurgency strategy in Darfur, the Sudanese government continued to arm and support Janjaweed militias in deliberately targeting civilians of the same ethnic origin as the Darfur rebels.[6] As a result of three years of massacres, mainly through summary executions and 'ethnic cleansing', 1,800,000 Darfurians were internally displaced, with another 207,000 Sudanese finding refuge in eastern Chad[7] – the vast majority of them Fur, Masalit and Zaghawa,[8] a minority tribe from which President Déby hailed. Once again, civilians were the victims of a conflict strongly fuelled by the self-centred motives of politicians.

As noted above, the porosity of borders also applied to CAR, which has over the years been unable to control significant parts of its territory. In early 2000, during President Ange-Felix Patassé's rule, the Sudanese army passed through Central African territory to attack the Sudan People Liberation Movement (SPLM) in Southern Sudan. Under Bozizé, meanwhile, Chadian rebels in April 2006 made use of the northeast of the country as they travelled from Darfur to

---

[3] Tubiana, J. (2008), 'The Chad–Sudan Proxy War and the "Darfurization" of Chad: Myths and Reality', Small Arms Survey, Graduate Institute of International Studies, Geneva.

[4] Ibid.

[5] United Nations (2005), 'Sudan Peace Agreement Signed 9 January Historic Opportunity, Security Council Told', Meetings Coverage and Press Releases, 8 February.

[6] Human Rights Watch (2004), 'Darfur in Flames: Atrocities in Western Sudan', A Human Rights Watch Report, Vol. 16, No. 5(A), April.

[7] UNHCR (2006), 'Operational Briefing on the Special Operations for Chad and Sudan', UNHCR, May.

[8] UNHCR (2006), 'Ethnicity of Sudanese Refugees – Eastern Chad', UNHCR Map, January.

execute their coup attempt in Chad.[9] Although the regime in CAR lacked resources to influence the geopolitics in the tri-border area, the easy accessibility to its largely uncontrollable territory made CAR a party to a 'triangular' political suspicion in the sub-region.

While the Sudanese government seemed to take a more offensive strategy in this game of influence and hegemony, its Chadian rival opted for a more defensive and destabilizing approach. Tension along the border reached its apex in early December 2005 with a joint operation by Sudanese government troops, Janjaweed militias and Chadian rebels on the Changaya headquarters of SLM commander Khamis Abdullah Abaker in West Darfur. Later, on 18 December, Chadian Rally for Democracy and Liberty (RDL) rebels led by Mahamat Nour attacked Adré, a strategic Chadian town along the Chad–Sudan border where armed groups drawing support from both countries had proliferated. Chadian troops repelled the RDL assault, with the Chadian government alleging that Nour could not have mounted his action without the support of the Sudanese government.[10] On 23 December 2005, Chad declared a 'state of belligerence' with Sudan.[11] Facing a rising menace from Darfur, the Chadian government sought defensive alliances with Darfurian rebel groups, with the aim of protecting its territory from Sudan government's backed militia attacks.

Attacks in eastern Chad went beyond refugee camps, with surrounding villages also targeted. The massacre of mid-April 2006 represented another serious call for local, regional and international attention. On 13 April, a major attack orchestrated by Sudanese Janjaweed militias and local Chadian villagers was staged against a group of Chadian villages in Dar Sila department (south-eastern Chad). These attacks against surrounding villages alarmed those who had made it to refugee camps and were still struggling to improve their own security.

Despite some efforts to contain these violent attacks the situation did not improve. On 16 June, more than 1,000 people fled attacks in south-eastern Chad and entered Darfur. Beating and other abuses, including systematic looting, were carried out by unidentified militiamen in the course of these attacks.[12]

[9]   Berg (2008).
[10] *Sudan Tribune* (2005), 'Chad in State of Belligerence with Sudan: Official', 24 December. Available online: https://www.sudantribune.com/spip.php?article13198 (accessed 28 August 2018).
[11] Reliefweb (2010), 'Chad Declares State of Belligerence with Sudan', 23 December. Available online: https://reliefweb.int/report/chad/chad-declares-state-belligerence-sudan (accessed 28 August 2018).
[12] Médecins sans Frontières (2006), 'Over 10,000 People Flee Violence in Chad', Press Release.

Vulnerable populations in unsafe shelters

Amidst all of this, concerns over alleged rebel activities in refugee camps in eastern Chad continued to grow due to the proximity of the conflict-affected border and the fact that many Darfur rebels had family ties in the camps.[13] Disturbing allegations of forced recruitments within eastern Chad refugee camps reached local authorities and the international humanitarian community trying to protect civilians from harm. According to UNHCR's statistics, approximately 4,700 refugees were recruited from refugee camps in eastern Chad into Sudanese rebels forces, risking the militarization of the camps and exposing vulnerable populations to abuse.[14] While UNHCR reported that a considerable number of refugees voluntarily joined the SLM rebel movement, Human Rights Watch upon investigation found that recruitment was indeed coercive in nature.[15]

The level of vulnerability in the refugee camps was not gender neutral. While men were vulnerable as they could be easily killed or targeted for forced recruitments into rebel or militia ranks, women were victims of sexual violence as well as other crimes. Both inside and outside refugee camps, women and girls were exposed to repeated acts of rape,[16] particularly when travelling outside of camps to cater for family needs, such as gathering firewood for cooking.[17] Since 2003, over 142,000 women had fled the insecure Darfur region, seeking safety in neighbouring eastern Chad.[18]

Humanitarian and human rights workers and advocates found it difficult to holistically address sexual violence related issues, as victims were often reluctant to report such egregious acts for fear of being stigmatized in highly patriarchal societies. Married women are often shunned or abandoned by their husbands, while unmarried girls who have been raped encounter serious difficulties finding

---

[13] UNHCR (2005), 'Perceptions of Refugee Security in Chad (Based on Information Received During ESS Mission, 12–17 July 2005)', UNHCR Internal Document.

[14] Human Rights Watch (2006), 'Violence Beyond Borders: The Human Rights Crisis in Eastern Chad', June, No. 4.

[15] Ibid.

[16] Report of the UN Secretary-General, 14 July 2009, para.19, 42, 44 and 51; Physicians for Human Rights, Nowhere to Turn: Failure to Protect, Support and Assure Justice for Darfuri Women, May 2009.

[17] Amnesty International (2009), 'No Place for Us Here: Violence against Refugee Women in Eastern Chad', Amnesty International Publications: 4.

[18] As of 31 March 2009, there were 252,488 Sudanese refugees in the twelve refugee camps in eastern Chad, 22.1 per cent of them were young girls, between five and seventeen years of age. Women and girls constituted 56.5 per cent or 142,682 of the total refugee population, UNHCR report, March 2009, on file with Amnesty International.

a husband. As the victims of sexual violence persisted in their silence, perpetrators took advantage to commit further related crimes which went unpunished. Impunity did not, however, emanate only from the silence of the victims, but also from the relatively low attention given by local authorities to cases of sexual violence.

UN and AU sporadic responses

At the height of the humanitarian crisis and up to 2006, UN involvement within individual countries and across the Central African region was sporadic and short term, with mixed results. I recall visiting CAR in late 2000, at the tail end of a UN Peacekeeping mission called MINURCA, which had been operating for nearly two years to help stabilize a volatile situation plagued by multiple mutinies and coup attempts, and to organize elections.[19] The Security Council decided to close the mission following the elections that brought to power then President Ange-Felix Patassé for a six-year term. The purpose of my visit to CAR at the head of a UN multi-disciplinary team was to propose to President Patassé – who was deeply unhappy about the Council's decision to terminate MINURCA – the establishment of a small UN successor arrangement aimed at consolidating some of the fragile gains achieved by the departing peacekeeping mission. That proposed arrangement was later to be called the UN Integrated office in the CAR, known by its French acronym BINUCA. The President, following several rounds of negotiations we had with his defence minister, reluctantly agreed to BINUCA's presence (which he termed as political baby-sitting), warning that the Security Council would regret closing the mission. The international community would return to CAR 'galloping', he said, given the security vacuum the premature departure of MINURCA would leave behind, which various disgruntled armed factions opposed to his regime would not hesitate to fill. Subsequent events proved him right. In 2003, he was removed in a coup perpetrated by his Army Chief of Staff François Bozizé who, in turn, was toppled ten years later by an armed rebellion[20] in which once again the main victims were invariably innocent civilians.

---

[19]   RFI Afrique (2010), 'Les Dates Clé de la République Centrafricaine', 11 August. Available online: http://www.rfi.fr/fr/afrique/20100811-dates-cle-republique-centrafricaine (accessed 26 August 2018).

[20]   *The New York Times* (2013), 'President is Said to Flee as Rebels Seize Capital of the Central African Republic', 24 March. Available online: https://www.nytimes.com/2013/03/25/world/africa/rebels-seize-capital-of-central-african-republic.html (accessed 26 August 2018).

The UN at that time had no presence in the equally unstable neighbouring countries of Chad and Sudan, until the establishment in 2007 of MINURCAT in eastern Chad and north-east CAR, and the deployment of a Joint UN-African Union Mission in Darfur (UNAMID) the same year.

The African Union did not adopt a meaningful, proactive role in mitigating crises in the troubled region, nor did it help normalize relations between Chad and Sudan. Instead, it was Libya, under President Muammar Gadhafi, that wrestled with the problem, trying to quench the fast-burning flame between its two faithful allies, the presidents of Chad and Sudan. During the February 2006 mini-summit[21] in Tripoli, under the auspices of Gadhafi, both belligerents signed an agreement to resume harmonious bilateral relations and end support to their respective proxy rebel groups and militias, which had devastated their respective border towns. Barely two months after the agreement was signed, however, a rebel attack was carried out in N'Djamena, once again straining Chad–Sudan relations.[22] While the AU, in a February 2007 communiqué,[23] condemned the rebel attacks in Chad and CAR as an unconstitutional move that was in violation of the Lomé Declaration and the Constitutive Act of AU, it was reluctant to take part in the October 2007 Sirte agreement, once again hosted by Libya.

UN protection peacekeeping mission without a political mandate

It was this cross-border humanitarian crisis that compelled international human rights and humanitarian organizations to increase pressure on the international community to take action, targeting in particular the UN Security Council. Humanitarian actors called on the Council to move from statements to action, pursuing the idea contained in para 9(d) of Resolution 1706 (September 2006) regarding the establishment of an international, multi-dimensional presence to improve the security situation along the borders between Sudan and Chad, and between Sudan and CAR.[24] However, the main host country, Chad, was not keen

---

21 The summit was also attended by Nigerian President Obasanjo, CAR President Bozizé, and AU Chairperson of the Commission Konaré, as well as Burkina Faso President Compaoré, who was also at the time chairing the Community of the Sahelo-Saharan States (CEN-SAD).

22 Lacey, M. (2006), 'Chad Severs Ties with Sudan as Tensions Escalate', *The New York Times*, 14 April.

23 Communiqué of the Peace and Security Council of the African Union (AU), at its seventieth meeting held on 12 and 13 February 2007.

24 United Nations (2006), 'Security Council Expands Mandate of UN Mission in Sudan to Include Darfur, Adopting Resolution 1706 by Vote Of 12 in Favour, with 3 Abstaining', Meetings Coverage and Press Releases, 31 August.

on such an all-encompassing presence. What it had requested was an international civilian presence with the sole mandate of supporting the police and rule of law structures in managing refugee camps and internally displaced persons' sites.

Towards the end of 2006, in order to help the Security Council make an informed decision on what action it should take, the United Nations Department of Peacekeeping Operations (DPKO) fielded a multi-disciplinary, technical assessment mission to CAR and Chad. However, the mission was not able to visit the affected tri-border areas connecting Sudan, Chad and CAR due to the ongoing hostilities and generalized insecurity created by rebel and criminal activities.

In the report the Secretary-General presented on 22 December 2006 (S/2006/1019)[25] to the Security Council, he conveyed the findings and recommendations of the assessment mission, including an analysis of the humanitarian and security situation in the affected areas of Chad and CAR. In addition to painting a worrisome picture of the humanitarian situation, the report recounted a meeting the mission held with the President of Chad in early December 2006. During the meeting, the President had reportedly signalled his agreement, in principle, to the deployment of an international presence at the border with Sudan so as to strengthen security in the area and ensure the protection of refugees and internally displaced persons. At a similar meeting in late November 2006, the President of CAR indicated he would welcome the establishment of a UN peacekeeping presence in the north-eastern part of his country and stressed the need for its rapid deployment.

The report further informed the Security Council that the assessment mission was unable to ascertain the views of the armed opposition groups. However, the opposition parties the team had contacted indicated that armed opposition would regard a UN operation along the border areas as partial and supportive of the governments in Chad and Sudan. In the absence of an inclusive political process, the report observed 'a United Nations multi-dimensional presence would therefore face considerable security risks'.[26]

In the recommendation section, the report offered two options for the Security Council's consideration. The first was a monitoring, multi-dimensional presence to observe the situation in the border area and improve security through confidence-building and preventive measures. The second was a

25 United Nations (2006), 'Report of the Secretary-General on Chad and the Central African Republic pursuant to paragraphs 9 (d) and 13 of Security Council resolution 1706 (2006)', S/2006/1019, 22 December.
26 United Nations (2006) 'Report of the Secretary-General on Chad and the Central African Republic pursuant to paragraphs 9 (d) and 13 of Security Council resolution'.

monitoring and protection multi-dimensional presence with a robust military component that would, within its capability, 'provide protection to civilians under imminent threat'.[27]

After reviewing the risks involved in pursuing either option in the absence of a meaningful political settlement among the parties concerned, the report concluded that 'conditions for an effective peacekeeping operation do not seem to be in place' and that 'if the Security Council decides to pursue the idea … a robust monitoring and protection mission should be considered' which is 'contingent upon cessation of hostilities and agreement by all parties'.[28] The Security Council deliberations preceding the establishment of MINURCAT were charged, emotional and critical of the UN Secretariat's advice. While Council members shared concerns about the deteriorating security and humanitarian situation along the Chad/Sudan and CAR tri-border area, they were divided over the wisdom of deploying a fully-fledged UN peacekeeping mission in the absence of a political process and the consent of all parties. Ultimately, the majority of members yielded to the persistent calls for urgent deployment of a multidimensional presence. Chad reluctantly agreed following pressure from the French government, which had brokered the deployment of a bridge European Union military force (EUFOR) for one year. The force would become an integral part of the resolution that was to establish MINURCAT.

At the time, the UN Mission was in the process of being established, there were already 281,000 refugees in Chad originating from Sudan and CAR, and another 150,000 internally displaced people.[29] It was this grave humanitarian situation that prompted the UN Security Council, through Resolution 1778 of 25 September 2007, to create MINURCAT for an initial period of one year. MINURCAT's mandate was 'to help create the security conditions conducive to voluntary, secure and sustainable return of refugees and displaced persons, *inter alia* by contributing to the protection of refugees, displaced persons and civilians in danger, by facilitating the provision of humanitarian assistance in eastern Chad and the north-east Central African Republic and by creating favourable conditions for the reconstruction and economic and social development in those areas'.

The resolution was adopted despite the Secretary-General's observation in his 23 February 2007 report (S/2007/97)[30] – following a second technical assessment

---

27 Ibid.
28 Ibid.
29 Ibid.
30 United Nations (2007), 'Report of the Secretary-General on Chad and the Central African Republic', S/2007/97, 23 February.

mission – that Chad was not 'a conventional peacekeeping environment' given the ongoing hostilities between the government and various armed opposition groups, and that it would be imperative to obtain from these groups assurances that would 'recognise the impartial character of United Nations presence'.[31] From a DPKO perspective, the basic conditions necessary for establishing a peacekeeping operation, as expounded in the Brahimi Report and reinforced in subsequent doctrinal developments, were not present.

By this founding resolution, two multilateral presences were created, a UN Mission (MINURCAT) and a European Union Military force (EUFOR) operating under a single mandate. The UN presence, initially staffed by civilians, was responsible for police training and reinforcing judicial infrastructure, and working with Chadian forces to reinforce safety for refugees, Internally Displaced Persons (IDPs) and aid agencies in the eastern camps. EUFOR, with its 3,700 troops, was tasked with providing general security for civilians and facilitating the free movement of humanitarian assistance and personnel. EUFOR was authorized, under Chapter VII of the Charter, to use military force as needed, whereas MINURCAT was not under the same original mandate.

After a year of uneven performance, largely due to logistical challenges and repeated delays in the deployment of its staff, MINURCAT's mandate was renewed for another year in September 2008 by resolution 1834.[32] By the terms of that resolution, the Council expressed its intention for EUFOR, which had experienced its own deployment difficulties,[33] to transfer authority to a UN military component. This transfer took place on 15 March 2009, when EUFOR's mandate expired. Under a new resolution (1861) on 14 January 2009, which extended MINURCAT for an additional year (i.e. until 15 March 2010), the mission was authorized to have a military component of 5,200 troops, despite the Secretary-General in his report recommending nearly 11,000 in light of the assessment missions' findings. The lower number was decided in order to address President Déby of Chad's objection to a strong military footprint on his territory.[34] The President's concerns and his reluctant consent would later plague the mission throughout its deployment phases and operations, as would the

---

[31] Ibid.

[32] United Nations (2008), 'Security Council Adopts Resolution Extending Mandate of United Nations Mission in Central African Republic and Chad until 15 March 2009', Meetings Coverage and Press Releases, 24 September.

[33] Murphy, R. (2011), 'Post-UN Withdrawal: An Assessment of Peacekeeping in Chad', *Irish Yearbook of International Law*, Vol. 4–5.

[34] In late 2008, President Déby was reportedly unhappy with EUFOR for not engaging the rebel advance on N'Djamena earlier in the year (https://fas.org/sgp/crs/row/RS22798.pdf).

tardy arrival on the ground of force multipliers and enablers, such as helicopters. Absent in the mandate of MINURCAT throughout its various iterations was any political role, including good offices, as had been recommended in the Secretary-General's 2006 report. All the mission was asked to do was liaise closely with national and regional stakeholders 'to exchange information on emerging threats to humanitarian activities in the region'.[35] These constraints resulted in a peacekeeping operation being deployed solely for the purpose of protecting civilians, with no authority given to accompany or facilitate any peace process. Those involved in the planning exercise confirmed the immense pressure exerted by key Council members to deploy a peacekeeping operation 'at all costs', in a context where there was no peace to keep.

It was therefore no surprise that the third report of the Secretary-General on the humanitarian situation in eastern Chad, dated 10 August 2007, removed from its recommendations anything that did not meet with the approval of the Chadian government. The report, for example, no longer recommended a political mandate, which had sought to address the root causes of insecurity, such as 'facilitation of improvement of relations between Chad and Sudan, and CAR and Sudan; supporting the efforts of the Government of Chad (GoC) to establish a sustained political dialogue with unarmed opposition groups and assistance in the development of a ceasefire between the GoC and armed opposition groups'.[36]

When it finally took over from EUFOR in March 2009, the role of MINURCAT police and military, as outlined in the concept of operations (CONOPS), was to 'contribute to protecting civilians in danger, particularly refugees and displaced persons ... and to contribute to protecting United Nations personnel, facilities, installations and equipment.' Meanwhile, the international civilian component of the mission was tasked with promoting human rights and supporting the application of the rule of law in eastern Chad. A small military presence was also established in north-eastern CAR, in the town of Birao, to provide *in extremis* extraction to humanitarian actors operating in the area.

Throughout the successive resolutions renewing its yearly mandate, the core mission of MINURCAT remained the protection of civilians. There was no mention of stabilizing the border areas between Chad and Sudan, nor was there

---

[35]   United Nations (2007), 'Security Council Authorizes Establishment of "Multidimensional Presence" in Chad, Central African Republic, Unanimously Adopting Resolution 1778 (2007)', Meetings Coverage and Press Releases, 25 September.
[36]   United Nations (2007), 'Report of the Secretary-General on Chad and the Central African Republic'.

any intimation that the mission would be allowed to play any political role. The vigilance of the Chadian authorities was such that successive Secretary-General's reports presented to the Security Council on Chad purposefully avoided any analysis or opinion on the internal political situation in the country.

As a result of the compromises and concessions dictating the terms of its mandate, MINURCAT was, from its inception, a flawed, 'better than nothing' mission. Though the deployment of UN troops started in March 2008, the UN only became fully responsible for military assignments in 2009.[37] As noted above, despite Resolution 1861(2009) mandating the establishment of a 5,200-strong United Nations military component by the end of 2009, that number was revised downwards to 4,700 troops. In late March 2010, when I arrived to negotiate the terms of MINURCAT's exit, the force stood at 3,422, largely as a result of multiple logistical and other impediments.

The overall deployment of civilian staff was also delayed. Mr Victor Angelo, the SRSG and head of MINURCAT, was appointed[38] six months into the mission and staff were not in place until nine months after the resolution for the mission was approved. Many of the delays were attributed to a lack of logistical arrangements and life-support facilities for staff in eastern Chad, a rather austere, desert-like environment.[39] Preparations for the creation of the mission were without doubt problematic. Thus, in addition to the enduring humanitarian crisis, MINURCAT was also challenged by its lack of planning and adequate preparation.[40]

Delays were also recorded with respect to establishing an important component of MINURCAT's mandate, a special UN-supported Chadian gendarmerie-like unit called *Détachement Intégré de Securité* (DIS). The DIS was expected to provide security in refugee camps, sites with concentrations of IDPs and key towns in neighbouring areas,[41] in addition to assisting with the restoration of the rule of law (legal protection) in eastern Chad and the promotion of inter-community dialogue[42] (political protection).

[37]   Between March 2008 and March 2009 MINURCAT was supported by EUFOR, under European Union command.
[38]   United Nations (2008), 'Secretary-General Appoints Victor Da Silva Angelo of Portugal to Head United Nations Mission in Central African Republic and Chad', Meetings Coverage and Press Releases, 31 January.
[39]   MINURCAT II Final Draft Report (2010), 'Lesson Learned', 6 November: 10.
[40]   Murphy (2011).
[41]   Boutellis, A. (2013), 'Chad and the Central African Republic', in J. Boulden (ed.), *Responding to Conflict in Africa. The United Nations and Regional Organizations*, New York: Palgrave Macmillan, 121–44.
[42]   United Nations (2010), 'Fonds d'Affectation Spéciale des Nations Unies au Profit du Détachement Intégré de sécurité', MINURCAT UNPOL, Interoffice Memorandum, 11 November: 3.

It was not until 2009 that the training of the mandated 850 DIS members was complete, with their programmed deployment to eastern Chad then delayed due to a lack of vehicles and police stations. This had angered the GoC, which was of the firm view that the newly created DIS was a far more viable option for the protection of civilians than the military contingent of MINURCAT which, as noted above, was slow to deploy.

The Mission's relationship with the Chadian authorities was further constrained by the nature of the official interface it had with the government-designated structure called CONAFIT (*Coordination Nationale d'Appui à la force Internationale à l'est du Tchad*), headed by a four-star army general, Oki Dagache and comprised predominantly of military personnel. Although there were frequent meetings with CONAFIT, the Mission had limited contact with the President and other high-level government officials. Information and advice on MINURCAT matters reaching the President and his senior advisors tended to be filtered through a military lens. Government dissatisfaction and at times impatience with the slow deployment of logistical support for the DIS was regularly expressed during meetings my predecessor and I had at the time of our respective encounters.

MINURCAT's response to such complaints was to over-compensate and bend backward to 'please' the GoC at all costs. This led at times to key principles – as well as established administrative and other procedures governing UN peacekeeping – being breached. The mission was more often than not concerned with providing material assistance to the DIS at the expense of its own logistical requirements. An internal DPKO evaluation report on MINURCAT stated, 'the need to stay on the good side of CONAFIT and the President of Chad guided the way the mission reported, prioritized activities and allocated assets ... the provision of equipment and supplies to DIS became MINURCAT's number one priority, even raison d'être, to the detriment of the mission's own security and operational capacity.' MINURCAT essentially became a 'service provider' for DIS.

MINURCAT at the exit door

Adding to the above account about the birthing and growing pains of MINURCAT, what follows is a cursory review of the salient additional factors that converged to explain the Chadian government's 15 January 2010 request for the 'premature' departure of MINURCAT. The move, while infuriating some members of the Security Council and a number of influential international non-governmental humanitarian and human rights organizations,[43] in reality represented the moment the sword of Damocles finally fell.

The first reason behind Chad's request was – not accidental – the signing on 15 January 2010 of an agreement between Chad and Sudan normalizing their bilateral relations and providing for the deployment along their common border of a joint force under a joint command, denying cross-border movement of armed elements and stemming their criminal activities. As noted above, from 2003 to 2009 the governments of Chad and Sudan engaged in a fierce proxy war waged through the provision of material support to each other's rebel groups and armed opposition forces. By May 2009, however, frustration and fatigue as well as other factors were affecting both regimes' willingness to continue proxy conflicts.[44] In late 2009, a serious rapprochement began between the two countries, particularly after Khartoum moved Chadian opposition forces away from the border. Chad reciprocated by asking in January 2010 for the withdrawal of MINURCAT and in May 2010 by expelling from its territory the Darfur Justice and Equality Movement (JEM) and its Chairman.[45] These actions were followed by an exchange of ambassadors. The rapprochement was duly noted by the Secretary-General[46] and subsequently welcomed by the Security Council.[47] By June 2010, a 3,000-strong joint force was in place and fully operational.

Secondly, there had been a marked improvement in the security situation, with the Chadian government also becoming increasingly politically independent, and financially and militarily self-reliant.[48] The government thus felt ready to assume full sovereignty throughout its territory and, as such, viewed the continued presence of external forces as an impediment to this. By late 2009, the government had succeeded in regaining and securing key parts of its territory, and declared itself ready to protect vulnerable civilian populations and humanitarian workers.[49] To this effect, it made known its intention to increase

---

[43]   Amnesty International (2010), 'Chad: We too Deserve Protection. Human Rights Challenges as UN Mission Withdraws', Amnesty International Publications.

[44]   Tubiana, J. (2011), 'Renouncing the Rebels: Local and Regional Dimensions of Chad–Sudan Rapprochement', Small Arms Survey, Graduate Institute of International and Development Studies, Geneva.

[45]   Ibid.

[46]   United Nations (2010), 'Report of the Secretary-General on the United Nations Mission in the Central African Republic and Chad', S/2010/217, 29 April.

[47]   United Nations (2010), 'Security Council Extends Mandate of Mission in Central African Republic and Chad, Calls on Secretary-General to Complete Withdrawal by 31 December', Meetings Coverage and Press Releases, 25 May.

[48]   Hicks, C. (2014), 'Clay Feet: Chad's Surprising Rise and Enduring Weaknesses', *World Politics Review*, 13 November.

[49]   Karlsrud, J. and R. Solhjell (2010), 'An Honourable Exit for MINURCAT?' Norwegian Institute of International Affairs: 2.

the size of the DIS contingent from 850 to 1000, with a view to deploying them to vulnerable locations in southern and south-western Chad.[50]

Thirdly, the GoC entertained the firm belief that, given the circumstances that initially militated for its deployment had changed, MINURCAT had become obsolete.[51] This is consistent with its repeated criticism of the mission's ineffectiveness due to its slow deployment. By the end of 2009, only 3,749 out of the 5,200 (revised downward in 2009 to 4,700) authorized troops and less than half of the pledged helicopters were on the ground.[52] The lack of helicopters and other enablers meant that UN troops adopted a 'zero risk' attitude, and were not, according to some Chadian officials, venturing out of their comfort zone except to protect their own lives and the mission's assets. Chad had hoped that MINURCAT, in addition to protecting civilians, would generate financial support for reconstruction and economic development in the east of the country, as the founding Security Council Resolution had intimated. Instead, they said, the mission's massive footprint had caused roads to deteriorate and raised the price of basic commodities such that locals could no longer afford them.

Fourthly, and this is perhaps the straw that broke the proverbial camel's back, were the unfulfilled promises that had been made early in the life of the Mission in exchange for the GoC accepting a UN Mission with a military component. These promises included the construction or rehabilitation of several aprons in N'Djamena's and Abéché's airports heavily used by the UN Mission and EUFOR before it. In relation to this, what was still vivid in the Chadian President's memory was the inaction of EUFOR and the French contingent permanently stationed in Chad when, in 2008, well-armed rebels swept into the capital N'Djamena and encircled the presidential palace, before retreating.

Following the initial request of 15 January 2010, the Permanent Representative of Chad to the UN informed the Security Council in a letter[53] dated 3 March 2010 that his government had decided to reconsider the original deadline for the withdrawal of MINURCAT, and was willing to agree to a two-month extension starting 16 March 2010. This welcome change of mind was brokered by the then head of DPKO Alain Le Roy following his mission to Chad at the end of February 2010. The letter further indicated that the military component should

---

[50] Ibid.
[51] Villaverde, J. (2010), MINURCAT: 'Achievements, Disappointments and Fragile Future', Institute of Studies on Conflict and Humanitarian Action, February: 3.
[52] New York University Center on International Cooperation (2011), Annual Review of Global Peace Operations, Boulder: Lynne Rienner Publishers.
[53] United Nations (2010), 'Letter dated 3 March 2010 Addressed to the President of the Security Council by the Permanent Representative of Chad to the United Nations', S/2010/115, 3 March.

be reduced while 'maintaining the civilian component as needed,'[54] which was an option that the government had consistently favoured over a militarized presence. In response to the letter, the UN Secretariat sent a technical mission to negotiate the modalities of MINUCAT's mandate. The government considered the technical mission as 'low level' for a sensitive matter of national importance. The outcome of the mission was inconclusive. A subsequent high-level mission was dispatched, led by the head of DPKO, Alain Le Roy, the positive outcome of which paved the way for my own mission to Chad, detailed in the next chapter.

For its part, the CAR authorities did not want MINURCAT to leave, warning that its eventual departure from the north-east in Birao would leave a security vacuum that the various armed movements would seize, taking advantage of the logistical assets that MINURCAT would no doubt have to leave behind. The President, when I visited him, complained that CAR had always been treated as '*le parent pauvre*' (the poor parent), despite CAR constituting the middle name of the mission!

The situation on the ground on arrival

The multi-disciplinary mission I was asked to lead in March 2010 was the third in a row tasked with brokering an orderly and less precipitous exit.

By the time I arrived in Chad in late March 2010, the humanitarian situation in north-eastern CAR was still fragile. The prolonged presence of a large number of refugees and IDPs stretched to the limit the meagre natural resources to be found around the refugee camps – especially firewood and water. The assessment visit of the Under-Secretary-General for Humanitarian Affairs and Emergency Relief Coordinator to eastern Chad in late May similarly revealed difficult living conditions in refugee camps and IDP sites. However, as noted above, the factors sustaining violence and generating mass forced displacement in eastern Chad had significantly abated following improved relations between Chad and Sudan and the deployment of the joint cross-border force.

What had not improved, however, and what I did not fully comprehend at the time, was the depth of the mistrust, disdain and even resentment felt by Chadian officials towards the Security Council and towards MINURCAT's military component in particular. After the initial one-on-one courtesy meetings, I

---

[54]   Ibid.

realized that my mission was not a technical one, but eminently political. Thus, I set out with due haste, albeit patiently, to address the trust deficit I had found.

The silver lining throughout negotiations was the universal appreciation by local authorities and communities of the excellent work carried out by the civilian component of MINURCAT in eastern Chad under the leadership of my able and indefatigable Deputy, Rima Salah, whose advice and counsel I ceaselessly sought throughout the negotiations and afterwards.

In addition to the political and humanitarian situations detailed above, I found the mission and its staff – particularly in its headquarters in N'Djamena – to be both restive and anxious given MINURCAT's uncertain future. When I arrived as the head of the UN delegation to negotiate the practical modalities of the exit, the sitting SRSG, Mr. Angelo, was preparing to retire at the end of March 2010. I discovered that most of the professional international staff in his front office, which would become part of my own office when I took over the helm of the mission a month later, had already left or were preparing to leave for other UN missions. The local staff, nearly a thousand of whom had been clamoring for a number of entitlements and back pay, were in defiant mood. They too were understandably concerned about their professional future once the mission departed and, to make their voices heard, went on strike twice early on in my tenure.

In sum, what I found upon my arrival in N'Djamena was a fragile humanitarian situation, a combative, triumphalist government keen to see the back of a peacekeeping presence it did not want in the first place, and anxious and dispirited UN Mission staff whose employment future was uncertain.

How did I prepare for this assignment before departing for Chad? What leadership challenges did I face throughout the negotiation phase and after I was confirmed as head of MINURCAT on 1 June 2010? How were these challenges overcome? How did we organize ourselves to continue implementing MINURCAT's residual mandate while drawing down? How were the legitimate demands of local staff met and their future job prospects addressed? What actions were taken, under the leadership of my Deputy, to lay the foundations for the sustainability of the achievements of MINURCAT's civilian component in eastern Chad? Responses to these and other pertinent questions, as well as an overview of the lessons learned from this unhappy peacekeeping experiment, are the subject of the following chapter.

6

Leading MINURCAT to the Exit Door

'Once you finish with the mission, if it does not finish you, you will have to invent a new definition of the word "challenge". So told me an informed colleague upon hearing of my assignment to MINURCAT.'

As my three-year assignment to Burundi neared its end, I was looking forward to a well-deserved retirement where making up for lost time with my family and teaching were to be the main priorities of my post-UN life. Little did I know that, barely two months after leaving Bujumbura, I would be called on by UN Secretary-General Ban Ki-Moon to take up another assignment.

On 15 March 2010, the then head of the Department for Peacekeeping Operations (DPKO), Alain Le Roy, confirmed that the Secretary-General had decided I should lead a UN multi-disciplinary technical team to negotiate a less rushed exit of the UN peacekeeping operation in Chad and the Central African Republic (MINURCAT). The Chadian government had first requested the operation's withdrawal in a *'note verbale'*[1] dated 19 January 2010, in which the UN was asked to commence 'negotiations' regarding the withdrawal of MINURCAT, effective 15 March 2010. As mentioned in the previous chapter, two successive UN senior envoys were dispatched to N'Djamena, Chad's capital, in order to persuade the Chadian authorities to agree to a less precipitous withdrawal. While the first was inconclusive, the second – led by Alain Le Roy himself – culminated in President Déby's consenting to a two-month technical extension of the mandate. This was to allow for further discussions on the gradual withdrawal of the MINURCAT military force alongside the possible continuation of its civilian component. The Security Council approved a two-month extension of MINURCAT until 15 May 2010,[2] subsequently extending

---

[1] A *note verbale* is a piece of diplomatic correspondence prepared in the third person and unsigned.
[2] United Nations (2010), 'Resolution 1913 (2010), adopted by the Security Council at its 6283rd meeting, on 12 March 2010', S/RES/1913 (2010), 12 March.

this for an additional two weeks to give more time to consider the outcome of negotiations.[3] These short roll-over extensions, while necessary, created further uncertainty among staff and accelerated the exodus of international staff to other UN missions.

I started the negotiation on MINURCAT's exit on 23 March 2010. On 1 April I was also appointed Acting Special Representative of the Secretary-General (SRSG), head of mission, following my predecessor's retirement. Negotiations were concluded on 23 April, with a timetable agreed for the gradual withdrawal of the Mission. On 1 June, I was confirmed in my position as SRSG and led MINURCAT throughout the various drawdown phases negotiated with the Chad and CAR authorities, culminating in the closure of the Mission on 31 December 2010.

This chapter describes the factors that enabled me to carry out the negotiations for MINURCAT's withdrawal to their logical conclusion, and outlines the leadership challenges arising from the implementation of the Mission's mandate, while preparing for its exit. It also offers lessons learned that future UN peacekeeping missions mandated with protecting civilians may wish to heed, particularly when the host nation's initial consent for such a mandate is fragile.

Preparing the ground for negotiating MINURCAT's exit

When I arrived in N'Djamena on 21 March 2010, my predecessor, Victor Da Silva Angelo, was preparing to leave on retirement at the end of the month. On 23 March, I commenced the negotiations with the head of the *Coordination Nationale au Deploiement de la Force Internationale* (CONAFIT), General Oki Yaya Dagache. CONAFIT, as explained in the previous chapter, was the coordinating structure created by the GoC as the main interlocutor with MINURCAT, with a particular focus on the operational activities of its military and police components.

Several key factors facilitated my task as negotiator, eventually earning me the grudging good will of the host government and its cooperation in a negotiation process that ultimately led to a mutually agreeable outcome.

The first factor was the intense, albeit short, preparations I had engaged in prior to my deployment. These included an analysis of the circumstances leading

---

[3]   United Nations (2010), 'Resolution 1922 (2010), adopted by the Security Council at its 6312th meeting, on 12 May 2010', S/RES/1922 (2010), 12 May.

to the mission's establishment, as well as the subsequent local, regional and international developments that had contributed to the Chadian government demanding the mission's premature departure. Much of this contextual information is contained in the previous chapter. Of particular help to me was an informal (private) consultation with the Security Council arranged by Alain Le Roy, during which he briefed the Council on previous discussions with the GoC regarding MINURCAT's withdrawal, including his own in late February 2010. The consultations also afforded Le Roy the opportunity to brief Council members on the mission entrusted to me by the Secretary-General, and for me to hear their views and expectations.

The second factor was the invaluable briefing notes from MINURCAT that had been prepared under the able guidance of Rima Salah, the Mission's Deputy Special Representative of Secretary-General, who subsequently became my Deputy after I took over as acting SRSG. Among the briefing notes was a substantive summary of informal interviews she had conducted with local and national government officials in eastern Chad and N'Djamena. This had been done with the aim of ascertaining their views and perceptions regarding MINURCAT's achievements and shortcomings, and of how best to manage UN–government relations during and after negotiations.

The third factor was the quality of the thirteen-strong, multi-disciplinary technical team that came with me from New York. However, they were unable to accompany me to most of the meetings I had with my Chadian interlocutors, led by General Dagache, the Special Representative of the President of Chad and head of CONAFIT. The General, who preferred one-on-one conversations with no interpretation, was uncomfortable having interlocutors who did not speak French, let alone Arabic, the other official language of Chad. Unfortunately, very few of the team spoke French, and none Arabic. Nevertheless, they continued to work diligently behind the scenes, providing me with valuable and timely advice that enabled me to secure incremental agreements. These eventually paved the way for the final comprehensive '*aide memoire*' or memorandum of understanding that crowned the month-long negotiations. What immensely facilitated our collective task was the time and energy we spent as a team both before leaving New York, and then after arrival, developing a shared understanding of the negotiation objectives and the principles that should guide them. Also helpful were the debriefing meetings we held at the end of each day, in which we updated our contingency planning and developed our negotiating position in anticipation of snags.

The fourth factor, unbeknownst to me until much later in my stay, was the fact that I was Tunisian. This reportedly motivated the Chadian authorities to give me the benefit of the doubt and help me carry out my assignment to its logical conclusion. This was done with the support of my Deputy Rima Salah, an Arabic speaker like myself, who already enjoyed their trust.

Last, but not least, was a healthy dose of humility and a capacity to listen with the intention of understanding the worldview of my interlocutors. All this without rushing to strike a deal or taking personally severe criticisms that were levelled at the UN, at times undeservedly. This ability to wield the power of listening was to stand me in good stead during my tenure in Chad, as will be explained below.

The negotiations

The meetings with my Chadian counterparts were often arduous. They were frequently resentful and mistrustful, determined to show they no longer needed MINURCAT and repeatedly hammering home that they were prepared to assume their sovereign responsibility to protect civilians on their territory. They could not understand why the mission could not simply pack up and leave. This contrasted with the views of a sceptical Security Council, which was bent on demonstrating that the GoC was not up to the task and therefore misguided in asking for MINURCAT's premature departure.

Before getting into the substance of the negotiation, I spent the best part of the first week listening to Chadian views on MINURCAT's future in order to gain an unfiltered, granular understanding of why the relationship between the Mission and the GoC had soured. In doing this, I suspended many of the preconceived notions I had taken on through the various briefings I had received in New York. The bulk of complaints revolved around MIMURCAT's slow deployment, its inability to deliver logistical support for the *Détachement Intégré de Sécurité* (DIS) – a local community policing contingent charged with protecting vulnerable populations in refugee camps and IDP sites – and, as mentioned in the previous chapter, its reneging on commitments to construct airport aprons and other infrastructure works. Other complaints related to the negative impact the mission's massive physical presence had had on the population in eastern Chad, particularly in the main town of Abeche where MINURCAT's forward headquarters was located. However, the one constant leitmotif was that the view that the UN had let itself become the instrument of outside pressures and geopolitical interests. According to my government interlocutors, the UN had pushed for a solution (a peacekeeping mission) that dealt with the symptoms of a problem rooted elsewhere, namely in the Darfur region of neighbouring Sudan.

Throughout most of this listening phase of the negotiations, I was accompanied by a French-speaking colleague from the mission who was known to and trusted by my interlocutors, and who took copious notes throughout. These notes helped inform the approach and substance of much of what my team and I proposed during the three-week-long negotiations/consultations that followed.

As indicated above, when exercised judiciously the power of listening creates space for interlocutors to focus on the issues at hand, rather than on each other or the institutions they represent, thereby allowing trust to emerge. Genuine listening also facilitated agreement on the principles and objectives that should guide negotiations. In this regard, my Chadian counterparts and I agreed on the following parameters, namely that the discussions should:

- seek to secure agreement on practical modalities allowing for the orderly reduction of MINURCAT's military component a spirit of partnership and mutual flexibility;
- take into account: (i) the GoC's request for the continuation of MINURCAT's civilian component; (ii) the UN's assessment of the military elements of MINURCAT required for the security of staff carrying out their activities as well as securing mission assets and property; and (iii) the operational requirements of humanitarian workers in their areas of deployment;
- focus on the support MINURCAT should provide, particularly for the DIS, in order to consolidate the gains achieved since its deployment in 2007, and lay the foundation for the sustainability of its operations, post-MINURCAT.

The second parameter was particularly helpful in pushing back on the government's offer that its security forces provide protection to UN staff in return for accelerating the drawdown of the military component. We argued that the number of troops to be maintained should be commensurate with the needs of UN staff on the ground. In the end, a compromise was found whereby the security of UN staff would be ensured by the remaining UN troops. In return, the mission would provide full support to the DIS in order to allow it to more effectively ensure security around refugee camps and IDP sites.

On 23 April 2010, an informal memorandum of understanding (MoU), containing agreement on the major elements of an exit strategy for MINURCAT, was signed by the head of CONAFIT and myself. Following consultation with CAR authorities, an addendum to the MoU was drafted, containing several options regarding how best to gradually withdraw the 300-strong MINURCAT military contingent from north-eastern CAR (located in Birao) without creating a security vacuum. The informal nature of the memorandum was stressed throughout the consultations, and it was made clear to my Chadian and CAR interlocutors that whatever was agreed with the UN on the ground would have to be presented to the Security Council, which would have the final say.

It was primarily on the basis of this MoU that the 29 April 2010 Secretary-General's report to the Security Council on the work of MINURCAT and its possible future was prepared.[4] On 7 May 2010, I presented the report to the Council on behalf of the Secretary-General in my capacity as acting SRSG. After formal and informal deliberation among Council members, Resolution 1923 of 25 May 2010 on MINURCAT's new mandate was unanimously adopted, with 31 December 2010 set as the final exit date, despite the *aide memoire* recommending 31 March 2011.[5] The Resolution also specified the UN had until 30 April 2011 to liquidate mission assets.

In order to help my Chadian negotiation partners fully understand the Council's decision-making process and the constraints under which I was labouring, I arranged for General Dagache of CONAFIT and a delegation of three of his key collaborators, including the Commander of the DIS, Col. Chanan Issaka Acheikh, to travel to New York. They attended various formal and informal meetings on the margins of the presentation of the October 2010 Secretary-General report. Their interactions included informal meetings with Council members, representatives of troop-contributing countries, and other stakeholders wanting to gauge the GoC's commitment and capacity to take over MINURCAT's protection of civilian mandate. The meetings also helped dissipate lingering apprehensions on the part of certain Council members who felt strongly that the Council was abdicating its responsibility under the Charter by agreeing to prematurely pull out a peacekeeping mission from a situation still deemed to be a threat to international peace and security. These Council members were also concerned that Chad's withdrawing of its consent for the continued presence of a peacekeeping mission might create a precedent for other countries hosting similar missions.

The above interactions and the social gatherings I helped organize for the Chadian delegation contributed to clearing up some of misunderstandings that

---

[4]   United Nations (2010), Report of the Secretary-General to the Security Council on the UN Mission in the Central Africa Republic and Chad (MINURCAT), S/2010/217.
[5]   United Nations (2010), 'Resolution 1923 (2010), adopted by the Security Council at its 6321st meeting, on 25 May 2010', S/RES/1923 (2010), 25 May.

had arisen, and cemented the relations of trust I had painstakingly built with them thus far. There was also the hope that upon their return from New York, the Chadian delegation would help foster a more cooperative attitude on the part of some hardliners on General Dagache's team that had not made the trip.

The council extends MINURCAT's mandate

As mentioned above, on 25 May 2010, the Security Council revised the mandate of the Mission and set its exit for 31 December 2010. Under the new mandate, the GoC was to assume full responsibility for the protection of civilians, under international norms, with MINURCAT beginning the gradual withdrawal of its military component as of 27 May 2010. The new mandate stipulated that the civilian component of the mission would work with the GoC and UN agencies on the ground to consolidate the gains achieved by the mission, as well as help develop plans for their sustainability after MINURCAT's departure on 31 December 2010.

The Resolution also took note of the commitment of the GoC, as outlined in the 21 May 2010 letter of the Permanent Representative of Chad to the President of the Council,[6] to assume full responsibility for the security and the protection of the civilian population in eastern Chad. This included refugees, internally displaced persons, returnees and host communities, with a particular focus on women and children, and UN and humanitarian personnel and assets.

Through Paragraph 4, the Council approved the agreement reached between the GoC and the UN to establish a joint high-level working group to assess on a monthly basis the situation on the ground with respect to the protection of civilians and the capacity of the DIS to provide security inside and around refugee camps and IDP sites.

With respect to the drawdown of MINURCAT's military component, the Council decided it would be reduced from a total of 3,300 to 2,200 military personnel (1,900 in Chad and 300 in the CAR), with initial drawdown to be completed by 15 July 2010 and final withdrawal to take place between 15 October and 31 December 2010. The Council further decided that MINURCAT should include a maximum of 300 police officers and an appropriate number of civilian personnel.

---

[6]   United Nations (2010), 'Letter dated 21 May 2010 from the Permanent Representative of Chad to the United Nations addressed to the President of the Security Council' S/2010/250, 21 May.

By the terms of the same resolution, the Council also called upon the Secretary-General to implement the withdrawal of all uniformed and civilian MINURCAT components, other than those required for the mission's liquidation, by 31 December 2010. The resolution outlined in great detail the tasks to be performed by MINURCAT's military and civilian components throughout the various phases of its drawdown. Particular emphasis was put on the residual work that needed to be performed by the civilian component of the mission in eastern Chad. This included supporting national and local authorities to resolve local tensions and promote local reconciliation efforts; contributing to the monitoring, promotion and protection of human rights, and promoting the rule of law, including support for an independent judiciary and strengthened legal system in close coordination with UN agencies. All these activities, as originally designed, were meant to create a protective environment supplementing the physical protection provided by the DIS, with the support of MINURCAT.

The resolution also welcomed the agreement in the MoU, to organize "humanitarian forums" fostering dialogue and collaboration, with a view to reaching a common understanding of roles and responsibilities on issues relating to protection of civilians, humanitarian access, and the safety and security of humanitarian actors.

The CAR government which did not wish the departure of the mission from its north-eastern enclave of Birao, felt it had been treated throughout the process as *le parent pauvre* (the poor parent). While it was not in favour of another international force to take over[7] from MINURCAT, it expressed the wish to be provided with bilateral support for its armed forces which was, regrettably not forthcoming. It finally had to settle for whatever physical assets the mission would be relinquishing upon withdrawal, leaving it to the small UN integrated office in CAR (BINUCA) to help the government mobilize that bilateral support. BINUCA closed its door in 2014 and was replaced by the current stabilization peacekeeping mission MINUSCA.

As mentioned in the previous chapter on the unusual circumstances surrounding the creation and deployment of MINURCAT, Resolution 1923, not unlike preceding resolutions, confined MINURCAT's mandate to the protection of civilians with no political role to play in helping address

---

[7]　Sebahara, P. (2011), 'Bilan en Demi-Teinte d'une Opération de Paix: La MINURCAT en Centrafrique et au Tchad', Groupe de Recherche et d'Information sur la Paix et la Sécurité, 11 February: 6.

the enduring underlying political causes that created the humanitarian crisis in the first place.

Shortly after the Security Council decided on a final extension of MINURCAT's mandate, a good number of non-governmental organizations, including Amnesty International[8] thought the Council's decision came at a time when MINURCAT had started to make a difference in protecting vulnerable population in eastern Chad. The negotiation process that led to the withdrawal agreement was criticized for failing to safeguard the human rights and guarantee the security of refugees and internally displaced persons camped around the eastern part of Chad. The agreement was also deemed flawed as it was not based on inclusive consultations with the affected communities and lacked a credible plan of action that would allow enough time for the Chadian to fully undertake security responsibilities where the refugees and the displaced were located.

In response, the GoC repeatedly declared itself as having sufficient capacity to protect refugees and IDPs, and ensuring their safe return to their original places of residence. On 18 May 2010, Emmanuel Nadingar, the then Prime Minister, encouraged IDPs to return to their areas of origin, stating that the GoC was in a better position to ensure their security through, *inter alia*, the Joint Border Force set up by Chad and Sudan.[9] On the same day, the refusal by Chadian immigration officials to grant entry to Darfurian rebel leader Khalil Ibrahim, whose forces had used Chad as a base of operations,[10] illustrated the determination of the Chadian government to maintain good relations with Sudan, thereby cementing the two countries' determination to ensure security across their joint border and mitigate the sources of threats to civilian safety.

Notwithstanding the above, the prolonged presence of a large number of refugees and IDPs continued to place a burden on the host population as their scramble for limited natural resources – especially firewood and water – increased. The assessment visit to eastern Chad from 22 to 26 May of the then Under-Secretary-General for Humanitarian Affairs and Emergency Relief Coordinator, John Holmes, revealed similar difficult living conditions in both refugee camps and IDP sites.[11]

---

[8] Amnesty International (2010), 'Chad: We too Deserve Protection. Human Rights'.
[9] United Nations (2010), 'Report of the Secretary-General on the United Nations Mission in the Central African Republic and Chad', S/2010/409, 30 July: 6.
[10] Ploch, L. (2010), 'Instability and Humanitarian Conditions in Chad', Congressional Research Service: 4.
[11] United Nations (2010), S/2010/409: 3.

Implementing the exit process

Soon after I was confirmed as SRSG, head of MINURCAT, on 1 June 2010 – a function I was carrying out on ad-interim basis since 1 April 2010 – I set myself a number of priorities regarding implementation of the new mandate contained in Security Council Resolution (SCR) 1923. These included:

- conducting an information and sensitization campaign on SCR 1923, particularly regarding the respective responsibilities of the GoC and MINURCAT in the area of protection of civilians, among MINURCAT staff, the UNCT, the diplomatic and humanitarian communities at the central and local levels. This would also help create a more nuanced and less negative perception in certain Chadian government circles of MINURCAT as it drew down. An important component of this communication strategy would be addressing the anxiety of mission staff who had lived months of uncertainty since the GoC had requested the mission's departure;
- creating the conditions for a secure and dignified drawdown of MINURCAT, in particular helping ensure that the retrenchment of national and international staff be carried out in a gradual, orderly, dignified and transparent manner;
- setting up a revised integrated security mechanism for UN staff and humanitarian workers, as well as for the protection of civilians in imminent danger, in close collaboration with the UN country team and the GoC at central and local levels;
- reconfiguring the activities of the civilian component in eastern Chad, with a view to helping the GoC at central and local levels consolidate achieved gains and lay the foundations for their sustainability, in close collaboration with the UN country team and other international partners;
- setting up and supporting the proper functioning of the various joint GoC/ UN coordination and consultation mechanisms, including the High-Level Working Group and the humanitarian dialogue forums, and ensuring the timely preparation of SG reports to the Security Council;
- helping ensure the mandated infrastructure projects in support of the DIS were implemented with minimum delay, and ensuring the sustainability of this community policing force after the departure of MINURCAT;
- enhancing the overall management of the mission, despite internal and external limitations arising from the circumstances surrounding the creation of MINURCAT and the nature of its mandate;

- drawing up and executing a plan specifying the physical assets to be handed over to the governments of Chad and CAR, as part of the UN's contribution towards sustaining MINURCAT's gains, as well as the assets to be repatriated during the liquidation phase, according to UN rules and regulations.

In pursuit of the above priorities, I put in place various processes for overseeing the timely implementation of the new mandate. This included setting up the joint GoC/UN high-level working group tasked with monitoring the overall implementation of the withdrawal, and establishing internal mechanisms for managing the various administrative and logistical aspects of the withdrawal. Though I followed the drawdown of the military component in order to ensure it complied with the requirements of the new resolution, I paid closer attention to the substantive/civilian components of the mission working in eastern Chad, under the able leadership of my Deputy, Rima Salah. She was entrusted with carrying out not only the residual tasks mandated by SCR 1923 in the areas of human rights, rule of law and inter-community reconciliation, but also helping ensure – in close collaboration with the UN country team on the ground – their sustainability post-MINURCAT.

Addressing the communication gap

Soon after my arrival in the mission area in March 2010, I noted there was a serious communication deficit not only within the mission but also with respect to the world outside the UN compounds where we worked and lived. This deficit was something I felt I had to address as a matter of priority during the negotiations and after the adoption of SCR 1923.

Throughout the negotiations, I made a point of keeping UN headquarters and Security Council members regularly informed, mostly through their bilateral Ambassadors in N'Djamena, Chad's capital city. When I took over the mission's reins on an interim basis on 1 April, I organized a series of information sessions aimed at the mission's national and international staff, both in N'Djamena and Abeche. I needed to assuage the anxiety they were feeling, given the uncertain future of the mission. This anxiety was particularly acute among the 1,000 strong national staff who feared joblessness after the closure of the mission, while also feeling wronged by perceived injustices on the part of MINURCAT's administrative and personnel services. This is a subject that will be returned to later in this chapter.

As the head of MINURCAT, my office was located in N'Djamena, 750 km from Abeche. This, however, did not prevent me undertaking regular overnight visits to speak and listen to staff in various outlying sectors, where working and living conditions were particularly harsh. The air assets at the mission's disposal made these otherwise onerous journeys possible.

During these visits, I also interacted with humanitarian workers from various UN agencies and local and international NGOs, in order to gain first-hand information about their protection of civilian activities. I was often accompanied by my Deputy Rima Salah or by MINURCAT Force Commander Major – General Elhadji Mahamadou Kandji, depending on the nature and objectives of the field trip

At times, when the objective of a visit was to organize the humanitarian forums mandated by the new resolution, I was also accompanied from N'Djamena by the head of CONAFIT and some of his staff. The purpose of these forums was to foster a shared understanding among local authorities, the DIS and humanitarian actors of their roles and responsibilities regarding the protection of civilians, as well as the safety and security arrangements of humanitarian actors, once MINURCAT ceased operations. The operational concept of protection of civilians issued in April 2010 by the Department of Peacekeeping[12] served as a useful basis for these sensitization forums, which intensified towards the last quarter of 2010.

The trips also included several visits to MINURCAT's contingent in Birao, in north-eastern CAR, in order to explain the mission's new mandate, the schedule for the military component's drawdown, and how this would affect their activities. I also visited CAR's capital, Bangui, to meet with the country's authorities at the highest level, bringing them up to date on the Council's decision regarding MINURCAT's future, and more importantly listening to their views on how they intended organizing themselves to fill the security vacuum resulting from the withdrawal.

I also held weekly virtual meetings from my location in N'Djamena with senior staff in Abeche, using the mission's video teleconferencing facilities. This virtual interface enabled discussion of logistical and other challenges facing the mission throughout the various phases of the drawdown, and helped address the communication and coordination lacunae between the mission's different components, be they civilian, police, military or administrative. The same

---

[12] Draft DPKO/DFS Operational Concept on the Protection of Civilians in United Nations Peacekeeping Operations.

technology proved equally helpful in maintaining the timely support of the backstopping entities at Headquarters in New York. These discussions with New York colleagues proved crucial during the planning and execution of the handover of physical assets to the Chadian and CAR authorities, in accordance with the complex UN General Assembly rules and regulations governing such an exercise. It also proved crucial, as will be explained later in the chapter, in addressing several longstanding grievances of local staff.

Most importantly, this communication strategy – both virtual and in person – enabled the mission's leadership team to monitor the morale of local and international staff, who were expected to implement the residual tasks dictated by the new mandate while at the same time effectively working themselves out of a job. During my interactions with them, whether in town hall meetings or casual gatherings, I hammered home two key messages. The first was that our impact would be measured by what the Chadians did with what remained, meaning that every activity MINURCAT engaged in henceforth should be planned and executed with a view to ensuring sustainability. The second was that, despite the distance separating us, Ms Salah and I formed a single leadership team, and my Deputy had full authority to lead the substantive components of the mission. I felt this was necessary, as I became aware early on in my tenure that there was some discord between the office of the SRSG in N'Djamena and Ms Salah's office.

In addition to the above, I directed MINURCAT's public information team to design multi-media outreach programmes to inform the general public about the mission activities in the east, which were generally appreciated and about the Mission's new mandate, so as to manage expectations that could not be fulfilled and to create a safe environment for the Mission's drawdown and asset removal.

The DIS, without frills, a viable local solution

The creation of the DIS was a unique experiment in building national capacity for the protection of civilians as a sovereign responsibility of the state. The DIS was built on an earlier corps of locally recruited community police, jointly created two years earlier by the GoC and UNHCR for the protection of humanitarian space in eastern Chad.[13] It was this rather low-cost operation that

---

[13]   Grünewald, F. and C. Olivia (2009), 'L'Espace Humanitaire à L'Est Du Tchad', *Groupe URD*: October.

the Chadian authorities had wanted strengthened, rather than the dispatch of a peacekeeping operation with a military contingent. As mentioned previously, this explains in part why the GoC acceded to MINIUCAT's establishment only under duress, with the explicit understanding that priority would be given to transforming these community police into a full-fledged national protection force, eventually called the DIS.

SCR 1923 requested MINURCAT continue to provide training, mentoring and support towards achieving DIS's self-sustainability as a professional law enforcement/protection of civilian entity. This support included the recruitment of additional DIS members and the initiation of infrastructure projects, such the construction of police stations and rehabilitation of a police school.[14]

To facilitate implementation, I set up the joint GoC/MINURCAT technical working group, the primary task of which was reviewing the key tasks required to strengthen DIS capacity and developing a plan for the progressive handover to the GoC of the administrative, financial and logistical support being provided.

When I took over MINURCAT, the DIS was already deployed in a number of locations in eastern Chad, and had, since February 2009,[15] been fulfilling its responsibilities regarding community policing in refugee camps and IDP sites, as well as escorting humanitarian workers, albeit limited to a 10 km radius from their locations. DIS elements were accompanied in all their activities by UN police, who, as mentioned above, were tasked with training, mentoring and supervising them. Although the Mission still had a long way to go in fulfilling the support required by the new resolution, much had already been done, including the recruitment and training of hundreds of new officers, as well as the provision of office and accommodation containers and dozens of brand new pick-up trucks. By the time I left the Mission on 31 December 2010, many of the remaining key requirements for the autonomous functioning of the force were in place, notwithstanding the multiple challenges that were overcome thanks largely to the leadership of MINURCAT Police Commissioner Mamadou Mountaga Diallo and the Head of Administration Guy Siri, with financial support from the EU Delegation in Chad.

From its inception, the DIS presented the mission with multiple challenges relating to selection of elements of the force, as well as the specific training and

---

[14] United Nations (2010), 'Report of the Secretary-General on the United Nations Mission in the Central African Republic'.
[15] République du TCHAD Présidence de la République Commission Nationale du Déploiement des Forces Internationales au TCHAD – CONAFIT Détachement Intégré de Sécurité (DIS), No. 1, Spring 2009.

support required to operate in harsh climates and the hard-to-reach areas of eastern Chad. Due to repeated delays in the deployment of MINURCAT's military component, which at no point reached it mandated strength, the Chadian authorities insisted on giving priority to upgrading DIS capabilities to international standards. As a result, the Mission ended up creating, in the words of an astute local observer, 'a Rolls-Royce amidst broken or antiquated cars' – that is, a community policing model more suited to European standards than the realities of eastern Chad, which had no long-term sustainability plan. Once MINURCAT's exit date was fixed, the GoC was pressed to produce just such a plan, which it finally presented to the international community in October 2010, both in N'Djamena and New York.[16]

One of the plan's key provisions was the establishment of a dedicated DIS administrative and management unit from January 2011, with approximately 130 personnel and an annual budgetary requirement of some $21 million. The GoC had committed to funding all DIS personnel costs (salaries, stipends and various allowances), estimated at approximately $7 million, or 33 per cent of the budget. It was, however, seeking $14 million in donor assistance to support logistical requirements (estimated at $12.6 million) and the building of the remaining national police structures (estimated at $1.4 million).

Following MINURCAT's closure, administrative and logistical support to the DIS was transferred to the United Nations Development Program (UNDP) and UNHCR.[17] Both endeavoured, in close collaboration with the relevant national authorities, to establish a mechanism for mobilizing and managing donor support as of 1 January 2011. UNDP and UNHCR designed a package of additional technical and operational support for the DIS covering 2011. It was not, however, feasible to replicate the level of support provided by MINURCAT.

The issue of the DIS will be returned to in the final, lessons learned, section of this chapter.

Challenged by local staff grievances

During my visits to eastern Chad, I was appalled by the living and working conditions of Mission staff, particularly those deployed close to the border with

---

[16] United Nations (2010), 'Letter dated 15 October 2010 from the Permanent Representative of Chad to the United Nations addressed to the President of the Security Council', S/2010/536, 18 October.

[17] United Nations (2010), 'Report of the Secretary-General on the United Nations Mission in the Central African Republic and Chad', S/2010/611, 1 December.

Sudan. There were situations where three staff members were forced to share a single small container with only beds and mattresses. At times, this container was also used for cooking and working. I was informed a lack of mission support planning and the mismanagement of support contracts were to blame. Also responsible was that much of the Mission's limited logistical resources had been directed at meeting the pressing needs of the DIS, thereby appeasing the disgruntled GoC. Regardless of the explanation, I was presented at every stop with a list of grievances, most of which were legitimate. In addition to the poor working and living conditions, local staff also complained about the long working hours they had to endure without proper compensation. I did not want these grievances to embitter them further, given the already palpable low morale occasioned by the job uncertainties they would be facing once the mission closed down. While these visits were universally appreciated, compassion alone was clearly not the answer.

After each visit I huddled with logistics, finance and personnel representatives, many of whom accompanied me on these visits, and directed them to come up with corrective actions that had a clear timetable. They were keenly aware that we had at least six months to go and many tasks to deliver before the mission closed, and that this could not be achieved with demoralized staff whom we had been encouraging to stay the course. With the active support of colleagues from headquarters, we were able to secure authorization to compensate local staff for overtime and improve some working conditions.

While I was busy addressing the urgent needs of staff in the east, little did I know that bigger staff trouble was brewing in the west, specifically in MINURCAT's rear headquarters, where my office and the heads of the Police and Administrative components, together with a small military security contingent, were located. The headquarters was situated a few miles from the centre of N'Djamena and my residence.

One morning in early June 2010, as I was approaching the MINURCAT compound, the head car of my security detail radioed my car, directing us to access the compound through a rear door without attracting attention. The reason, it turned out, was a general strike by MINURCAT local staff, who had gathered in large numbers at the main entrance gate, assertively blocking access to the compound. They were protesting, I was informed, about the lack of response to their longstanding grievances regarding employment conditions, which they feared would remain unanswered now that MINURCAT was leaving the country.

Once word got around that I had made it to my office, I received word that the strikers wanted to talk to me. I requested they send a delegation accompanied by the chairperson of the local staff union, with whom I had interacted on a few occasions and who had warned me about the rumblings. As my request was making its way to the front door, I heard shouts. Upon inquiry, I was told that an international security officer who had been dealing with the situation since early morning had infuriated the crowd by using language they felt was insulting and humiliating, bordering on racist. A scuffle ensued. I disregarded the advice to call the host country police, and instead sent my trusted Chief of Staff to calm the situation and escort the delegation to the room adjoining my office.

At my request, the Chief of Staff asked the Chief of Administration or Director of Mission Support (DMS) and his senior personnel and finance staff to join us. Once everyone was seated, I joined them, though not before I asked my jittery close-protection detail to be at ease and look relaxed.

We spent an hour listening to the delegation's grievances, during which I instructed my colleagues to interject only if they had questions of clarification. Once they had finished, I acknowledged their views, which were duly noted, summarizing the main categories of their complaints. I then asked them to put in writing all what they had just told us, and hand it to my Chief of Staff the following day, if possible. I also asked them to consult their fellow national staff in the east and ensure that their views were fully reflected. I then promised that we would seriously study their complaints and provide them with initial answers in one week's time.

Once the meeting was over, I spoke a couple of sentences in Arabic to underscore my empathy, essentially saying, 'only those who step on hot coals feel the pain'. I then asked them to brief their colleagues outside the gates, and expressed hope that they could convince them to clear the entrance to the compound and return to their duties. I added that those who wished to go home for the remainder of the day to calm down or work on their grievance document could do so without penalty, provided they came back bright and early the following day. Most of them did not trust the DMS, and some of his staff gave me the benefit of the doubt as a newcomer, convincing the recalcitrant among those amassed outside to disband. Many went home, but the majority opted to return to work.

The written document we received the following day presented, in an organized fashion, what the staff delegation had shared with us. The complaints were similar to those I had heard from their fellow national staff, ranging from poor health insurance to unpaid overtime to disbelieved assurances they would collect their pension contribution. What came through as a leitmotiv, though, was their anxiety about their professional future once the mission closed. They wanted to be considered for UN jobs in other peacekeeping missions, to be trained to compete in a saturated local job market, and to be given guarantees that they would be hired by UN agencies on the ground as vacancies became available.

I asked my Chief of Staff to work with the DMS and his staff in proposing credible answers to their grievances, many of which seemed reasonable and legitimate, stressing that I had worked with personnel services in my earlier professional incarnations and that I knew how much could be done without bending the rules. I added that they should focus as a matter of priority on areas where the Mission, under its delegated authority, had influence and/or control to act. I also asked that a small committee of Administration staff be formed to address those grievances the solutions to which required the cooperation of New York colleagues in the Department of Field Service (DFS), and further requested that the DFS designate the right people to work with our local committee.

I added that, as MINURCAT drew down and international staff started leaving the mission in search for long-term employment opportunities with other UN field missions, we would be increasingly reliant on our local colleagues. I also stressed that as the protective shield provided by our military component got thinner on the ground, particularly in outlying areas where we were still operating, our collective safety as well as the security of our physical assets would be in their hands. Therefore, we must do the right thing.

Once I was satisfied that the majority of proposed solutions under the first tier (i.e. under the Mission's control) were genuine, despite some imperfections, we proceeded as planned. I met with the majority of the local staff in a town hall meeting format, where my colleagues and I shared with them what we could immediately offer. We also communicated what we would be working on with our New York colleagues (e.g. on back pay and retrieval of pension contributions), and what would not be feasible, namely job placements or guarantees with other UN agencies or local employers. Under this last item, however, I promised that a mission-wide training and development strategy for local staff would be devised, following consultation with the Administration and particularly my Deputy, Rima Salah. This face-to-face, frank and constructive interaction helped show our good faith in finding solutions to grievances, and even contemplating actions which we were under no obligation to fulfil.

It was thus that we were able to diffuse a tense situation that could have soured intra-mission relations and complicated the Mission exit, which was already fraught with predictable and unpredictable challenges. Once again, this episode demonstrates the power of listening without condescension, particularly when tensions are high and solutions are not readily available. It creates the psychological space that allows people to feel heard and respected, thus unleashing good will for a common purpose, despite residues of past hurt and mistrust.

Another important factor that enabled the Mission to manage this challenge relatively successfully was the surge capacity team that our DFS colleagues in New York sent to N'Djamena to support the Mission's personnel and financial team in coping with the increased volume of work generated by the timely redress of staff grievances. This surge team also played a critical role in placing international staff in other UN missions in an orderly manner, without jeopardizing the Mission's capacity to deliver on its residual mandate. They also managed to send a select number of local Chadian staff with specific skills on short-term assignments to other UN field missions.

Earning local good will during the last mile

As promised, we developed and implemented a strategy to enhance the re-employment chances of around 600 local staff. This strategy included professional development programmes in such areas as CV writing, interview taking, and basic and advanced IT training, and was followed by a job fair organized in N'Djamena. During the job fair, national staff had the opportunity to meet and be interviewed by potential recruiters from the private and public sector, including national and international NGOs and UN Agencies active in Chad. In preparation for the job fair, my Deputy's office also coordinated the creation of a roster for MINURCAT national staff members, which was subsequently sent to interested potential employers. The roster was also shared with the National Office for the Promotion of Employment (ONAPE), for publication on its official website. National staff members were also invited, through MINURCAT broadcast facilities, to register with ONAPE in order to be included in their job bank. The planning and implementation of this strategy would not have been possible without the cooperative leadership of the senior leadership team, particularly – given the amount of travel required to ferry staff to and from N'Djamena – those in charge of aviation and logistics. Special credit goes to the Director of Mission Support, Guy Siri, who despite our differences measured up to the task.

Looking back on these staff-related challenges, the responses we improvised to address them earned more good will among local staff and national authorities for the Mission and the UN generally than perhaps all the activities invested in the DIS across its entire life span.

Addressing management anomalies, extracting mission assets, consolidating gains

Addressing management anomalies

Early in my tenure, I made a conscious decision to adopt a collaborative, inclusive leadership style that would empower staff to carry on with their work without micro-management. This, however, would involve a unified command structure, supported by a robust communication strategy. My frequent visits to localities around eastern Chad and the weekly video teleconferences mentioned above would not have produced some key outcomes if I had not taken steps to devolve decision-making and unleash the leadership potential of my Deputy and her senior staff.

In pursuit of the above strategy, I had to take corrective measures addressing some management anomalies that I had inherited. When I took over the helm of MINURCAT, the bulk of the mission leadership was concentrated in N'Djamena, despite most of the Mission's work was being carried out in eastern Chad, nearly 800 kilometers away. Collaboration between the two headquarters was not smooth, and as mentioned above, there was a palpable trust deficit between the office of the SRSG and that of the Deputy SRSG, Rima. As part of the overall communication strategy, I continued to hammer home that the Mission had a single civilian leadership that spoke with a single voice, represented by my Deputy and myself, with the former having overall responsibility for the programmatic aspects of the mission. I instructed my front office staff to consult Rima and seek her views on decisions affecting her portfolio, and extend her unstinting support in my absence, when she would officiate as officer in charge of the entire Mission.

With the separation of DPKO into two entities early in the tenure of Ban Ki-Moon – one substantive (DPKO) and one logistical/financial (DFS) – the Administrative component of the Mission tended to take major decisions without reference to the office of the SRSG. These included decisions on staffing and budgets, which were worked out directly in consultation with the relevant entities in New York. I felt strongly that certain aspects of staffing and budgeting were highly sensitive and required political oversight during the critical transition the Mission was experiencing. Without imposing additional bureaucratic layers, I put in place the consultative mechanisms necessary to achieve this imperative.

Extracting mission assets

Among the priorities I had set for myself, two were particularly challenging in their planning and execution. The first involved reconfiguring the activities of the Mission's civilian component in eastern Chad and laying the foundations for their sustainability. The second involved drawing up a plan outlining the gradual closure of our camps and sites in the east, specifying which assets the Mission could hand over to the governments of Chad and CAR, and those that needed to be repatriated during the Mission's liquidation phase, set to be concluded by the end of April 2011.

The implementation of these priorities meant that my senior mission leadership team and I had to carry out the Mission's residual activities while gradually reducing the contingent of international staff and preparing to hand over these activities and assets to the government, in a context where staff morale was low.

The political and financial considerations of asset disposal meant I had to familiarize myself with the key UN General Assembly rules and regulations governing the operation. I learned, for example, that the Mission can only write off or bequeath equipment classified as category 5. This is equipment that had depreciated over time and would cost threefold its original value to dismantle and ship out of the country. Any other category of equipment (i.e. items that could be sold locally) had to secure the express approval of the UN Controller in New York before being disposed of locally.

This familiarization proved helpful for two reasons. The first was it enabled me to understand the financial and programmatic arguments that had to be made to the UN Controller as to which movable or immovable assets could be handed over to the local authorities. This usually required some form of cost-benefit analysis demonstrating that the UN would incur higher costs dismantling and shipping some of the fixed assets, such as hard-wall accommodation containers. Chad being a land-locked country, and given the vast distances separating the various camps where we had deployed, such costs tended to be prohibitive. The second reason was that it enabled us to explain to the governments of Chad and CAR why certain assets and sensitive equipment, such as computers, could not be handed over. Based on this familiarization and in order to avoid any misunderstanding, we prepared several information sheets that were handed over to our staff and to local authorities, on whose cooperation we relied to safely extract the assets.

Throughout this operation, we had to contend with relentless pressure from the GoC, and particularly the country's aviation authorities, which wanted to take back parts of Abeche airport ahead of our scheduled withdrawal from the facility, considered neutral UN territory under the bilateral status of forces agreement. A solution was eventually found that allowed for an uncomfortable co-habitation, which created additional legal and security challenges that plagued the Mission throughout part of the liquidation phase. In February 2011, weeks after she had left the Mission, my former Deputy Rima, by then retired, had to be dispatched to Chad to help address some of the still-lingering challenges.

This camp closure and asset disposal task would have been far more delicate had we not addressed the grievances of local staff, on whose cooperation we had to rely, particularly in outlying areas. What also stood me in good stead was my brief but informative exposure to asset disposal in Burundi, when I had overseen the tail end of the peacekeeping operation's withdrawal.

Consolidating gains

Another challenge was developing an overall strategy for the consolidation and sustainability of the Mission's achievements in the east, and the handover of its substantive programmes to the GoC and its partners. Under the able supervision of my Deputy and her senior staff, an exit strategy guided by the principles of partnership and integration was devised. This aimed at ensuring that all actions taken were consistent with the needs and priorities of national and local actors, including the UN system. The Programme of Consolidation of MINURCAT's Gains handed over to the UN country team included human rights, rule of law and good governance, child protection, the campaign against gender-based violence, the return of IDPs, and HIV/AIDS projects. As MINURCAT completed its mandate on 31 December 2010, the UN country team in eastern Chad assumed most of these activities.

Lessons learned from a troubled mission

Many lessons can be learned from the trajectory of this Mission, from its troubled start to its precipitated exit, some of which have been incorporated into the

1 December 2010 report[18] of the Secretary-General to the Security Council. The findings and lessons summarized below are drawn from the findings of an internal DPKO management review of the mission performance as it was drawing down.

Local expectations and mission mandate were not aligned

Local expectations and the mandate of the mission were not in alignment. As the mandate was not clearly communicated or understood, Chad expected both more direct military support and greater financial support for economic development. The Mission was neither resourced nor mandated for the scale and type of these activities, notwithstanding some language in MINURCAT's founding resolution[19] relating to economic recovery and development in affected regions. Over time, the gap between the high visibility and heavy footprint of the Mission on one hand, and its actual ability to deliver on expectation on the other, proved to be the main driver of deteriorating relations between MINURCAT and the GoC. Early attempts to bridge this gap by making informal commitments to improve public infrastructure and expanding civilian support to rule of law and the DIS were hampered by the slow deployment of the Mission, further discrediting it in the eyes of the government. Quick Impact Projects (QIPS) benefiting local communities helped somewhat in mitigating this disgruntlement.

The lesson to draw here is that commitments made to gain favour with a recalcitrant government should be realistic and appropriate to the context. Mission resources or operational capacity should not be used to curry favour or for narrow political purposes.

Failure to communicate

The absence of a communications and outreach strategy impaired the Mission's ability to narrow the gap between expectation and reality. The main lesson learned is that such a strategy must be developed at the initial stage of a mission's deployment. An effective communication strategy should have been central to enhancing confidence and reducing misunderstandings as to the Mission's role and purpose in Chad and CAR.

---

[18]   United Nations (2010), 'Report of the Secretary-General on the United Nations'.
[19]   United Nations (2007), Security Council Resolution S/RES/1778, 25 September.

Nurturing consent

Sustained consent by and effective cooperation with a host government are essential to a mission implementing its mandate and attaining its objectives. Even when freely given, the consent of a host government should be nurtured in order to ensure sustainability. Consent is reversible, especially when the conditions in the country and/or sub-region change significantly during the life of a mission. An operation such as MINURCAT, conceived and deployed under duress, can become hostage to pressures and contradictions that distract it from its intended objectives, resulting in its overall performance and credibility being eroded. In order to address the GoC's reservations about an operation that was not in accordance with its wishes and objectives, the Mission resorted to a number of coping and mitigating strategies, including making concessions and promises just to 'please' the government. A recent study by the Stimson Center[20] contains a number of useful recommendations on how the UN Secretariat and Member States can best detect early signs of deteriorating host-state consent, and take proactive steps to address them.

In a talk I gave at IPI in October 2010,[21] while I was serving as SRSG, it was suggested that the Security Council or the Secretariat should set up a barometer to monitor the consent level of nations hosting UN peacekeeping operations and take corrective action as and when needed.

Shared understanding of POC

No clear strategy was devised as to how the mandate would harmonize with or complement the work of UN Agencies and NGOs. Moreover, the DPKO Framework on Protection of Civilians (POC) was only issued in April 2010. Consequently, MINURCAT was entrusted with a POC mandate without an integrated strategy as to how this mandate should be implemented in a multidimensional context.

Thus, in an integrated strategy elaborated in the pre-deployment planning phase, a shared and practical understanding of the protection of civilians must be developed and the contributions of key partners identified. Once a mission is

---

[20]   UN Peacekeeping and Host-State Consent (2018), Stimson Center.
[21]   International Peace Institute (2010), 'Mahmoud: "At Times, We Leave in Humiliating Circumstances"', 21 October. Available online: https://www.ipinst.org/2010/10/mahmoud-at-times-we-leave-in-humiliating-circumstances (accessed 2 August 2018).

deployed, such a strategy should be routinely reviewed on the ground with the host government, the UN country team and other humanitarian stakeholders, in order to take into account local and regional developments without jeopardizing organizational values and norms.

Planning for a harsh operational environment

Remoteness, harsh terrain, extreme climate and the virtual absence of infrastructure and appropriate support structures should be fully taken into account in the planning and management of a mission, especially during its start-up phase. MINURCAT committed to projects or timelines for delivery that were largely impossible to meet given the physical conditions on the ground, the late deployment of mission assets, and the distances that had to be travelled to deliver them.

DIS, an unsustainable community policing model

The sustainability requirements of creating a force such as the DIS should be prepared at the initial stage of the mission's conception, with principles stringently adhered to throughout development.

Originally envisaged as purely a community police force, the DIS concept evolved to incorporate more robust tasks (particularly the provision of security escorts), owing in part to operational humanitarian and security necessities. The technological sophistication employed in its further development was more suited to a European environment than eastern Chad. As a result, the UN had to commit to substantial projects that at times proved difficult or even impossible to carry out, further undermining the trust and confidence of the host government. To address this trust deficit, MINURCAT had to invest heavily in DIS by providing a level of support that proved difficult to sustain after the departure of the Mission.

---

6. Former colleagues' perspectives on my leadership in managing the departure of MINURCAT

'Leadership is very important because the leaders are those setting the vision. The leadership of Prof Mahmoud was very important, particularly with regard to the challenges we faced in the MINURCAT mission. It was the shortest mission, which was a good thing because we didn't want to stay like other missions for 20 or 30 years, the environment was very harsh, there was a lack of an integrated strategy. When we started in 2007, the concept of protection was not properly understood even within the DPKO. It was later that the concept became clearer. Leadership was very important because we needed a vision, that was what Prof Mahmoud brought when he joined the mission. He arrived when the mission was at its exit point as the government had asked the mission to be closed ...

'One of the qualities of Prof Mahmoud was the capacity and ability to translate challenges into opportunities. When there was problem of communication between the mission and the government, he suggested the establishment of the joint high-level working group to facilitate interaction between the government and the Mission/UN. In relation to challenges pertaining to humanitarian access, the security of humanitarians and that of internally displaced persons and refugees, Prof Mahmoud organized humanitarian field visits to five regions [to address the concerns of all concerned about the consequences of the mission departure].

'It was necessary to ensure a better involvement of the UN country team in the process. There was something done with the UNHCR. Nevertheless, we could have done a little bit more to make sure that all we left behind were properly used. Only two weeks after departure, we realized that what we had left at the northern part of CAR [Birao] had been taken over by rebels. We ought to have done enough to prevent such situation. What we left in eastern Chad has been reduced to nothing.'

Concluding observations

In his final report to the Security Council in December 2010, the Secretary-General said, 'MINURCAT has been an unusual and unique United Nations peacekeeping operation in that it was devoted solely to contributing to the protection of civilians, without an explicit political mandate. It has gone through the stages of planning, deployment and withdrawal in the short span of less than four years, enduring adversities in each.'

Alex Bellamy and Paul Williams have described[22] MINURCAT as one of a 'string of highly vulnerable, relatively weak and under-resourced peace operations made more problematic by their complex mandates and the inter-institutional relationships between the UN, EU, government, rebels and regional actors.'

From my point of view, MINURACAT was a mission that should not have been deployed, for all the reasons mentioned in the reports the Secretary-General

---

22   World Peace Foundation (2017), 'United Nations Mission in the Central African Republic and Chad (MINURCAT) /European Union Force (EUFOR)', short mission brief.

submitted to the Security Council in December 2006 and February 2007, following two successive technical assessment missions to Chad and CAR. In the December 2006 report,[23] the Secretary-General observed that in the absence of an inclusive political process, a UN multi-dimensional presence would be risky. In the subsequent report,[24] he remarked that Chad was not 'a conventional peacekeeping environment', given the ongoing hostilities between the government and various armed opposition groups. Both observations went unheeded when the Council decided to deploy MINURCAT,[25] which, despite costing nearly $700 million a year, did not have a political mandate or commensurate deterrent force. Also unheeded was the well-known position of the GoC, which had only consented to host an international civilian presence on the basis of it supporting the community police and rule of law structures in managing refugee camps and IDP sites.

In light of the above, the assessment of the Mission's travails by the Secretary-General and Bellamy and Williams, as well as others,[26] should not come as a surprise. Had the advice offered to the Security Council been heeded, the UN would not have militarized the protection of civilians while at the same time providing inadequate force to back it up. Instead, it would have led the UN to draw on the capacities of the GoC and those of humanitarian organizations already playing an essential role in the protection of civilians. Had the Security Council contented itself with sending a civilian mission, it would have been able to explore and leverage the positive contributions of unarmed civilian protection actors working to create a protective environment, in close collaboration with local communities. Recognizing that protecting civilians from organized violence and other imminent security threats requires, at times, the use of force, the DIS – designed differently and properly supported from the inception of MINURCAT – could have played that deterrent role, which it eventually did with the help of UN civilian police, albeit at great cost to the Mission and to a level that proved unsustainable.

It is heartening to note that in some of the peacekeeping missions currently in operation, the practice of unarmed protection of civilians is being increasingly explored as a result of the recommendations offered in the report of the High-Level Independent Panel on Peace Operations.[27]

23 United Nations (2006), S/2006/1019.
24 United Nations (2007), S/2007/97.
25 United Nations (2006), S/2006/1019.
26 Villaverde (2010).
27 Report of the High-Level Independent Panel on the United Nations Peace Operations (2015), Uniting our Strength for Peace – Politics, Partnership and People, 16 June.

The negotiations for the dignified and orderly exit of MINURCAT and the short nine months I spent as head of the Mission tested my understanding of the word "challenge" and the adaptive, resilient leadership skills I thought I had in abundance. I was confronted by challenges on all fronts, internally within the Mission, externally between the Mission and the GoC and between the latter and a sceptical Security Council.

What helped me with these challenges was the small, wonderful team that I had around me, particularly the shrewd, good-hearted and competent Deputy whose living compound in Abeche offered my Special Assistant and I respite for writing and reflection.

Most of all, I owe a great deal to the selfless and ever-caring, twelve-strong close-protection team from Portugal with whom I shared living quarters in N'Djamena. In addition to ensuring my security in a discreet and professional manner, they ensured I took time out for regular walks on most afternoons after the implacable N'Djamena heat had abated. It is this same team who took it upon themselves to find us a different home when one day the local authorities decided to demolish the house where we lived to make way for a new highway connecting the centre of the town to the airport. I will never forget the sweaty nights they had to spend in the steamy corridors outside my hotel room, where I found temporary refuge while they were looking for new living quarters.

It is in these challenging times that you realize your relative importance as an individual. However lofty your position may be, the cooperation, abnegation and trust of others – all of which must be willingly given and earned – are essential. Furthermore, once secured, these qualities need to be nurtured. My experience in Chad brought home the dictum that leadership for peace, however desired that peace may be, is not about just the leader. It is about the 'ship' that you, as leader, steer while unleashing the leadership potential of those best-placed to maintain it.

Figure 1 Cycling with the late President Pierre Nkurunziza of Burundi, November 2007.

Figure 2 A four-way peace embrace: with the late Ambassador Mamadou Bah to my left, the Minister of Social Affairs to my right and Agathon Rwasa, former FNL rebel leader on my extreme right, all watching a soccer match between Burundian security forces and FNL players International day of peace, September 2008.

Figure 3 With the Minister of Women Affairs and Social Solidarity, celebrating women's day, March 2007.

Figure 4 As SRSG MINURCAT arriving at Mongolian contingent base camp – Iriba province in Eastern Chad, June 2010.

Figure 5 Reviewing the honour guards of a contingent from the Ghana battalion (GHABATT) in Eastern Chad, June 2010.

Figure 6 Handing over ceremony of MINURCAT assets following the closure of its Iriba base camp in Eastern Chad, October 2010.

7

What It Would Take to Build Peace Better

This book represents a personal account of my leadership journey as a UN envoy and head of two successive peace operations in Central Africa, spanning four intense years at the tail end of a three-decade career at the UN. It has detailed some of the challenges I encountered in attempting to strike a balance between what the mandates entrusted to me dictated and what the realities on the ground allowed.

The purpose of this final chapter is to summarize the main lessons of the previous chapters, with a particular focus on how the dominant peacebuilding agenda can and should be retooled in a world where the operational space for the UN to build peace is shrinking. The final part of the chapter offers reflections on how I would exercise leadership differently were I to be head of a peace operation in the future. It also suggests avenues for further research on peace and leadership.

Make peace the end goal, but don't give it a shape

Chapter 1 attempted to question some of the assumptions that have informed the peacebuilding enterprise for the past four decades. While some scholars and practitioners continue to defend the relevance of the liberal values underpinning it, others reject them as a pathway to peace altogether. From an empirical standpoint, however, it can be asserted with some confidence that peacebuilding operations have not always had a successful track record in actually 'building' peace.[1]

A major critique levelled at the peacebuilding paradigm is that it has a very deterministic vision of what peace looks like. Peace has been moulded in the image of those Western democracies that have successfully refrained from

---

[1] Denskus, T. (2007), 'Peacebuilding Does Not Build Peace' *Development in Practice,* 17 (4–5).

fighting each other since the Second World War. Given the violent history of Western Europe for centuries prior to this, it is somewhat presumptuous to contend that 'democracies do not fight each other.'[2] Moreover, by the time peacebuilding really took off as a paradigm, the most pressing peace and security challenges involved intra-state rather than inter-state violence.

I failed to realize, until a few years after my retirement and upon deeper reflection, that the peacebuilding interventions in BINUB's mandate were determined by their instrumental value in achieving regional and international order rather than aiming at peace as a goal in its own right. Such an approach significantly altered the scope and definition of peace, as well as its sustainability. Under the sustaining peace paradigm discussed in this book,[3] peace should be treated as the end goal, though without imposing a pre-determined vision of what that peace should look like.[4] It should be largely defined by those who are deemed to be at the receiving end.

The priorities reflected in the liberal peace agenda do not necessarily align with the priorities of the population.[5] The peace settlements that informed BINUB's mandate (the 2000 Arusha Peace and Reconciliation Agreement Accord)[6] and the subsequent negotiations with Burundi's government were an elite affair, based on the assumption that those who agree to stop a war and are capable of winning elections are the same people who can imagine and create a just society. This is a vision that excludes most of the population, creating a legitimacy deficit my team and I tried to address in the design and implementation of the various peacebuilding projects financed by the UN Peacebuilding Fund. The race towards establishing a representative democracy often comes at the cost of meaningful participation, further entrenching exclusionary patterns.

In order to remedy the imposition of elite-driven priorities on the local needs of the population, building 'peace' should be seen as a participatory, inclusive exercise drawing on the priorities and objectives of the population. However, this proposition, key to any aspiration towards a more popular peace and a hallmark of the sustaining peace paradigm, invariably faces potential roadblocks and dilemmas.

---

[2]   Doyle, M. (1986), 'Liberalism and world politics', *American Political Science Review*, 80 (4).
[3]   Mahmoud, Y., L. Connolly and D. Mechoulan (2018), 'Sustaining Peace in Practice: Building on What Works', International Peace Institute, February.
[4]   Mahmoud and Makoond (2018).
[5]   Call, C. (2008), 'Building States to Build Peace? A Critical Analysis', *Journal of Peacebuilding and Development*, 4 (2).
[6]   Arusha Peace and Reconciliation Agreement for Burundi.

One of the dilemmas faced during my tenure in Burundi was how to engage directly with 'We the Peoples' without making government officials feel usurped.[7] The flip side of this dilemma is how to partner with these officials under the guise of national ownership without the latter capturing consultative processes or projects for narrow political gains, such as winning local elections or shoring up a real or perceived lack of performance legitimacy.[8]

Another dilemma was definitional and related to what constitutes 'local', given that this 'is not a homogenous entity, nor can it be approached uncritically'.[9] Just as at the national level, power and authority can be as contested locally, with not all local actors having capacities for peace,[10] particularly when acting as surrogates for elites at the central level. Moreover, there was a dearth of evidence as to which approaches external peacebuilders might use to help build peace from the bottom up. In this regard, the recent pioneering work of Autesserre[11] is illuminating, but would probably have gone unnoticed had it existed when I was in Burundi. Even then, my colleagues and I would have paid little attention, busy as we were implementing – under tight time-frames – externally driven mandates which contained no room for questioning the state-centric assumptions informing them.

Recognizing complexity, targeting resilience

Much of peacebuilding practice and policy, including the recent resolutions on sustaining peace,[12] are wedded to the notion that peace and conflict and peace are binary, with the factors associated with former understood to be the inverse of those leading to the latter. As a result, peacebuilding interventions are conceived as a package of interventions aimed at addressing the root causes of conflict,[13] on the basis that removing the causes of conflict will result in peace.[14] However,

[7] Van Tongeren, P., M. Brenk, M. Hellema and J. Verhoeven (2005), (eds), *People Building Peace II: Successful Stories of Civil Society*, Boulder: Lynne Rienner Publishers.

[8] Ibid.

[9] Paffenholz, T. (2015), 'Unpacking the Local Turn in Peacebuilding: a Critical Assessment towards an Agenda for Future Research', *Third World Quarterly*, 36 (5).

[10] Simons, C. and F. Zanker (2014), 'Questioning the Local in Peacebuilding', Working Papers of the Priority Programme 1448 of the German Research Foundation: 10.

[11] Autesserre, S. (2017), 'International Peacebuilding and Local Success: Assumptions and Effectiveness', *International Studies Review*, 0.

[12] United Nations (2016), 'Security Council Unanimously Adopts Resolution 2282 (2016) on Review of United Nations Peacebuilding Architecture', SC/12340, 27 April.

[13] De Coning, C. (2016), 'From peacebuilding to sustaining peace: Implications of complexity for resilience and sustainability', *Resilience*, 4 (3).

[14] Coleman (2012).

empirical research has shown that the processes of averting or mitigating the causes of destructive conflict are different from those that aim at building and sustaining peace.[15] Whereas addressing the root causes of conflict produces a negative peace (absence of war or violence), processes aimed at building peace are driven by broader conceptions of peace, such as justice, human rights, economic equality, and other aspects of human and social development that take a much longer time to nurture.

The above distinctions were not fully present in my mind when I was busy implementing statebuilding through discrete projects. Although these projects produced tangible short-term results – such as supporting critical reforms of the Burundian defence and security forces, and establishing Burundi's Independent National Commission on Human Rights – they failed to recognize that peace, rather than conflict, should be the starting point[16] for designing projects aimed at actively building peace. To this day, such distinctions continue to elude even more forward-thinking propositions for building and sustaining peace, which rightfully point out the need to prioritize prevention.[17]

The inevitability and even desirability of conflict in human social organization has been discussed at length since the early days of peace research, with scholars such as Jean Paul Lederach contending that conflict is in fact a driving force for innovation in society.[18] Violent conflict is an altogether different issue, but conflict – manifest in the competition between ideas or resources – is ultimately what motivates the emergence of new ideologies, systems and institutions. A recent resurgence of interest in complexity theory goes further, suggesting that a society's capacity for self-organization is nurtured by confronting conflict.[19] The liberal peacebuilding agenda, in attempting to control political and social spaces as a means of ensuring security and stability, has in fact undermined the emergence of self-organizing capacities within societies.

Recognizing that conflict is natural has led to a growing interest in resilience on the part of peacebuilding actors.[20] Rather than attempt to eradicate conflict, the focus should be on ensuring that societies have the capacity to address

---

[15] Diehl, P. (2016), 'Exploring Peace: Looking Beyond War and Negative Peace', *International Studies Quarterly*, 60 (1).

[16] International Peace Institute (2017), 'Sustaining Peace: What Does it Mean in Practice?

[17] World Bank (2018), 'Pathways for Peace: Inclusive Approaches to Preventing Violent Conflict', Washington, DC.

[18] Lederach, P. (2005), *The Moral Imagination: The Art and Soul of Building Peace*, New York: Oxford University Press.

[19] De Coning (2016).

[20] Ibid.

conflict in a constructive, non-violent manner. To some extent, this was already reflected and incorporated in BINUB's peacebuilding projects, which targeted the capacity-building of conflict-resolution institutions and mechanisms. Nonetheless, many of these capacity-building initiatives reproduced the deterministic stance of liberal peacebuilding by fostering a preconceived set of capacities.

A society's capacity to self-organize and respond to conflict constructively (rather than violently) is nurtured over time. Furthermore, while it can be supported by external actors, it must ultimately emerge from within, drawing on context-specific attributes.

Reflecting on my own experience, fostering resilience was not foremost on my mind. Although we used a plethora of sophisticated conflict-analysis tools, there were no readily available tools – much less research and development – for analysing resilience and local capacities for peace. Recent efforts to study peace proactively and develop frameworks for assessing resilience for peace[21] go some way to addressing this gap.

The sustainability challenge

While states can start and end conflict, they cannot build peace on their own.[22] Those who sign peace agreements are not necessarily those who can imagine and work for a peaceful society. While independent studies have demonstrated that, like a tree, peace grows from the bottom up, most external peacebuilding prescriptions tend to be top down, state-centric enterprises that at best have only a perfunctory outlook on what ordinary people think about peace or what they do to maintain it amidst adversity.

Since moving into the peace and security field over two decades ago, and even more so now, I have come to the firm belief that building peace is not what outsiders do, however well-intentioned or resourced they may be. In fact, resources not properly mobilized and managed may provide incentives for peacebuilding approaches that are ill-suited to a particular context.[23]

In pursuit of this belief as SRSG, I put a premium on engaging with civil society organizations and citizen networks – including women and youth

---

[21]   Interpeace, Frameworks for Assessing Resilience. Available online: http://www.interpeace.org/ programmes/far (accessed 3 September 2018).
[22]   Call (2008).
[23]   The Geneva Peacebuilding Platform, White Paper on Peacebuilding, 2015.

associations, religious and other leaders – without unwittingly triggering the government's ire. My purpose was to deepen my understanding of the local context and design, where possible, peacebuilding activities that could potentially add value to the lives of those who had experienced conflict. In my attempts to reach this goal, I had, however, to contend with many challenges and constraints.

One challenge to building sustainability was a lack of common understanding among national and international stakeholders of the key determinants of peace. In the case of Burundi, for example, external actors – including the UN Security Council mandated peace operations – essentially focused on three areas of peace: power sharing, security sector reform and transitional justice and the rule of law. This approach leaned heavily towards the liberal peace model discussed above, with electoral democracy seen as the means of legitimizing governance, and criminal prosecutions judged the best way of dealing with impunity and addressing legacies of past violence. It was based on the assumption that people emerging from conflict cannot focus on the future together if they are divided by a painful past. With respect to putting an end to impunity, for example, President Nkurunziza of Burundi argued against setting up the special tribunal foreseen in the Arusha Agreements, arguing this mechanism would re-ignite conflict, whereas the UN argued the opposite. These competing visions created a tense relationship between the Government of Burundi and BINUB.

Outside the country's capital Bujumbura, local communities understood peace primarily in terms of 'healing the heart', and that the reintegration of communities through healing and dialogue was more important than digging up the past. They shared the sense that insisting on any form of accountability, including criminal prosecution of elite actors, may simply re-ignite the conflict, and that the priority should be on rebuilding communities and rehabilitating lives.[24] BINUB's attempts to consult a sample of the local population on how best to come to terms with legacies of past violence were strictly controlled by the government, creating frictions between the latter and the Mission leadership.

A second challenge was the obsessive eagerness of donors, the Security Council and UN agencies to seek quick results on the basis of short-term performance indicators. In reality, the relevant peacebuilding activities normally take years, if not decades, to produce the desired impact. This focus limited the time for consultations and listening to the views of the most critical constituency: the beneficiaries. It also led international peacebuilding actors limiting their

---

[24]   Wielenga and Akin-Aina (2016).

engagement to those local NGOs that were based in urban centres, familiar with UN budgeting and programming processes, and whose staff spoke English or French. However, these NGOs often had no local base at the community level.

A third challenge, mentioned above, was an aversion by governments towards attempts by international actors to bypass line ministries and reach out directly to local NGOs. The argument often used by governmental detractors was that these organizations were not actually 'civil' society organizations, but rather Trojan horses serving as 'fronts' for retired or active members of the political opposition.

In order to circumvent some of these constraints in Burundi, I made it conditional – where possible – that no peacebuilding project should be financed from the Peacebuilding Trust Fund unless there was a grassroots organization legitimately representing the relevant local communities and involved in analysing the problem, designing the interventions, and implementing and monitoring planned activities.[25] This led to the creation of inclusive civil society advisory groups, which vetted projects before they were channelled for approval. If there were gaps in technical capacities, then training in project and program design were provided. These technical groups worked side by side with government officials representing the relevant ministries standing to benefit from the projects. While the transactional costs were at times high, these mechanisms allowed for greater national ownership and a better foundation for sustainability.

This methodology helped me, to some degree, strike a balance between fulfilling globally determined plans and targets, and locally driven needs and priorities.[26] It is the latter, though, that constitutes a better guide for ensuring bottom-up coherence[27] and a modicum of sustainability.

The above notwithstanding, it was not always easy to implement such a methodology, as I was often distracted by the custodians of global accountability mechanisms anxious to hear reports on success stories that would make the organization or the financial contributors to the Peacebuilding Fund look good. Paramount was short-term organizational success rather than the long-term impact of peacebuilding initiatives.[28] As a result, there was little room for

---

[25] Mahmoud (2010).

[26] *The Washington Post* (2015), 'What Burundi's Crisis Says about U.N. Capacity to Build Peace', 18 May. Available online: https://www.washingtonpost.com/news/monkey-cage/wp/2015/05/18/what-burundis-crisis-says-about-un-capacity-to-build-peace/ (accessed 4 October 2018).

[27] Campbell, S. (2008), '(Dis)integration, Incoherence and Complexity in UN Post-conflict Interventions', *International Peacekeeping*, 15 (4).

[28] I am grateful to Susanna Campbell whose excellent work I cited above and whom I interviewed for this chapter, for helping me articulate the above constraints that weighed heavily on our collective peacebuilding endeavours in Burundi.

innovation, let alone learning, with such practices often not prized, let alone incentivized.

In the case of MINURCAT, the sole mandate of its peacekeeping operations was to protect civilians, with sustainability absent from the planning, let alone implementation, of the Mission. Sustainability came to the fore only when the Mission was unexpectedly asked by the Government of Chad to leave the country.

Security Council mandate: floor or ceiling?

One of the challenges I faced as an SRSG was implementing a Security Council mandate the design of which neither I nor the host government had rarely a hand in. Early on, and inspired by the actions of those preceding me, I made a conscious decision to consider the mandate entrusted to me by the Security Council as a floor rather than an immovable ceiling.[29] This ultimately helped me manage the delicate web of relationships connecting me to the Security Council, the UN Secretary-General and the host country.

For example, when I took over as Executive Representative of the Secretary-General (ERSG) and Head of the UN Integrated Office in Burundi (BNUB), I inherited a mandate that had already been negotiated with the Burundian government and key officials from the UN Secretariat. A few months into my new functions, I realized that evolving realities on the ground – brought about by a government reshuffle and key developments in the inter-Burundian peace process – necessitated adapting the mandate, which was to be reviewed a year hence. To handle this challenge, I engaged in intense dialogue with the host government and other national stakeholders in order to develop a shared and dynamic understanding of the original mandate's letter and spirit. This process paved the way for the joint design of an implementation plan, providing for the flexible interpretation of the mandate.

In order to get the Security Council and the Secretariat support team on board, I used the periodic reports of the Secretary-General – whose original drafts were prepared by my team and myself in the field – as well as my oral briefings to the Security Council that accompanied their publication, to advocate for and secure endorsement of the plan. One of the plan's salient features was how to organize the UN system differently in order to provide integrated support to the mandated peacebuilding activities, including the establishment of a

---

[29]   Hochschild, F. (2010), 'In and Above Conflict. A Study on Leadership at the United Nations', Geneva.

transitional justice mechanism, and the DDR programme for the final Burundian rebel movement following the 2006 ceasefire agreement. This strategy served me well for over three years – until the Government of Burundi asked for my replacement, claiming that in the exercise of my political role I was biased in favour of the opposition.

Leadership for sustaining peace: what would I do differently?

In light of the above, the question arises: in terms of leading a UN Mission, what would I do differently with the knowledge I now have acquired?

As a first step, I would attempt to learn all I could about the UN. This would involve acquiring a deep understanding of the factors leading to its creation, its relative position in the multi-lateral governance system, the norms and values animating its work, and the challenges it is traversing at a time of heightened geopolitical tensions and pressure for reform. More importantly, I would actively learn how peace is constructed both as a process and as an outcome, how it is sustained, and why it fails to take hold in the immediate aftermath of conflict.[30] On a more pragmatic level, I have found that familiarity with the budgetary and administrative rules and regulations of the UN helps in reconciling the frustrating asymmetry between the political responsibility entrusted to the SRSG and the relatively limited authority they have over a Mission's financial and staff resources.

Secondly, I would make a point of remembering that in the changing and uncertain environment we live in, context and followers have increasingly become far more important than leaders. As a manager of a UN Mission, I would recognize the valuable benefits of drawing on the diverse expertise and perspectives of 'followers' whose values, belief systems, language and culture may be different from mine. In countries under stress, leaders emerge from many places and no society, however broken, is bereft of ideas and aspirations.

Thirdly, as an external peacebuilder, I would be guided by the simple, overarching principle that leadership for sustaining peace is not about you. Rather, it is about unleashing the leadership potential of those you are supposed to help, while resisting being captured by the country's elite under the guise of national ownership. As outlined above, this 'un-heroic' stance is easier said than done, given that the upward global accountability systems embedded in UN mandates

---

[30] Van Brabant, K. (2012) 'Leadership for Peace', Interpeace, Working Paper No. 2.

put a premium on leaders' and the organisation's success, leaving little room for local accountability towards the people whose lives you are trying to transform.

Fourthly, having observed what befell UN envoys when I was head of the front office of the UN Under-Secretary-General for Political Affairs, and later on as Director in the same department, I have learned that expecting to be declared *persona non grata* at some point in your career should be part of any UN high-representative's DNA. This is all the more important when such a representative is serving in a complex, post-conflict political environment, and is expected to take a principled stand when the values and principles of the UN Charter are routinely flouted by governing elites.

As a corollary to this, I have further learned that the juridical legitimacy conferred through being appointed by the UN Secretary-General – with the blessing of the Security Council when necessary[31] – is not sufficient for the proper discharging of the duties of a Special Representative of the Secretary-General (SRSG). Such legitimacy must be complemented by performance legitimacy. Borrowing from political science, I interpret performance legitimacy as formal, positional authority being judiciously exercised in such a way as to earn the willing acceptance of key stakeholders. In my case, the main stakeholders whose acceptance and collaboration I sought to cultivate were the Government of Burundi, which granted its initial consent for my appointment, and the various heads of UN agencies, funds and programmes operating on the ground, whose operational activities I was mandated to coordinate. In essence, I found that my legitimacy as SRSG and ERSG rested on three pillars: the trust of the Secretary-General, the blessing of the Security Council, and the continued consent of the host government. Of the three pillars, it is the last – as my experience in Burundi attests – that determines longevity of tenure, regardless of the approval quotient the two other pillars may furnish.

Fifthly, I would interrogate the paradigms informing whatever mandate I was given. At a minimum, I would question the unsubstantiated assumption that if one understands the pathology of war and the complexities of the causes driving and sustaining violent conflict, one will be able to foster and sustain peace. This entails rethinking how we analyse peace and conflict context: in addition to assessing the factors driving and sustaining violent conflict, we should also identify those capacities enabling afflicted communities to peacefully prevent or manage conflict, thereby nurturing a modicum of peace despite internal

---

[31]   United Nations (2006), 'Letter dated 22 December 2006 from the President of the Security Council addressed to the Secretary-General', S/2006/1021, 22 December.

vulnerabilities and external pressures. This requires a shift in the way prevention for sustaining peace is understood, with factors enabling peace included as units of analysis informing international action.

Sixthly, as a mission leader I would consciously assume the responsibility to do no harm. This includes gaining an understanding of how – despite short-term outcomes appearing to calm the ravages of violent conflict – outside efforts may end up raising expectations, creating dependence and undermining national self-organizing capacities for peace.

Lastly, and above all, I would be wary of certain emerging paradigms that espouse the notion that for the UN to remain relevant and 'fit for purpose', it must be more militarily robust. Legitimizing the use of force in the pursuit of peace and stability would risk, in my view, the further militarization of peace operations, creating in turn more lethal security threats against peacekeepers, whose perceived neutrality is already under stress.[32] More importantly, these securitized paradigms, if pursued indiscriminately, risk sapping the already drained credibility of the UN as a broker of peace,[33] at a time when prevention through war, rather than through diplomacy, seems to be the new norm.

Avenues for further research on peace and leadership

Below, I highlight gaps noted in the conceptual chapter and suggest some research avenues that may enhance our understanding of the theory and practice of leadership for peace.

Redefine leadership for sustaining peace and global crisis management

As intimated throughout this book, a key determinant for laying the foundations of durable peace is leadership, but not just any leadership. As can be seen in Chapter 1, much has been written about leaders (in terms of individuals who perform roles in a specific context) and about leadership (in terms of the

---

[32] Benson, J. (2016), 'The UN Intervention Brigade: Extinguishing Conflict or Adding Fuel to the Flames'? A One on Earth Future Discussion Paper, June.

[33] Karlsrud, J. (2018), '*The UN at War. Peace Operation in a New Era*', Switzerland: Palgrave Macmillan.

processes by which these individuals perform their roles). But with a few exceptions,[34] little has been written about leadership for the purposes of sustaining peace. As the manuscript of this book was being completed, the author made a modest attempt to expound on the latter subject in the form of a short article entitled 'What Kind of Leadership Does Sustaining Peace Require'.[35]

Essentially, I define leadership for sustaining peace as the processes that create and nurture an empowering environment, which in turn unleash the positive energy and potential existent within people, enabling them to resolve conflict non-violently and participate in charting a path towards positive peace. This definition is motivated by a more nuanced understanding of peace that taps into the human potential for peace,[36] rather than the overstated potential for war. It is also motivated by the belief that facilitative approaches drawing on local people's understanding of conflict and peace empowers them and strengthens the bonds that help preserve peace.[37] It is what is referred to in Chapter 1 as 'popular peace'. Readers and scholars are invited to further investigate this emerging nexus between leadership and sustaining peace, and what it means for peace studies and peace research endeavours.

As I was putting the final touches on this book, a novel health pandemic, the Coronavirus (Covid-19) broke out sweeping indiscriminately across over 190 nations with devastating consequences. Even though its humanitarian and economic toll has thus far been most visible in rich and emerging countries, it is expected that the fallout of this global crisis would be far worse in conflict-affected countries with fragile institutions and broken health systems. It is often said it is in crisis that the mettle of leadership is forged. This pandemic seems to have pushed to the limit the boundaries of what we understand leadership to be, including some of the tenets expounded in this book. It has also forced us to rethink what peace and security mean in the time of health pandemics and how to build and sustain them.

It behoves future researchers to look back at this crisis and study the types of leadership of those who were in the front lines, including women political leaders[38]

---

[34]   Amaladas, S. and S. Byrn (eds) (2018), *Peace Leadership, the Quest for Connectedness*, New York: Routledge.

[35]   Mahmoud, Y. (2019), 'What Kind of Leadership Does Sustaining Peace Require', Global Observatory, International Peace Institute, New York, USA, January.

[36]   Fry, D. (2005), *The Human Potential for Peace*, New York: Oxford University Press.

[37]   Kriesbert, L. (2015), *Realizing Peace: A Constructive Conflict Approach*. New York: Oxford University Press.

[38]   Fincher, L.H. (2020), 'Women Leaders Are Doing a Disproportionately Great Job at Handling the Pandemic. So Why Aren't There More of Them?', *CNN World*.

had to conjure up to mitigate the pandemic ravages, address the systemic inequities and social injustices it had revealed and actualize the new normal that was waiting to emerge. The outcome of such research would help induct the future generation of transformative leaders into not only how to anticipate and contend with the next pandemic or the next planetary, climate-change-induced crisis but also how to seize the opportunities global crises present to build more inclusive, just and peaceful societies.

Leadership for peace beyond the gender lens

Gendered approaches to leadership and peace are woefully absent, meaning much can be gained from understanding the gender dynamics of leadership for sustaining peace, divesting it of pervasive binary stereotypes of women as peacemakers and men as warmongers.[39] Despite a growing body of work in both academia and the policy realm, scholars, practitioners and students should aim to fill the significant remaining gaps in our understanding of gender and leadership. As such, two research streams are suggested. The first should focus on understanding the forms of power, influence, strategies and tactics that women utilize in their capacities as leaders for peace, beyond prescriptive gender essentialism linked to femininities and masculinities.[40] The second should focus on uncovering women's understanding of peace and security through an analysis of the multiple identities they inhabit, and in doing so suggest ways in which such perspective can help inform the work of men and women leaders dedicated to creating propitious environments for peace to take root.

Incorporate differing perspectives on peacebuilding and leadership

The reader may have noted that the literature survey contained in Chapter 1 is primarily based on theories and practices developed by thinkers and writers from the Northern hemisphere. Bringing in other perspectives, informed by differing human experiences and diverse cultures, could enrich the theory and practice of peacebuilding.

To give just one example, a paradigm that has resurfaced over the past two decades is the African concept of *ubuntu*. As a world view, *ubuntu* broadly means

---

[39] McElroy, L. and T. Dineen (1988), 'Women and Peace: A Dissenting View', *Canadian Women Studies*, 9 (1).
[40] Cook-Huffman, C. and A. Snyder (2018), 'Women, Leadership, and Building Peace' in S. Amaladas and S. Byrne (eds), *Peace Leadership: The Quest for Connectedness*, London: Routledge, 30–45.

that together we are one. It asserts that the common ground of humanity is greater and more enduring than the differences dividing us. As a philosophy, *ubuntu* can potentially help to bridge the gap between Western theories and approaches to peacebuilding and lesser-known approaches to achieving sustainable peace. Among its early proponents were Nelson Mandela and Desmond Tutu, and more recently Reuel Khoza – all from South Africa. Khoza has spoken and written extensively on the subject, including weaving it into his latest book, *Attuned Leadership*.[41] In order to build peace better (which is the title of this last chapter), it is imperative that we understand how peace is conceived, understood and promoted in different cultures, particularly in parts of the world that are often the targets of external peacebuilding interventions. *Ubuntu* is as good a place as any to start this open-minded exploration.

Why is peace treated as an exception?

An enduring, positive peace is at the heart of any endeavour seeking to address humanity's global challenges. Without it, pervasive governance and development deficits will persist unabated. Yet peace seems to be at a low ebb these days. Where it does exist, it tends to be treated as an exception, bounded by external normative moorings that tie its fortunes to the presence or absence of violent conflict.

Attempts to measure peace as a starting point and end goal are rare,[42] and studying the causes of peace in both peaceful and conflict settings is equally rare,[43] even at times shunned or viewed with suspicion. The question worth investigating is: Why does destructive conflict and war seem ever more seductive to observers and actors alike?[44] Furthermore, why do studies showing a historical decrease in violence[45] or chronicling multiple stories of people living together in peace in many corners of the world go unheeded or unreported? An exception to this trend is a recent piece in *The New York Times* declaring 2018 the best year in human history, despite the ills afflicting our planet.[46]

[41]   Khoza, R. (2011), *Attuned Leadership, African Humanism as Compass*, South Africa: Penguin.
[42]   Happy exception are currently pursued by Columbia University Sustaining Peace Project (http://ac4.ei.columbia.edu/research-themes/dst/sustainable-peace/), by the Kroc Institute for International Peace studies, (https://kroc.nd.edu/)
[43]   Uppsala University, (2014–), 'The Causes of Peace – The Botswana, Zambia and Malawi-Zone of Peace', Department of Peace Conflict and Research.
[44]   Olonisakin, F. (2018), 'Securing Peace in the Unromantic Context', Premium Times, Lagos, Nigeria, 31 July.
[45]   Pinker, S. (2012), *The Better Angels of Our Nature: Why Violence Has Declined*, Amazon Books.
[46]   Kristof, N. (2019), 'Why 2018 Is the Best Year in Human History', *The New York Times*, 5 January.

Increase understanding of peace in contexts under stress

As noted elsewhere, the binary relationship ascribed to conflict and peace means that stable societies with no violent conflict are excluded from the study of peace, when, in fact, they are the case studies most likely to unveil the factors associated with peace.

A meaningful investigation in this regard would attempt to unveil the domestic, regional and international threads that make countries such as Senegal, Ghana or Botswana relative oases of peace despite internal vulnerabilities and external pressures.

Going forward

It is my hope that by investigating some of the research avenues suggested above, current and future students, as well as scholars, will challenge our ingrained mental models of how peace is built and sustained, and contribute to a more holistic and practical understanding of the conditions that incubate positive peace and the tenets of leadership that can facilitate its emergence.

Concluding thought

Jean Monnet[47] liked to quote this saying from Dwight Morrow: 'The world is divided into people who do things, and people who get credit. Try, if you can, to belong to the first class, there is far less competition.' I like to think, on the basis of what I shared in this book, that I belong to the first breed, notwithstanding some of the errors that I fell prey to along the way. I have always tried, in good faith, to help peace take root, while resisting, where possible, the urge to prescribe its shape.

---

[47] Jean Monnet whom I quote in Chapter 1 is a French political economist and diplomat. An influential supporter of European unity, he is considered as one of the founding fathers of the European Union.

References

Advisory Group of Experts (2015), 'The Challenge of Sustaining Peace: Report for the 2015 Review of the United Nations Peacebuilding Architecture', The United Nations, June.

Ahmedou Ould, A. (2016), *Plutôt Mourir que Faillir*, Tunis: Sud Editions.

Amaladas, S. and S. Byrn (eds) (2018), *Peace Leadership, the Quest for Connectedness*, New York: Routledge.

Amnesty International (2009), 'No Place for Us Here: Violence against Refugee Women in Eastern Chad', Amnesty International Publications: 4.

Amnesty International (2010), 'Chad: We too Deserve Protection. Human Rights Challenges as UN Mission Withdraws', Amnesty International Publications.

Arusha Peace and Reconciliation Agreement for Burundi, Arusha August 2000.

Autesserre, S. (2017), 'International Peacebuilding and Local Success: Assumptions and Effectiveness', *International Studies Review*, 0: 1–19.

Barma, H. (2017), *The Peacebuilding Puzzle: Political Order in Post-Conflict States*, Cambridge: Cambridge University Press.

Basagic, Z. (2007), 'The Role of the United Nations in Making Progress towards Peace in Burundi'. Available online: https://www.diplomacy.edu/sites/default/files/23082010104120%20Basagic%20%28Library%29.pdf (accessed 25 March 2020).

Bennis, W and B. Nanus (1985), *Leaders: The strategies for taking charge*, New York: Harper and Row.

Benson, J. (2016), 'The UN Intervention Brigade: Extinguishing Conflict or Adding Fuel to the Flames?', A One on Earth Future Discussion Paper, June.

Bentley, K. and R. Southall (2005), *An African Peace Process: Mandela, South Africa-Burundi*, Cape Town: HSRC Press.

Berg, P. (2008), 'The Dynamics of Conflict in the Tri-Border Region of Sudan, Chad and Central African Republic', Friedrich Ebert Foundation.

Boshoff, H., W. Vrey and G. Rautenback (2010), 'The Burundi Process: From Civil War to Conditional Peace', Monograph 171.

Bouka, Y. (2014), 'Status and Dynamics of the Political Situation in Burundi', Central African Report, Institute for Security Studies, Issue 1.

Bouka, Y. (2017), 'Burundi: Between War and Negative Peace', in G.M. Khadiagala (ed.) *War and Peace in Africa's Great Lake Region*, 17–31, Switzerland: Palgrave Macmillan.

Bouka, Y and S. Wolters (2016), 'Battle for Burundi, Is there a Viable Solution?', Central Africa Report, Institute for Security Studies, Issue 7.

Boutellis, A. (2013), 'Chad and the Central African Republic', in J. Boulden (ed.), *Responding to Conflict in Africa. The United Nations and Regional Organizations*, 121–44, New York: Palgrave Macmillan.

Boutellis, A. (2013), 'Driving the System Apart? A study of United Nations and Integrated Strategic Planning', International Peace Institute, August.

Bureau Intégré des Nations Unies au Burundi (2008), 'Célébration de la Journée Internationale des Droits de l'Homme', No. 024, 10 December.

Bureau Intégré des Nations Unies au Burundi (2009), 'La Réinsertion durable des Soldats Démobilisés, Gage de Stabilité', BINUB, No. 026, February.

Bureau Intégré des Nations Unies au Burundi (2009), 'Journée Mondiale des Réfugiés', No. 030, 20 June.

Burns, J. (1978), *Leadership*, New York: Harper & Row.

Call, C. (2008), 'Building States to Build Peace? A Critical Analysis', *Journal of Peacebuilding and Development*, 4 (2): 60–74.

Campbell, S. (2008), '(Dis)integration, Incoherence and Complexity in UN Post-conflict Interventions', *International Peacekeeping*, 15 (4): 556–69.

Campbell, S. (2010), 'Independent External Evaluation of Peacebuilding Fund Projects in Burundi'. Available online: https://reliefweb.int/sites/reliefweb.int/files/resources/CABFEA3AB9A416D34925779C000EAE96-Full_Report.pdf (accessed 2 June 2020).

Campbell, S. (2015), 'What Burundi Crisis Tells Us About UN Capacity to Build Peace', *The Washington Post*.

Campbell, S. and A. Kaspersen (2008), 'The UN's Reforms: Confronting Integration Barriers', *International Peacekeeping*, 15 (4): 470–85.

Catalyst for Peace, Building Peace from the Inside Out. Available online: 2008–15, https://www.catalystforpeace.org/ (accessed 25 March 2020).

Centre for Strategies and Security for the Sahel Sahara, Biography Ahmedou Ould Abdallah. Available online: http://www.centre4s.org/en/index.php?option=com_content&view=article&id=47&Itemid=55 (accessed 5 March 2018).

Chandler, D. (2007), 'The State-Building Dilemma: Good Governance or Democratic Government?', in H. Aiden and N. Robinson (eds), *Statebuilding: Theory and Practice*, 70–88, London: Routledge.

Charter of the United Nations and the Statute of the International Court of Justice, San Francisco, 1945.

Chrétien, J-P. (1978), 'Le Commerce du Sel de l'Uvinza au XIXe Siecle: De la Ceuillette au Monopole Capitaliste', Revue Française d'Histoire d'Outre-Mer LXV.

Coleman, P. (2012), 'The Missing Piece in Sustainable Peace', General Earth Institute, 6 November.

Comprehensive Ceasefire Agreement between the Government of the Republic of Burundi and the PALIPEHUTU – FNL, Dar ES Salam, 7 September 2006.

Communiqué of the Peace and Security Council of the African Union (AU), at its 70th meeting held on 12 and 13 February 2007.

Cook-Huffman, C and A. Snyder (2018), 'Women, Leadership, and Building Peace' in S. Amaladas and S. Byrne (eds), *Peace Leadership: The Quest for Connectedness*, 30–45, London: Routledge.

Daley, P. (2006), 'Ethnicity and political violence in Africa: The challenge to the Burundi state', *Political Geography*, 25 (6): 657–79.

De Coning, C. (2016), 'From peacebuilding to sustaining peace: Implications of complexity for resilience and sustainability', *Resilience*, 4 (3): 166–81.

Denskus, T. (2007), 'Peacebuilding Does Not Build Peace', *Development in Practice* 17 (4–5): 656–62.

Diehl, P. (2016), 'Exploring Peace: Looking Beyond War and Negative Peace', *International Studies Quarterly*, 60 (1): 1–10.

Doyle, M. (1986), 'Liberalism and world politics', *American political science review*, 80 (4): 1151–69.

Draft DPKO/DFS Operational Concept on the Protection of Civilians in United Nations Peacekeeping Operations.

European Union, Emergency Humanitarian Aid Decision. Available online: https://ec. europa.eu/echo/files/funding/decisions/2005/dec_guyana_01000_en.pdf (accessed 28 February 2018).

Facts and Details, Mekong River Cambodia. Available online: http://factsanddetails. com/southeast-asia/Cambodia/sub5_2f/entry-3505.html (accessed 5 March 2018).

Fincher, L.H. (2020), 'Women Leaders Are Doing a Disproportionately Great Job at Handling the Pandemic. So Why Aren't There More of Them?', *CNN World*.

Fry, D. (2005), *The Human Potential for Peace*, New York: Oxford University Press.

Galtung, J. (1964), 'An Editorial', *Journal of Peace Research*, 1 (1): 1–4.

Galtung, J. (1975), 'Three Approaches to Peace: Peacekeeping, Peacemaking and Peacebuilding', in J. Galtung (ed.), *Peace, War and Defence – Essays in Peace Research*, Vol. 2: 282–304, Copenhagen: Christian Ejlers.

GCI (2011), 'In Memoriam: Mamadou Bah, le Représentant De L'UA au Burundi N'est Plus', 28 June. Available online: http://www.guineeconakry.info/article/detail/ in-memoriam-mamadou-bah-le-representant-de-lua-au-burundi-nest-plus/ (accessed 25 March 2018).

Ghali, B. (1992), 'An Agenda for Peace: Preventive Diplomacy, Peacemaking and Peace-keeping', Document A/47/277 – S/241111, 17 June, New York: Department of Public Information, United Nations.

GlobalSecurity.org. (2000), 'Burundi Civil War'. Available online:http://www. globalsecurity.org/military/world/war/burundi.htm (accessed 11 March 2018).

Grint, K. (2010), *Leadership: A Very Short Introduction*, New York: Oxford University Press Inc.

Grünewald, F. and C. Olivia (2009), 'L'Espace Humanitaire à L'Est Du Tchad', Groupe URD, October.

Guyana. A case study prepared by the Social Cohesion Programme (UNDP Guyana) for the UNDESA expert meeting on dialogue, New York 21–3 November 2005.

Hailey, J. (2006), 'NGO Leadership Development, A Review of the Literature', International Training and Research Centre Praxis Paper, 10 July.

Hicks, C. (2014), 'Clay Feet: Chad's Surprising Rise and Enduring Weaknesses', *World Politics Review*, 13 November.

History of Burundi#Kingdom of Burundi (1680–1966).

Hochschild, F.H. (2010), 'In and Above Conflict. A Study on Leadership at the United Nations', Geneva.

Holtkamp, M. (2014), 'Leadership Skills and the Role of Adaptability and Creativity in Effective Leadership: A Literature Review Geared toward an Integrative Model', University of Twente.

Human Rights Watch (2004), 'Darfur in Flames: Atrocities in Western Sudan', A Human Rights Watch Report, Vol. 16, No. 5 (A), April.

Human Right Watch (2006), 'Violence Beyond Borders: The Human Rights Crisis in Eastern Chad', No. 4, June.

Imburi Phare Media (2016), 'Burundi: Justice pour Ernest Manirumva, 7 Ans après sa Mort', 10 April.

Independent News (2009), 'Burundi's Election Needs International Support', United Nations Press Release, 11 December.

Institute for Security Studies (2008), '23 June 2008: The Return of Agathon Rwasa Could Signal Permanent Peace in Burundi', 23 June. Available online: https://ucdpged.uu.se/peaceagreements/fulltext/BUI%2020080610.pdf (accessed 1 July 2018).

International Archive (2007), 'Chronology for Hutus in Burundi', 10 January.

International Crisis Group (2003), 'Refugees and Internally Displaced in Burundi: The Urgent Need for a Consensus on Their Repatriation and Reintegration', 2 December.

International Crisis Group (2006), 'Burundi: Democracy and Peace at Risk', Africa Report No. 120–30, November 2006.

International Federation of Journalists (2006), 'Journalist Summoned by Prosecutor Goes Missing; IFJ Calls for End of Intimidation Campaign against Independent Journalism', 11 December.

International Listening Association, Listening Legend Interview, Dr. Ralph Nichols, Interview by Rick Bommelje, Listening Post, Vol. 84, Summer 2003.

International Monetary Fund (IMF) (2002), 'IMF Approves US $13 Million in Emergency Post-conflict Assistance for Burundi', 9 October Press Release No. 02/48, 9 October.

International Monetary Fund (IMF) (2007), 'Burundi: Poverty Reduction Strategy Paper', IMF Country Report No. 07/46, February.

International Peace Institute (2010), Mahmoud: At Times, We Leave in Humiliating Circumstances, 21 October. Available online: https://www.ipinst.org/2010/10/mahmoud-at-times-we-leave-in-humiliating-circumstances (accessed 2 August 2018).

International Peace Institute, Mission and History. Available online: https://www.ipinst.org/about/mission-history (accessed 20 January 2018).

International Peace Institute (2016), 'Armed Conflict: Mediation, Conciliation and Peacekeeping', Independent Commission on Multilateralism, Paper Issue, March.

International Peace Institute (2017), 'Sustaining Peace: What Does it Mean in Practice?', IPI, April.

Interpeace, 'What is Peace?', Available online: https://www.interpeace.org/what-we-do/what-is-peacebuilding/ (accessed 10 January 2018).

Interpeace, Frameworks for Assessing Resilience. Available online: See http://www.interpeace.org/programmes/far (accessed 3 September 2018).

IWACU (2011), 'Hommage à l'Ambassadeur Mamadou Bah', *La Voix du Burundi*, 27 July.

IWACU (2011), 'Chronique d'un Désamour', 30 July. Available online: https://www.iwacu-burundi.org/chronique-dun-dsamour/ (accessed 6 August 2018).

Jackson, S. (2006), 'The United Nations Operations in Burundi (ONUB)-Political and Strategic Lessons Learned', External Independent Study, Conflict Prevention Peace Forum, New York.

Jensen, D. and S. Lonergan (2012), *Assessing and Restoring Natural Resources in Post-Conflict Peacebuilding*, USA and Canada: Earthscan.

Karlsrud, J. (2018), '*The UN at War. Peace Operation in a New Era*', Switzerland: Palgrave Macmillan.

Karlsrud, J. and R. Solhjell (2010), 'An Honourable Exit for MINURCAT?', Norwegian Institute of International Affairs.

Kellerman, B. (2012), *The End of Leadership*, New York: HarperCollins.

Khoza, R. (2011), *Attuned Leadership, African Humanism as Compass*, South Africa: Penguin.

Kim, J. (2011), 'Leadership in Context. Lessons from a New Leadership Theory and Current Development Practice', The King's Fund.

Kotter, P. (1990), *A Force for Change: How Leadership Differs from Management*, New York: Free Press.

Kriesbert, L. (2015), *Realizing Peace: A Constructive Conflict Approach*. New York: Oxford University Press.

Kristof, N. (2019), 'Why 2018 Is the Best Year in Human History', *The New York Times*, 5 January.

Lacey, M. (2006), 'Chad Severs Ties with Sudan as Tensions Escalate', *The New York Times*, 14 April.

Lakovic, V. (2016), 'How to Become a Mindful Listener (and Avoid Giving Advice All the Time)', Peace Blog.

Lederach, P. (1997), *Building Peace: Sustainable Reconciliation in Divided Societies*, Washington, DC: US Institute of Peace Press.

Lederach, P. (2005), *The Moral Imagination: The Art and Soul of Building Peace*, New York: Oxford University Press.

Lemarchand, R. (1996), *Burundi: Ethnic Conflict and Genocide*, Cambridge: Woodrow Wilson Center Press and Cambridge University Press.

Lemarchand, R. (2006), 'Consociationalism and Power Sharing in Africa: Rwanda, Burundi, and the Democratic Republic of the Congo', *African Affairs*, 106 (422):1–20.

Lemarchand, R. (2009), *The Dynamics of Violence in Central Africa*, Philadelphia: University of Pennsylvania Press.

Liberation (1996), 'Entretien avec Ahmedou Ould Abdallah, Ancien Représentant de L'ONU au Burundi. "il Faut Imposer la Cohabitation"', 26 July. Available online: https://www.liberation.fr/evenement/1996/07/26/entretien-avec-ahmedou-ould-abdallah-ancien-representant-de-l-onu-au-burundi-il-faut-imposer-la-coha_176189 (accessed 2 March 2018).

Los Angeles (1997), 'Zaire Peace Drive a Coup for Mandela', 9 May. Available online: https://www.latimes.com/archives/la-xpm-1997-05-09-mn-57117-story.html (accessed 20 February 2018).

Lund, M. and S. McDonald (2015), *Across the Lines of Conflict: Facilitating Cooperation to Build Peace*, Woodrow Wilson Center Press with Columbia University Press.

Lussier, R. and C. Achua (2004), *Leadership: Theory, Application and Skill Development*, South-western: Thomson.

Mahmoud, Y. (2010), 'Partnership for Peacebuilding in Burundi: Some lessons Learned', in H. Besada (ed.), *Crafting an African Security Architecture*, 129–42, London: Ashgate.

Mahmoud, Y. (2019), 'What Kind of Leadership Does Sustaining Peace Require', Global Observatory, International Peace Institute, New York, January.

Mahmoud, Y. and A. Makoond (2018), 'Can Peacebuilding Work for Sustaining Peace?', IPI Global Observatory, 10 April. Available online: https://theglobalobservatory. org/2018/04/peacebuilding-work-sustaining-peace/ (accessed 8 August 2018).

Mahmoud, Y., L. Connolly and D. Mechoulan (2018), 'Sustaining Peace in Practice: Building on What Works', International Peace Institute, February.

Masciulli, J., M. Molchanov and W. Knight (2009), 'Political Leadership in Context' in Masciulli, J., M. Molchanov and W. Knight (eds). *The Ashgate Research Companion to Political Leadership*, 3–30, England: Ashgate.

Maxwell, J. (2005), *The 360° Leader Developing Your Influence from Anywhere in the Organisation*, Nashville, TN: Thomas Nelson.

Mbiatem, A. (2016), 'Leadership Emergence and Style: Fidel Castro of Cuba', *Leadership and Developing Societies*, 1 (1): 59–81.

McElroy, L. and T. Dineen (1988), 'Women and Peace: A Dissenting View', *Canadian Women Studies*, 9 (1): 34–6.

Médecins sans Frontières (2006), 'Over 10,000 People Flee Violence in Chad', Press Release.

Metcalfe, V., A. Giffen and S. Elhawaryf (2011), 'UN Integration and Humanitarian Space. An Independent Study Commissioned by the UN Integration Steering Group', Humanitarian Policy Group Overseas Development Institute, December.

MINURCAT II Final Draft Report (2010), 'Lesson Learned', 6 November.

Monnet, J. (1976), *Mémoires*, Paris: Librairie Arthème Fayard.

Murphy, A. (1941), 'A Study of the Leadership Process', *American Sociological Review*, 6 (5): 674–87.

Murphy, R. (2011), 'Post-UN Withdrawal: An Assessment of Peacekeeping in Chad', Irish Yearbook Of International Law, Vol. 4–5.

Nations Unies (2009), '6236e Séance', S/PV.6236, 10 December 2009.

Nations Unies, Commission de Consolidation de la Paix. Available online: http://www.un.org/en/peacebuilding/mandate.shtml (accessed 30 July 2017).

Ndikumana, L. (2005), 'Distributional Conflict, the State, and Peacebuilding in Burundi', Research Paper No. 2005/45, United Nations, University World Institute for Development Economics Research (UNU-WIDER).

New York University Center on International Cooperation (2011), Annual Review of Global Peace Operations, Boulder: Lynne Rienner Publishers.

Newbury, D. (2001), 'Precolonial Burundi and Rwanda: Local Loyalties and Regional Royalties', *International Journal of African Historical Studies*, 34 (2): 255–314.

Ngaruko, F. and J. Nkurunziza (2000), 'An Economic Interpretation of Conflict in Burundi', *Journal of African Economies*, 9 (3): 235–43.

Northouse, P. (2013), *Leadership: Theory and Practice*, sixth edition, Thousand Oaks, CA: SAGE.

OECD (2010). 'Peacebuilding and Statebuilding Priorities and Challenges. A Synthesis of Findings from Seven Multi-Stakeholder Consultations', Organisation for Economic Co-operation and Development, Paris.

OSCE (2003). Mission in Kosovo Newsletter, 3 (1):4.

Olonisakin, F. (2012), 'Leadership and Peacebuilding in Africa', ALC Working Paper, No. 3, 1 March: 16.

Olonisakin, F. (2017), 'Towards Re-Conceptualising Leadership for Sustainable Peace', *Leadership and Developing Societies*, 2 (1): 1–30.

Olonisakin, F. (2018), 'Securing Peace in the Unromantic Context', *Premium Times*, Lagos, Nigeria, 31 July.

Ould Adallah's reflections on the promise and limitations of preventive diplomacy in his book 'Burundi on the Brink 1993–1995' (2000). Available online: https://bookstore.usip.org/books/BookDetail.aspx?productID=51265 (accessed 10 March 2018).

Paffenholz, T. (2015), 'Unpacking the Local Turn in Peacebuilding: a Critical Assessment towards an Agenda for Future Research', *Third World Quarterly*, 36 (5): 857–74.

Panel Discussion: Panelist Presentation 1 The UN Integrated Approach –Toward Effective Humanitarian Assistance, Tomoya Kamino (Gifu University).

Peace Insight (2010), 'Human Rights Watch Representative Asked to Leave Burundi', 20 May. Available online: https://www.peaceinsight.org/blog/2010/05/human-rights-watch-representative-asked-to-leave-burundi/ (accessed 7 August 2018).

Pearce, C. and J. Conger (2003), 'All those years ago: the historical underpinnings of shared leadership' in C. Pearce and J. Conger (eds), *Shared Leadership: Reframing the Hows and Whys of Leadership*, 1–21, Thousand Oaks, New Delhi: SAGE.

Pinker, S. (2012), *The Better Angels of Our Nature: Why Violence Has Declined*, Amazon Books.

Ploch, L. (2010), 'Instability and Humanitarian Conditions in Chad', Congressional Research Service.

PressAfrik (2009), 'Burundi: Le Gouvernement Burundais Demande le Départ du Représentant de l'ONU', 20 November.

Project Ploughshares (2014), Armed Conflicts Report – Burundi.

Reliefweb (2002), 'Burundi: Interview with Mamadou Bah, AU Representative', 12 December. Available online: https://reliefweb.int/report/burundi/burundi-interview-mamadou-bah-au-representative (accessed 25 March 2018).

Reliefweb (2008), 'Mandate of the Burundi Peace Process Facilitator Extended', 8 February. Available online: https://reliefweb.int/report/burundi/mandate-burundi-peace-process-facilitator-extended (accessed 7 July 2018).

Reliefweb (2008), 'UN Integration in Burundi in the Context of the Peacebuilding office BINUB – Taking Stock and Lessons Learned from Jun 2006 to Nov 2007', 29 February. Available online: https://reliefweb.int/report/burundi/un-integration-burundi-context-peacebuilding-office-binub-taking-stock-and-lessons (accessed 5 May 2018).

Reliefweb (2010), 'Chad Declares State of Belligerence with Sudan', 23 December. Available online: https://reliefweb.int/report/chad/chad-declares-state-belligerence-sudan (accessed 28 August 2018).

Report presented to the Secretary-General on 16 June 2015 by the High-Level Independent Panel on Peace Operations.

Report of the UN Secretary-General, 14 July 2009, para.19, 42, 44 and 51; Physicians for Human Rights, Nowhere to Turn: Failure to Protect, Support and Assure Justice for Darfuri Women, May 2009.

Report of the High-Level Independent Panel on the United Nations Peace Operations (2015), Uniting our Strength for Peace – Politics, Partnership and People, 16 June.

Report of the Panel on United Nations Peace Operations (2000), 21 August, A/55/305–S/2000/809, 21 August.

République du Burundi, Assemblée Nationale, Commission d'Enquête Parlementaire sur la Vente de l'Avion Présidentiel 'Falcon 50', Bujumbura, July 2008. Available online: www.arib.info/An_RAppORT_venTe_FAlCOn50.pdf (accessed 16 March 2018).

République du TCHAD, Présidence de la République Commission Nationale du Déploiement des Forces Internationales au TCHAD – CONAFIT Détachement Intégré de Sécurité (DIS), Numéro 1, Spring 2009.

Reychler, L. and A. Stellamans (2005), 'Researching Peacebuilding leadership', 71 (2). Kwartaal.

RFI Afrique (2010), 'Les Dates Clé de la République Centrafricaine', 11 August. Available online: http://www.rfi.fr/fr/afrique/20100811-dates-cle-republique-centrafricaine (accessed 26 August 2018).

Roberts, D. (2010), 'From Liberal to Popular Peace', Opendemocracy.net, 29 October. Available online: https://www.opendemocracy.net/en/from-liberal-to-popular-peace/ (accessed 18 January 2018).

Roberts, D. (2011), 'Post-conflict Peacebuilding, Liberal Irrelevance and the Locus of Legitimacy, *International Peacekeeping*, 18 (4): 410–24.

Schiavo-Campo, S. (2006), 'Fighting Corruption and Restoring Accountability in Burundi', United States Agency for International Development.

Sebahara, P. (2011), 'Bilan en Demi-Teinte d'une Opération de Paix: La MINURCAT en Centrafrique et au Tchad', Groupe de Recherche et d'Information sur la Paix et la Sécurité, 11 February.

Security Council Report (2006), 'Africa Burundi', March 2006 Monthly Report.

Security Council resolution 2282 and General Assembly resolution 70/262.

Shields, P. (2017), 'Limits of Negative Peace, Faces of Positive Peace', *Parameters*, 4 (3): 5–14.

Simons, C. and F. Zanker (2014), 'Questioning the Local in Peacebuilding', Working Papers of the Priority Programme 1448 of the German Research Foundation: 10.

Sternberg, J., J. Antonakis and A. Cianciolo (2004), *The Nature of Leadership*, Thousand Oaks, CA: SAGE.

Sudan Tribune (2005), 'Chad in State of Belligerence with Sudan: Official', 24 December. Available online: https://www.sudantribune.com/spip.php?article13198 (accessed 28 August 2018).

The East African (2016), 'Burundi Rejects UN Police Force after Security Council Vote', 4 August. Available online: https://www.theeastafrican.co.ke/news/Burundi-rejects-UN-police-deployment-after-Security-Council-vote/2558-3330100-r7xmuy/index.html (accessed 20 August 2018).

The Geneva Peacebuilding Platform, White Paper on Peacebuilding, 2015.

The Guardian (2003), 'Sergio Vieira de Mello High-flying UN Diplomat who Fought for Peace in Global Trouble Spots across Three Decades', 20 August. Available online: https://www.theguardian.com/news/2003/aug/20/guardianobituaries.brazil (accessed 20 February 2018).

The Irish Times (1996), 'Mobutu Flies to Villa in South in France', 5 November. Available online: https://www.irishtimes.com/news/mobutu-flies-to-villa-in-south-in-france-1.102697 (accessed 28 February 2018).

The New York Times (1995), 6 January.

The New York Times (1997), 'Burundi Army Admits It Killed 126 Hutu Refugees', 12 January. Available online: https://www.nytimes.com/1997/01/12/world/burundi-army-admits-it-killed-126-hutu-refugees.html (accessed 11 March 2018).

The New York Times (2013), 'President is Said to Flee as Rebels Seize Capital of the Central African Republic', 24 March. Available online: https://www.nytimes.com/2013/03/25/world/africa/rebels-seize-capital-of-central-african-republic.html (accessed 26 August 2018).

The Washington Post (1994), 'Two African Presidents Are Killed in a Plane Crash', 7 April. Available online: https://www.washingtonpost.com/archive/politics/1994/04/07/two-african-presidents-are-killed-in-plane-crash/38ee6e5e-ba11-4d21-b17c-50a0c1d88516/ (accessed 2 March 2018).

The Washington Post (2015), 'What Burundi's Crisis Says about U.N. Capacity to Build Peace', 18 May. Available online: https://www.washingtonpost.com/news/monkey-cage/wp/2015/05/18/what-burundis-crisis-says-about-un-capacity-to-build-peace/ (accessed 4 October 2018).

Trask, J. (2016), 'Servant Leaders: Empowering Followers' PennState, 15 April. Available online: https://sites.psu.edu/leadership/2016/04/15/servant-leaders-empowering-followers/ (accessed 19 January 2018).

Tubiana, J. (2008), 'The Chad–Sudan Proxy War and the "Darfurization" of Chad: Myths and Reality', Small Arms Survey, Graduate Institute of International Studies, Geneva.

Tubiana, J. (2011), 'Renouncing the Rebels: Local and Regional Dimensions of Chad–Sudan Rapprochement', Small Arms Survey, Graduate Institute of International and Development Studies, Geneva.

UK Foreign and Commonwealth Office (2005), 'Country profiles: Burundi'.

UMOYA, Grandes Lagos; Semaine du 28 janvier au 1er février 2008, 5 February. Available online: https://umoya.org/2008/02/05/grandes-lagos-semaine-du-28-janvier-au-1er-fie.r-2008 (accessed 4 August 2018).

UN News (2006), 'As Blue Helmets Prepare to Leave Burundi, UN Officials Pledge Continued Support', 20 December: https://news.un.org/en/story/2006/12/204102-blue-helmets-prepare-leave-burundi-un-officials-pledge-continued-support.

UN Peacekeeping and Host-State Consent (2018), Stimson Center.

UN Press Release of 31 October 2014, SG/SM/16301-SG/A/1521-PKO/451. Available online: https://www.un.org/press/en/2014/sgsm16301.doc.htm (accessed 29 July 2017).

UNHCR (2005), 'Perceptions of Refugee Security in Chad (Based on Information Received During ESS Mission, 12–17 July 2005)', UNHCR Internal Document.

UNHCR (2006), 'Ethnicity of Sudanese Refugees – Eastern Chad', UNHCR Map, January.

UNHCR (2006), 'Operational Briefing on the Special Operations for Chad and Sudan', UNHCR, May.

United Nations Peacebuilding. Available online: https://www.un.org/peacebuilding/ (accessed 10 January 2018).

United Nations Transitional Authority in Cambodia. Available online: https://en.wikipedia.org/wiki/United_Nations_Transitional_Authority_in_Cambodia (accessed 2 February 2018).

United Nations (1996), 'Secretary-General Appoints Raymond Chretien of Canada as Special Envoy to Great Lakes Region', SG/A/624/Rev.1, 30 October.

United Nations (1997), 'Mohamed Sahnoun of Algeria Nominated UN/OAU Special Representative for Great Lakes Region of Africa', SG/A/626, 27 January.

United Nations (2001), 'Statement by the President of the Security Council', S/PRST/2001/5, 20 February.

United Nations (2003), 'Secretary-General Appoints Behrooz Sadry of Iran Deputy Special Representative for Democratic Republic of Congo', SG/A/832-AFR/564, 18 February.

United Nations (2004), 'Second Report of the Secretary-General on the United Nations Operation in Burundi', S/2004/902, 15 November.

United Nations (2005), 'Sudan Peace Agreement Signed 9 January Historic Opportunity, Security Council Told', Meetings Coverage and Press Releases, 8 February.

United Nations (2005), 'Security Council Establishes UN Integrated Office in Sierra Leone to Further Address Root Causes of Conflict', SC/8487, 31 August.

United Nations (2006), 'Security Council Expands Mandate of UN Mission in Sudan to Include Darfur, Adopting Resolution 1706 by Vote Of 12 in Favour, with 3 Abstaining', Meetings Coverage and Press Releases, 31 August.

United Nations (2006), 'Sixth Report of the Secretary General on the United Nations Operation in Burundi', S/2006/163, 21 March.

United Nations (2006), 'Seventh Report of the Secretary-General on the United Nations Operation in Burundi', S/2006/429, 21 June.

United Nations (2006), 'Resolution 1692 (2006), adopted by the Security Council at its 5479th meeting, on 30 June 2006', S/RES/1692 (2006), 30 June.

United Nations (2006), 'Seventh Report of the Secretary-General on the United Nations Operation in Burundi', S/2006/429/Add.1, 14 August.

United Nations (2006), 'Secretary-General Appoints Youssef Mahmoud of Tunisia as Deputy Special Representative for Burundi', SG/A/1021-BIO/3809, 22 September.

United Nations (2006), 'Eighth Report of the Secretary-General on the United Nations Operation in Burundi', S/2006/842, 25 October.

United Nations (2006), Resolution 1719 (2006), adopted by the Security Council at its 5554th Meeting', S/RES/1719, 25 October.

United Nations (2006), 'Ninth Report of the Secretary-General on the United Nations Operation in Burundi', S/2006/994, 18 December.

United Nations (2006), 'Letter dated 22 December 2006 from the President of the Security Council addressed to the Secretary-General', S/2006/1021, 22 December.

United Nations (2006), 'Report of the Secretary-General on Chad and the Central African Republic pursuant to paragraphs 9 (d) and 13 of Security Council resolution 1706 (2006)', S/2006/1019, 22 December.

United Nations (2007), 'Report of the Secretary-General on Chad and the Central African Republic', S/2007/97, 23 February.

United Nations (2007), 'First Report of the Secretary-General on the United Nations Integrated Office in Burundi", S/2007/287, 17 May.

United Nations (2007), 'First session Burundi Configuration. Identical letters dated 21 June 2007 from the Chairman of the Burundi configuration of the Peacebuilding Commission to the President of the Security Council, the President of the General Assembly and the President of the Economic and Social Council', PBC/1/BDI/4, 22 June.

United Nations (2007), Security Council Resolution S/RES/1778, 25 September.

United Nations (2007), 'Security Council Authorizes Establishment of "Multidimensional Presence" in Chad, Central African Republic, Unanimously Adopting Resolution 1778 (2007)', Meetings Coverage and Press Releases, 25 September.

United Nations (2007), 'Resolution 1791 (2007), adopted by the Security Council
    at its 5809th Meeting, on 19 December 2007', S/RES/1791 (2007),
    19 December.

United Nations (2008), 'Secretary-General Appoints Victor Da Silva Angelo of Portugal
    to Head United Nations Mission in Central African Republic and Chad', Meetings
    Coverage and Press Releases, 31 January.

United Nations (2008), 'Annual session 2008 16 to 27 June 2008, Geneva Item 4 of the
    provisional agenda UNFPA – Country programmes and related matters',
    DP/FPA/2008/6, 28 March.

United Nations (2008), 'Security Council Adopts Resolution Extending Mandate of
    United Nations Mission in Central African Republic and Chad until 15 March 2009',
    Meetings Coverage and Press Releases, 24 September.

United Nations (2008), 'Fourth Report of the Secretary-General on the United Nations
    Integrated Office in Burundi', S/2008/745, 28 November.

United Nations (2008), 'Seventh Report of the Secretary-General on the United Nations
    Integrated Office in Burundi', S/2010/608, 30 November.

United Nations (2008), 'Secretary-General Urges Parties to Burundi Ceasefire
    Agreement to Summon "Political Will and Courage" to Overcome Outstanding
    Issues, in Message to Regional Summit', SG/SM/11983-AFR/1785, 4 December.

United Nations (2008), 'Resolution 1858 (2008), adopted by the Security Council at its
    6057th Meeting, on 22 December 2008', S/RES/1858 (2008), 22 December.

United Nations (2008) 'Third Report of the Secretary-General on the United Nations
    Integrated Office in Burundi', S/2008/330, 15 May.

United Nations (2009), 'Fifth Report of the Secretary-General on the United Nations
    Integrated Office in Burundi', S/2009/270, 22 May.

United Nations (2009), 'Sixth Report of the Secretary-General on the United Nations
    Integrated Office in Burundi', S/2009/611, 30 November.

United Nations (2009), '6236th Meeting', Thursday, 10 December.

United Nations (2009), 'Resolution 1902 (2009), adopted by the Security Council at its
    6245th Meeting, on 17 December 2009', S/RES/1902 (2009), 17 December.

United Nations (2010), 'Secretary-General Appoints Bo Schack of Denmark Deputy
    Special Representative for Central African Republic',
    SG/A/1214-AFR/1928-BIO/4157, 5 January.

United Nations (2010), 'Resolution 1913 (2010), adopted by the Security Council at its
    6283rd meeting, on 12 March 2010', S/RES/1913 (2010), 12 March.

United Nations (2010), 'Letter dated 3 March 2010 Addressed to the President of the
    Security Council by the Permanent Representative of Chad to the United Nations',
    S/2010/115, 3 March, S/2010/115.

United Nations (2010), 'Report of the Secretary-General on the United Nations Mission
    in the Central African Republic and Chad', S/2010/217, 29 April.

United Nations (2010), 'Resolution 1922 (2010), adopted by the Security Council at its
    6312th meeting, on 12 May 2010', S/RES/1922 (2010), 12 May.

United Nations (2010), 'Letter dated 21 May 2010 from the Permanent Representative of Chad to the United Nations Addressed to the President of the Security Council' S/2010/250, 21 May.

United Nations (2010), 'Resolution 1923 (2010), adopted by the Security Council at its 6321st meeting, on 25 May 2010', S/RES/1923 (2010), 25 May.

United Nations (2010), 'Report of the Secretary-General on the United Nations Mission in the Central African Republic and Chad', S/2010/409, 30 July.

United Nations (2010), 'Letter dated 15 October 2010 from the Permanent Representative of Chad to the United Nations addressed to the President of the Security Council', S/2010/536, 18 October.

United Nations (2010), 'Fonds d'Affectation Spéciale des Nations Unies au Profit du Détachement Intégré de sécurité', MINURCAT UNPOL, Interoffice Memorandum, 11 November.

United Nations (2010), 'Report of the Secretary-General on the United Nations Mission in the Central African Republic and Chad', S/2010/611, 1 December.

United Nations (2010), 'Security Council Extends Mandate of Mission in Central African Republic and Chad, Calls on Secretary-General to Complete Withdrawal by 31 December', Meetings Coverage and Press Releases, 25 May.

United Nations (2016), 'Security Council Unanimously Adopts Resolution 2282 (2016) on Review of United Nations Peacebuilding Architecture', SC/12340, 27 April.

United Nations (2016), 'Resolution adopted by the General Assembly on 27 April 2016', A/RES/70/262, 12 May.

United Nations (2016), 'Adopting Resolution 2303 (2016), Security Council Requests Secretary-General Establish Police Component in Burundi to Monitor Security Situation', SC/12469, 29 July.

United Nations Development Programme (2016), 'Issue Brief, Peace and Development Advisors', Joint UNDP-DPA Programme on Building National Capacities for Conflict Prevention.

United Nations Development Operations Coordination Office (2017), 'Interim Technical Guidance The Assessment of Results and Competencies for Resident Coordinators and UN Country Teams', September.

United Nations Development Assistance Framework Guidance 2017.

United Nations Integrated Office in Burundi (2008), 'Strategic Framework for Peacebuilding in Burundi Highlights and key lessons learned', Tokyo, 25 July.

United Nations Official Document. Available online: http://www.un.org/en/ga/search/view_doc.asp?symbol=S/PV.6138 (accessed 2 August 2018).

United Nations Peacebuilding Fund, 'Burundi Overview', www.unpbf.org/countries/burundi.

United Nations Peace Operations (2008), 'UN Integration in Burundi in the Context of the Peacebuilding Office BINUB Taking Stock and Lessons Learned from June 2006 to November 2007', BINUB Bujumbura, February.

United Nations Security Council Resolution 1959 (2010).

UNSC Resolution 1270 (1999), Operative Paragraph 14, on the Mandate of UNAMSIL.

Uppsala University, (2014), 'The Causes of Peace – The Botswana, Zambia and Malawi-Zone of Peace', Department of Peace Conflict and Research.

Van Brabant, K. (2012), 'Leadership for Peace', Interpeace, Working Paper No. 2.

Van der Lijn, J., T. Smit and T. Höghammar (2016), 'Peace operations and conflict management', in SIPRI Yearbook 2016: *Armaments, Disarmament and International Security*, Oxford: Oxford University Press.

Van Tongeren, P., M. Brenk, M. Hellema and J. Verhoeven (2005) (eds), *People Building Peace II: Successful Stories of Civil Society*, Boulder: Lynne Rienner Publishers.

Vansina, J. (1967), 'Note sur la Chronologie du Burundi Ancient', Bulletin de l'ARSOM 38.

Villaverde, J. (2010), MINURCAT: 'Achievements, Disappointments and Fragile Future, Institute of Studies on Conflict and Humanitarian Action', February.

Weiss, T. (2012), *What is Wrong with the UN and how to Fix It?* Second Edition, Polity Press, USA.

Wielenga, C. and S. Akin-Aina (2016), 'Mapping Conflict and Peace in Burundi, An Analysis of the Burundi Conflict Terrain', ResearchGate.

Wolpe, H. (2011), 'Making Peace after Genocide. Anatomy of the Burundi Process', United States Institute of Peace.

World Bank (2011), 'World Development Report 2011: Conflict, Security and Development', Washington DC.

World Bank (2018), 'Pathways for Peace: Inclusive Approaches to Preventing Violent Conflict', Washington DC.

World Peace Foundation (2017), 'United Nations Mission in the Central African Republic and Chad (MINURCAT)/European Union Force (EUFOR)', Short Mission Brief.

Yale-UN Oral History Sir Marrack Goulding, James S. Sutterlin, interviewer June 30, 1998 Oxford, England.

Annex

Letter from the Government of Burundi to the UN Secretariat asking for my replacement at the end of my third year as head of BINUB.

REPUBUQUE DUBURUNDI   Bujumbura, le 24 Décembre 2009

Ministère des Relations Extérieures
Et de la Coopération Internationale

N° 204.05/ 3390 / RE: (2009)

Le Ministère des Relations Extérieures et de la Coopération Internationale de la République du Burundi présente ses compliments au Secrétariat Général des Nations Unies, à New-York, et a l'honneur de l'informer que le Gouvernement du Burundi voudrait demander le remplacement de Monsieur Youssef MAHMOUD, comme Représentant Exécutif du Secrétaire Général des Nations Unies pour le Burundi à la tête du BINUB.

En effet, après avoir exercé les fonctions de Coordonnateur Résident, de Représentant Spécial Adjoint du Secrétaire General et de Représentant Résident du PNUD au Burundi, Monsieur Youssef MAHMOUD a été proposé au poste de Représentant Exécutif du Secrétaire Général des Nations Unies au Burundi le 14Décembre 2006 pour faire suite à la résolution 1719 (2006), qui mettait en place le Bureau intégré des Nations Unies au Burundi, à partir du 1 Janvier 2001, le Gouvernement de la République du Burundi a accepté cette nomination le 21 Décembre 2006.

Sur base du mandat de la Résolution 1719 que l'Organisation des Nations Unies, par l'intérimaire du BINUB, a signé avec le Gouvernement du Burundi, la Stratégie Intégrée d'appui des Nations Unies à la Consolidation de la Paix au Burundi pour 2007-2008 et dont la mise en œuvre a été effective sous L'égide du Département du Maintien de la Paix.

De commun accord, l'Organisation des Nations Unies et le Gouvernement du

Burundi ont prolongé la mise en œuvre de cette stratégie de rnême que le partenariat avec le Département du Maintien de la Paix pour poursuivre la mise en œuvre *de* l'Accord de paix entre le Gouvernement du Burundi et les F.N.L. ainsi que le désarmement des populations civiles.

Compte tenu de l'issue heureuse de ces deux programmes comme l'ont reconu les partenaires en décidant de mettre fin au Partenariat pour la Paix au Burundi au 31 Décembre 2009, le Gouvernement a, pour se conformer aux axes de la nouvelle stratégie intégrée a appui des Nations Unies au Burundi pour 2010-2014, demande au Secrétaire Général des Nations Unies que le Département de Maintien de la Paix soit relaye dans sa mission au Burundi par le Département des Affaires Politiques.

Pour l'année 2010 pour laquelle le mandat du BINUB a été prolongé, son travail est décrit à l'alinéa 5 de la résolution 1902 (2009) et est conforme à la nouvelle stratégie intégrée.

De ce fait, le Gouvernement de la République du Burundi estime qu'il faut un autre profil que celui du Représentant Exécutif actuel pour mettre en œuvre le contenu du mandat du BINUB pour 2010.

Au demeurant, le Gouvernement de la République du Burundi réitère sa reconnaissance vis-à-vis de l'Organisation des Nations Unies pour son accompagnement engage auprès du Burundi dans le processus de consolidation de la Paix.

De même, ii tient à adresser de nouveau ses félicitations et ses remerciements à l'égard de Monsieur Youssef MAHMOUD, Représentant Exécutif du Secrétaire General de l'Organisation des Nations Unies au Burundi pour son implication active dans la Consolidation de ta Paix.

Le Gouvernement de la République du Burundi saisit cette opportunité pour renouveler au Secrétariat Général des Nations Unies, à New York, les assurances de sa haute considération.

Bujumbura. le 24 Décembre 2009,

A

AU SECRETARIAT GENERAL DE L'ORGANISATION
DES NATIONS UNIES

Index

Page numbers: Figures are given in *italics* and notes as [page number] n. [note number].